IMAGES
of America

WINSTON-SALEM'S HISTORIC WEST END

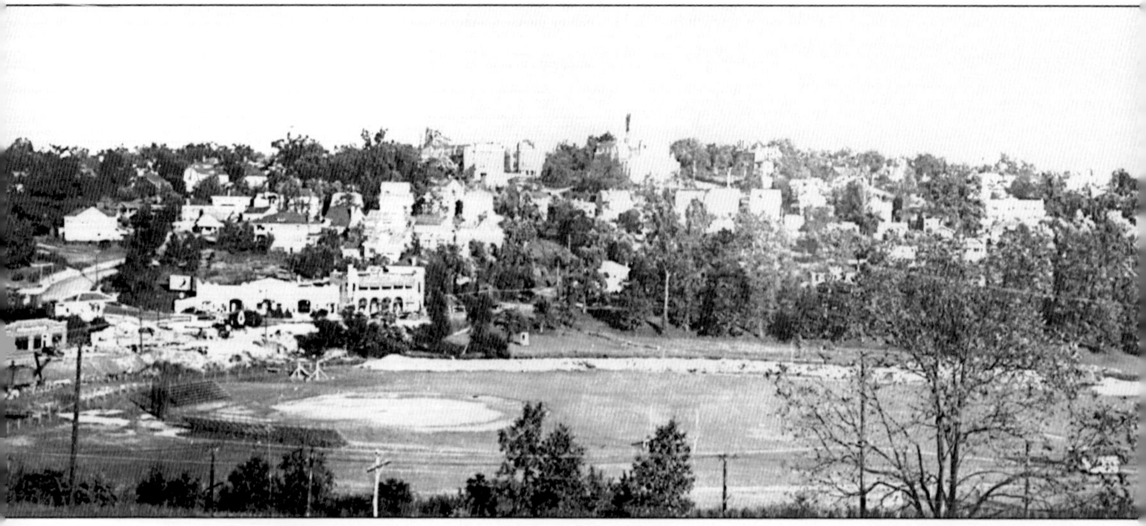

West End is seen here from the west about 1934. Peters Creek, in the valley at front, was the western edge of the original Salem tract developed by the Moravians after 1766. West End lies at the western end of a ridge running east–west through the center of the former town of Winston, just north of old Salem. (Courtesy of The North Carolina State Archives, hereafter listed as NCSA.)

IMAGES
of America

WINSTON-SALEM'S HISTORIC WEST END

J. Eric Elliott

ARCADIA
PUBLISHING

ISBN 978-0-7385-1682-0

Published by Arcadia Publishing
Charleston, South Carolina

Printed in the United States of America

Library of Congress Catalog Card Number: 2004106572

For all general information contact Arcadia Publishing at:
Telephone 843-853-2070
Fax 843-853-0044
E-mail sales@arcadiapublishing.com
For customer service and orders:
Toll-Free 1-888-313-2665

Visit us on the Internet at www.arcadiapublishing.com

Contents

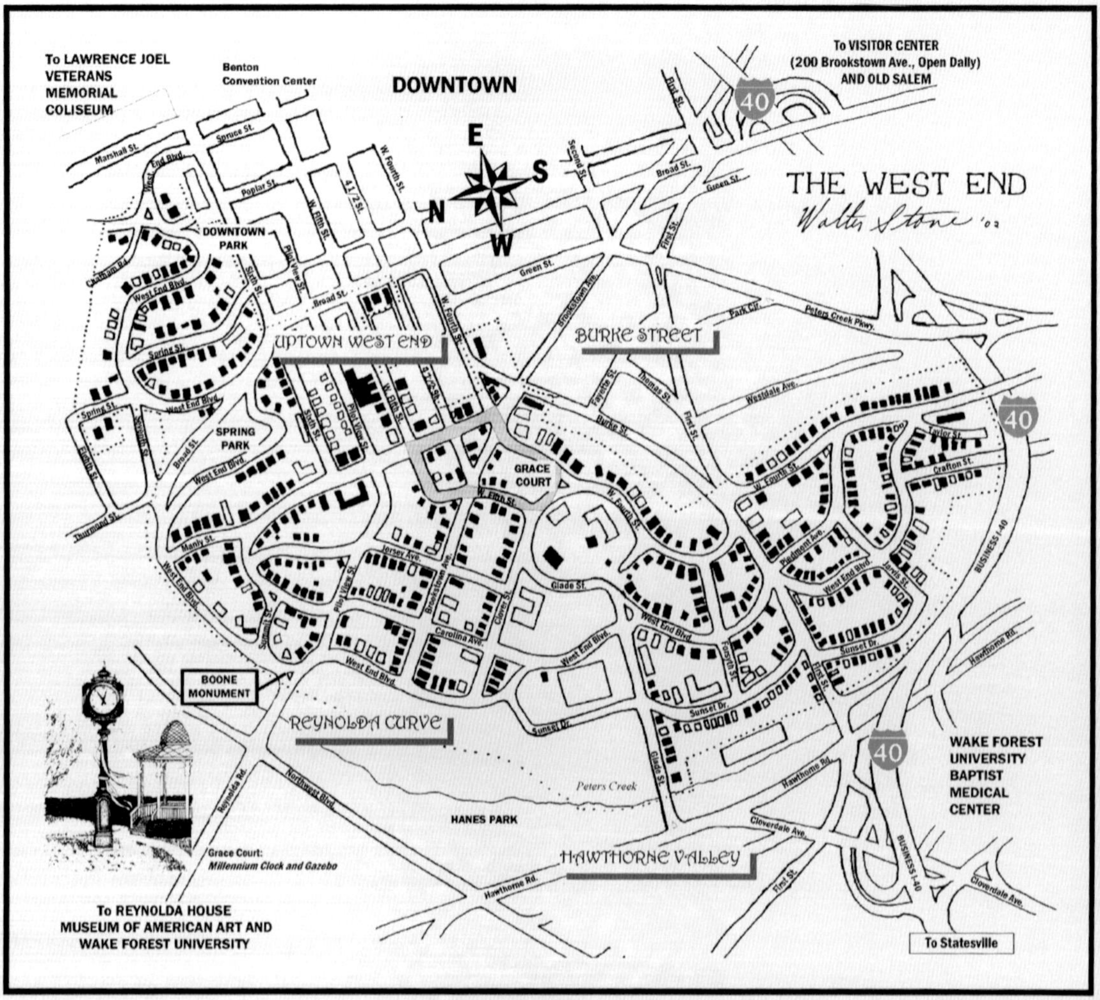

This visitor's map shows present-day West End, a National Register Historic District and a Winston-Salem Local Historic District. Contributing structures are shown in solid black; light gray highlights a walking tour where the four principal house styles in the neighborhood can be seen. The Hotel Zinzendorf would have been immediately to the west of Grace Court at the map's center. (Map by Walter Stone; composition by Eric Elliott/Echidna Design.)

Front cover: This photo shows a construction crew at the site of the Hotel Zinzendorf in late 1891 or early 1892. (Courtesy of the Collection of the Wachovia Historical Society, Old Salem, Inc.; hereafter listed as WHS/OS.)

Preface

This book will serve for many of you as a first introduction to an important part of the story of Winston-Salem. Many visitors to our community know of our area's Moravian heritage through the interpretative history at two premiere local attractions: the village of Old Salem and Historic Bethabara Park. Others know of the prominent role our community has played in education through such institutions as Salem College, Wake Forest University, and Winston-Salem State University. And yet the story of the town's most important growth in the early 20th century—years during which resources were assembled from tobacco and textile manufacture to make possible the later establishment of Old Salem and Wake Forest, and the growth of Bethabara, Salem, Winston-Salem State, or a myriad of other community resources—may not be known to the casual visitor.

When Winston-Salem's industrial growth exploded after the turn of the last century to make the city the largest municipality in the state, the neighborhood that was home to many of the decision-makers and leaders of the day was West End. Indeed, because of the wide influence of its decisions, not a few commentators have noted that during its heyday, West End was the most important neighborhood in the state. In recent years, West End residents have helped preserve the architectural legacy of those days; in so doing, they have given us all as close a collective view of the streetscape of Old Winston as we have in one concentrated area in the city. They have helped remind us that as we move forward as a community, we ought to always remember to take the best of our past with us.

So enjoy learning about this treasured part of our community story amidst our many fine neighborhoods. You may find yourself wanting to visit the West End's twisty streets, historic homes, and charming shops, inns, and restaurants. As this book shows, the assembly of those charms was no accident. Enjoy your visit to our community in these pages.

Mayor Allen Joines
City of Winston-Salem

ACKNOWLEDGMENTS

Historian Nan Tilley relates that one of the casualties of the 1893 Panic in Winston-Salem was the loss of the H.H. Reynolds tobacco company, whose signature "Red Elephant" product line had the marketing slogan "a thousand spits in every chew." While the imagery isn't particularly appealing to this writer's taste buds, I think the modern equivalent claim might be "satisfying and lasts a long time." I know I've bitten off more than I can chew with this project. I just hope there's more than a few good spits in it.

My thanks go to the many individual providers of photographs in this book for their willingness to make available this unique form of treasure. I would like to thank the staffs of each of the archives mentioned in this work, including Jennifer Bean Bower, Sue Choate, Todd Crumley, Trudy Cox, Steve Massengill, and Richard Starbuck. I would especially like to thank the staff of the North Carolina Room of the Forsyth County Public Library, notably Molly Rawls of the photograph collection. My thanks to the photographers unknown and known (like Frank Jones, Tom Hege, Jim Keith, H.A. Lineback, and Allie Brown) whose work can be found in such archives. Julie Harris at the library of the *Winston-Salem Journal* was helpful in allowing access to the paper's files on the area. A thank you, too, to those writers who took time along the way to write down part of our community's story: W.A. Blair, Fam Brownlee, Rev. Bill Bumgarner, Chester Davis, Bill East, Adelaide Fries, Ed Hendricks, Jo White Linn, Michael Shirley, James Howell Smith, Larry Edward Tise, Nan Tilley, Frank Tursi, Manly Wade Wellman, Mel White, Alan Willis, and Douglas Young, as well as West Enders Jane Hill, Nancy Stockton Martin, Robina Mickle, Laura Phillips, Bess Gray Plumly, Gwynne Taylor, and Terrell Young. Thanks to Tom Angelo, Betty Beeson, Linwood Davis, Richard Gibson, Linda Hamilton, Catherine Hendren, Wava Howard, Paul McGraw, Tommy McNulty, Joan Meier, Andrew and Donna Mickle, Rick Pardue, Kristin Scheve, Caroline Singletary, Jule Spach, John Still, Dick Stockton, Bill Womble, and Rev. Ellen Yarborough for sharing so much in person; and thanks to June Dinkins and Robin Voiers for sharing their papers on the neighborhood and Mayor Allen Joines for his kind words. Detailed bibliography and notes for this text can be found at a website I have prepared about the neighborhood, www.w-sfrontporch.com.

My appreciation for their review goes to Barry Miller and Gwynne Taylor, for their forbearance and labors to Arcadia's Adam Latham and Laura New, and to my own crew at home. Laura, Norma, John, and Zachary have had to endure more than they should with this work (and elsewhere as well). I appreciate greatly their love, support, and encouragement. Mom and Dad, again, thanks.

My apologies to those whose family stories have been an important part of the West End story but whose pictures are not part of this history due to lack of space or access to materials. The advice I give myself every day about car keys also works for historic photographs: "Please leave them where I can find them." Lastly, this book is dedicated to all those whose hard work and hopes have kept West End the vital, interesting place that I call home.

J. Eric Elliott
Independence Day 2004
Winston-Salem, NC

One

The Spa on the Ridge *1890–1909*

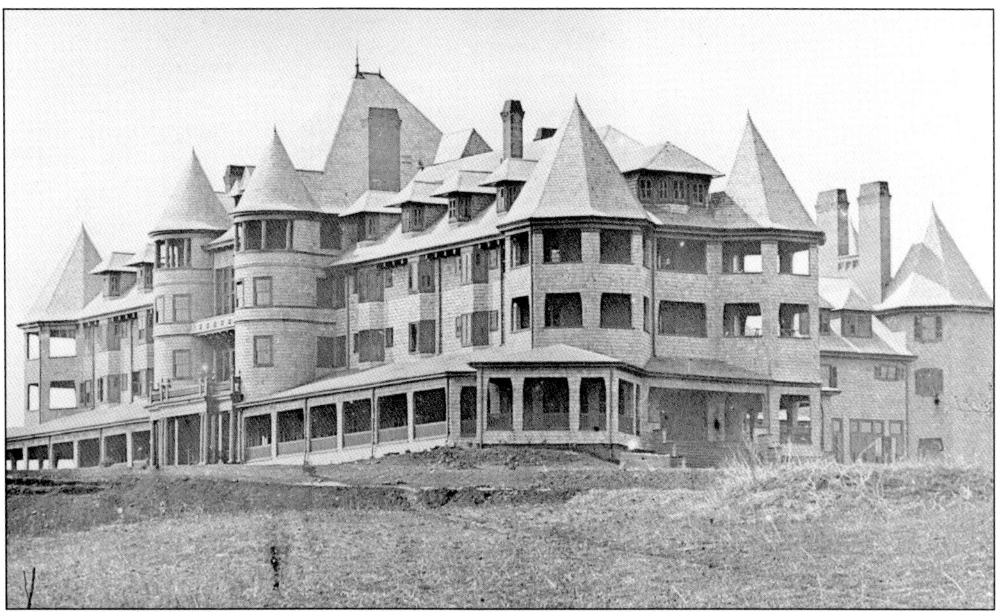

Winston-Salem's West End was to be no ordinary neighborhood. Envisioned as the showcase of a new "Piedmont Metropolis," West End could have been one of the South's finest health resorts. To understand why it was not, one has to know the story of "the spa on the ridge." Here is the Hotel Zinzendorf seen from the northeast, under construction in 1891 or 1892. (Courtesy WHS/OS.)

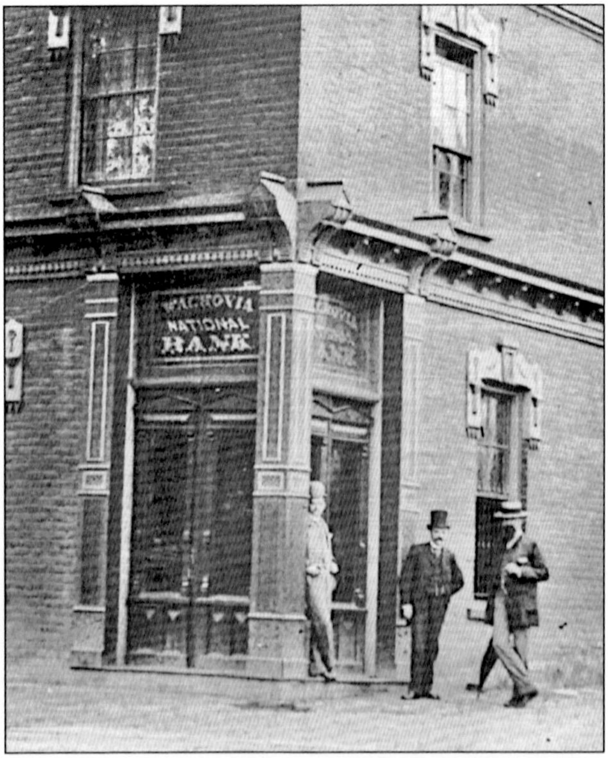

The town of Winston blossomed with the growth of tobacco warehousing and manufacture. Established in 1849 as the seat of Forsyth County when sister town Salem refused hangings on the public square, Winston had but one tobacco warehouse in 1872. By 1890, it had 31 tobacco factories. Here in 1887, banker James A. Gray, center, consults with entrepreneur R.J. Reynolds, at right. (Courtesy Wachovia Corporation Corporate Archive; hereafter listed as WCCA.)

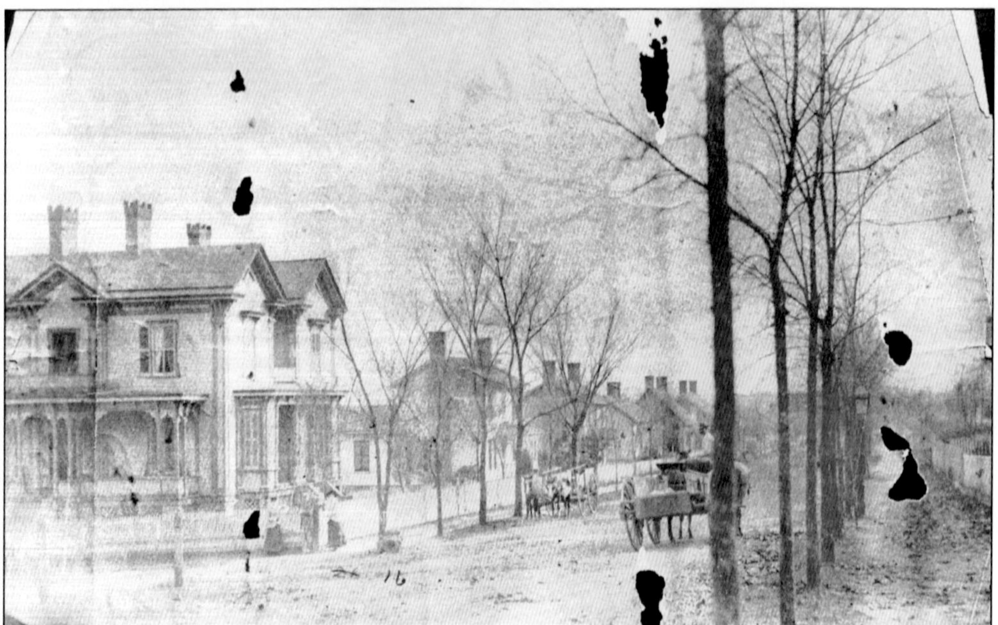

The "Elegant Eighties," as Harvard-trained publisher and local school administrator W. A. Blair called them, were years of great creativity and institution building in Winston-Salem. New wealth built fine homes along Cherry and Marshall Streets, north and south of the dividing line between Winston and Salem at First Street. Here is the view at Cherry and Third around 1882. (Courtesy Old Salem, Inc.)

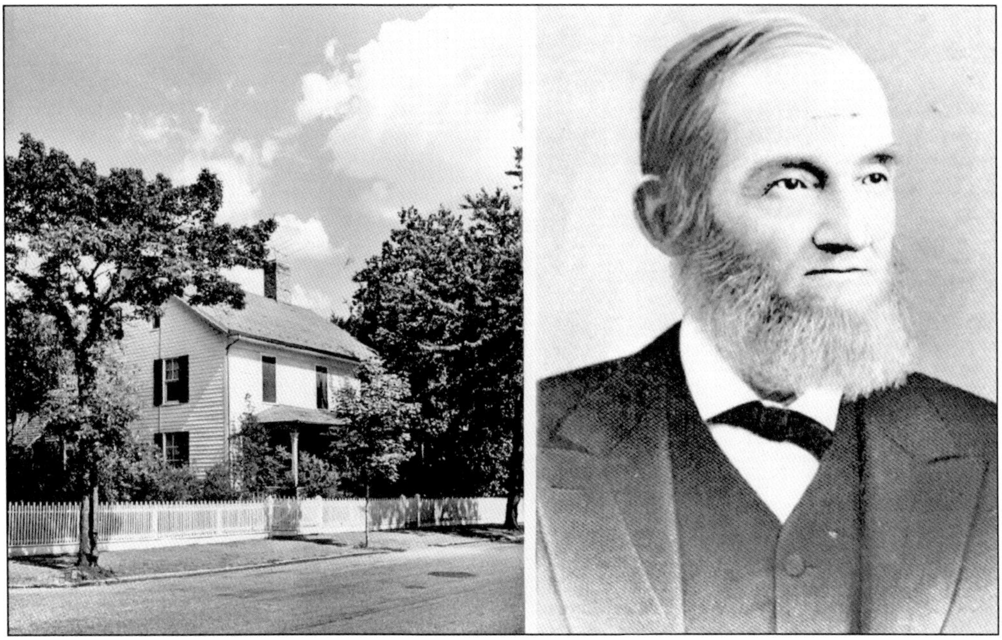

Rev. Calvin H. Wiley D.D. was the general superintendent of common schools in North Carolina from 1852 to 1865. In the 1880s, he helped Winston leaders establish a system of public schools for the town. Wiley's home at 523 Spruce Street was a local landmark until its removal in the 1950s. (Courtesy Forsyth County Public Library Photograph Collection; hereafter listed as FCPL.)

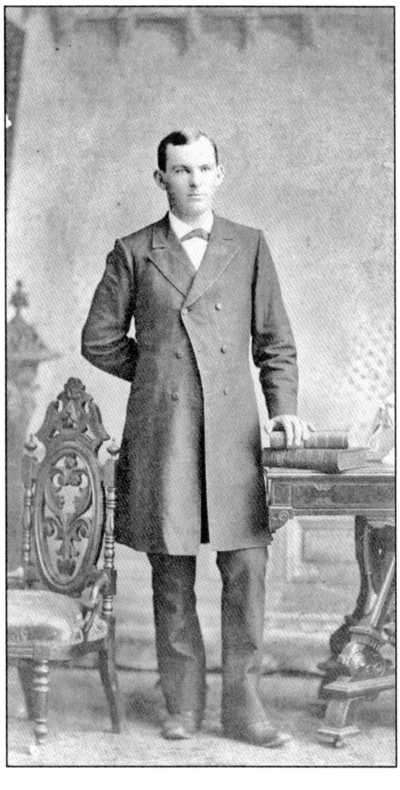

Charles Duncan McIver, fresh from organizing public schools for Durham, North Carolina, became in February 1884 the first principal of the Winston Graded School. Disturbed by the state's inattention to women's education, he left Winston for Raleigh after only two years, organizing the State Normal and Industrial School for women, later known as the Woman's College of the University of North Carolina, in 1891. (Courtesy University Archives, the University of North Carolina at Greensboro.)

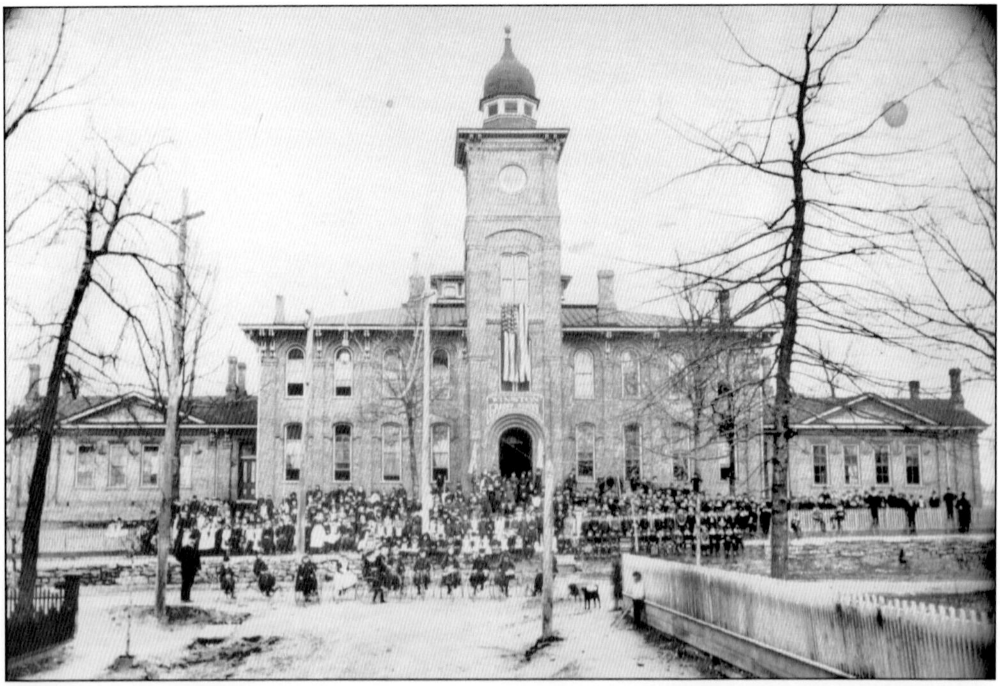

The Winston Graded School was founded at the northwest corner of Fourth and Broad in 1884. The view here is looking north from Pond Street, later known as Green Street. Three other town public school facilities, including one for black youth, were built within a decade. (Courtesy Moravian Archives, Winston-Salem, North Carolina; hereafter listed as MA.)

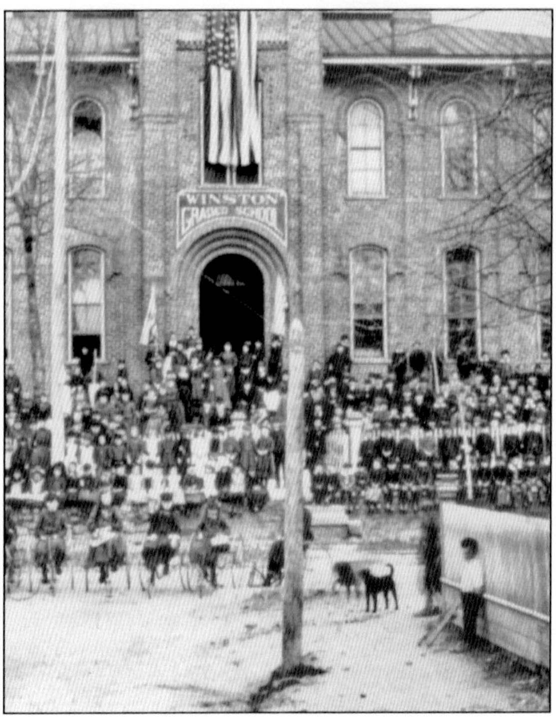

The little boy at the lower right of this 1884 close-up leans against a fence that surrounds the home of Robert Glenn, of the firm of Watson and Glenn, attorneys for the City of Winston. As other schools were added in Winston, this school became known as the West End Graded School (Courtesy MA.)

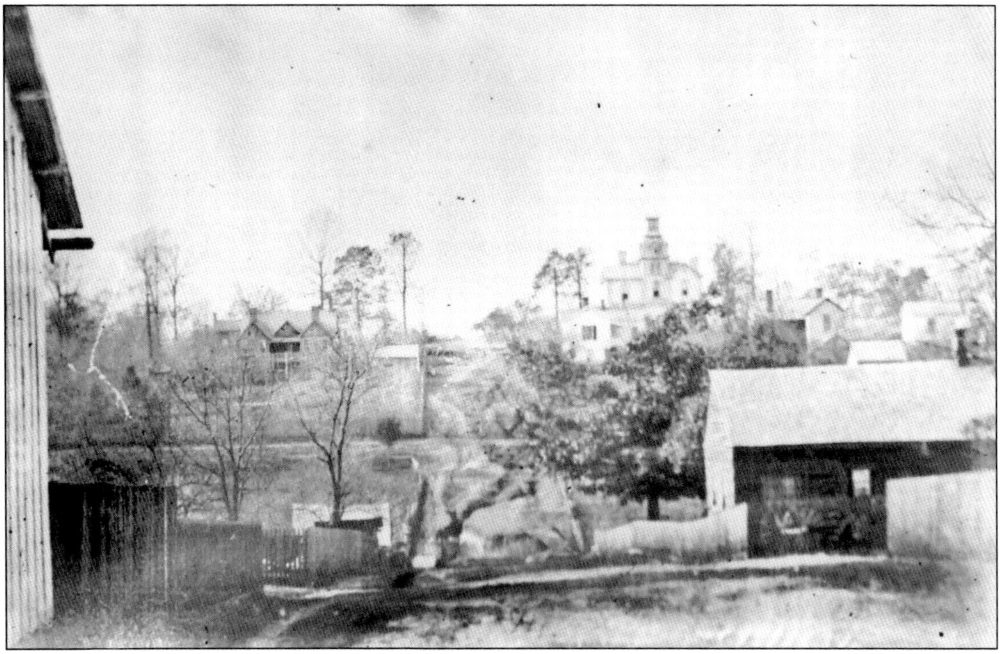

By 1890, downtown Winston reached the blocks bounded by Spruce and Poplar Streets, with homes becoming scattered farther west. Here is an undated westward view of First Street from Liberty Street. The "West End" in this book includes both the current Historic District and Winston's Fifth Street west of Poplar, which became a central entrance to the town's West End residential district. (Courtesy WHS/OS.)

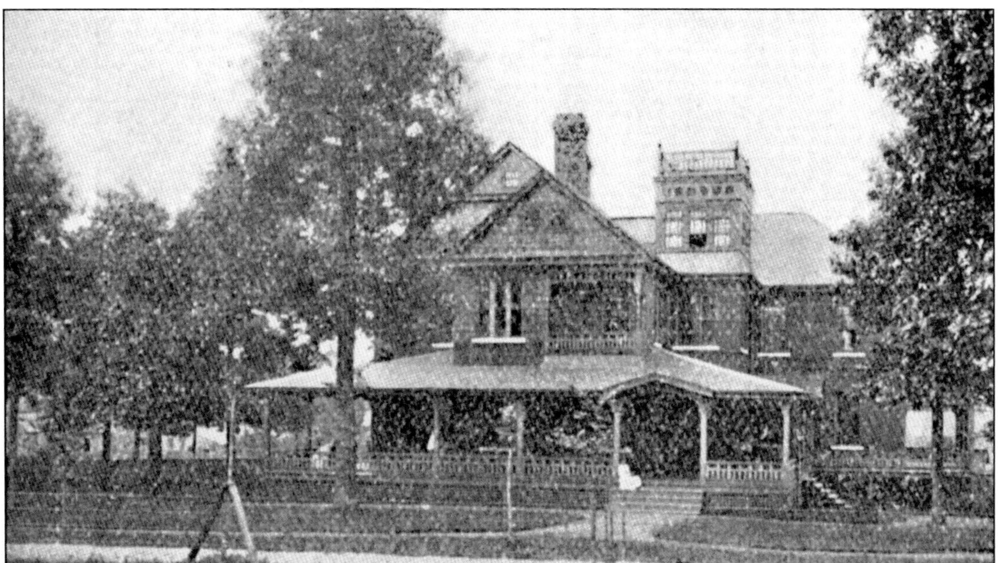

Many of the town's elite gathered for a New Year's week costume party in 1886 at the home of M.N. Williamson, on Fifth Street just west of Poplar. During the celebrations, reported on in great detail by the paper, guests decided that what Winston needed was a first-class hotel: good for business and tourists and good for further celebrations. Local writer Bill East says West End was born this night. (Courtesy FCPL.)

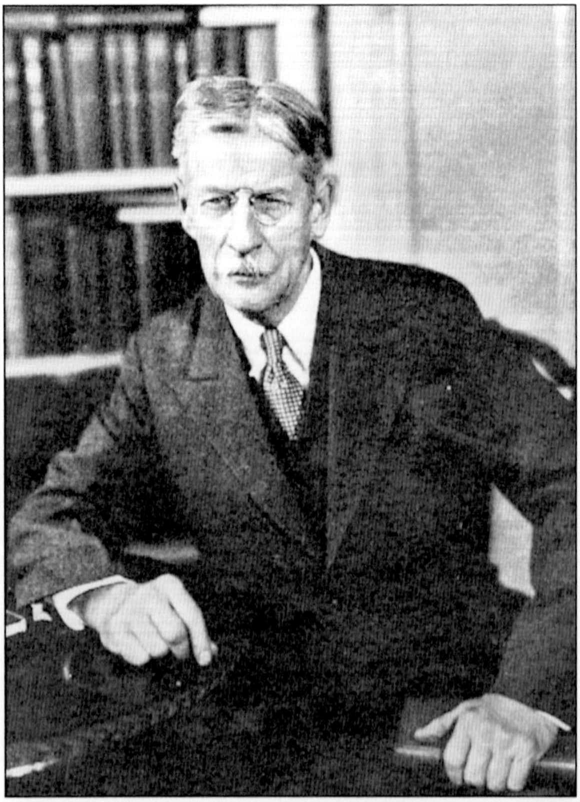

Frank Sprague, shown here in the 1920s, worked with Thomas Edison in the 1880s. He developed a motor and suspension that enabled previously horse-drawn streetcars to climb hills with the aid of an electric power grid. Sprague left Edison to found his own company, installing the first electric trolley in Richmond, Virginia, in 1887. Within three years, more than 100 municipalities had expressed interest in a Sprague streetcar. (Courtesy the author.)

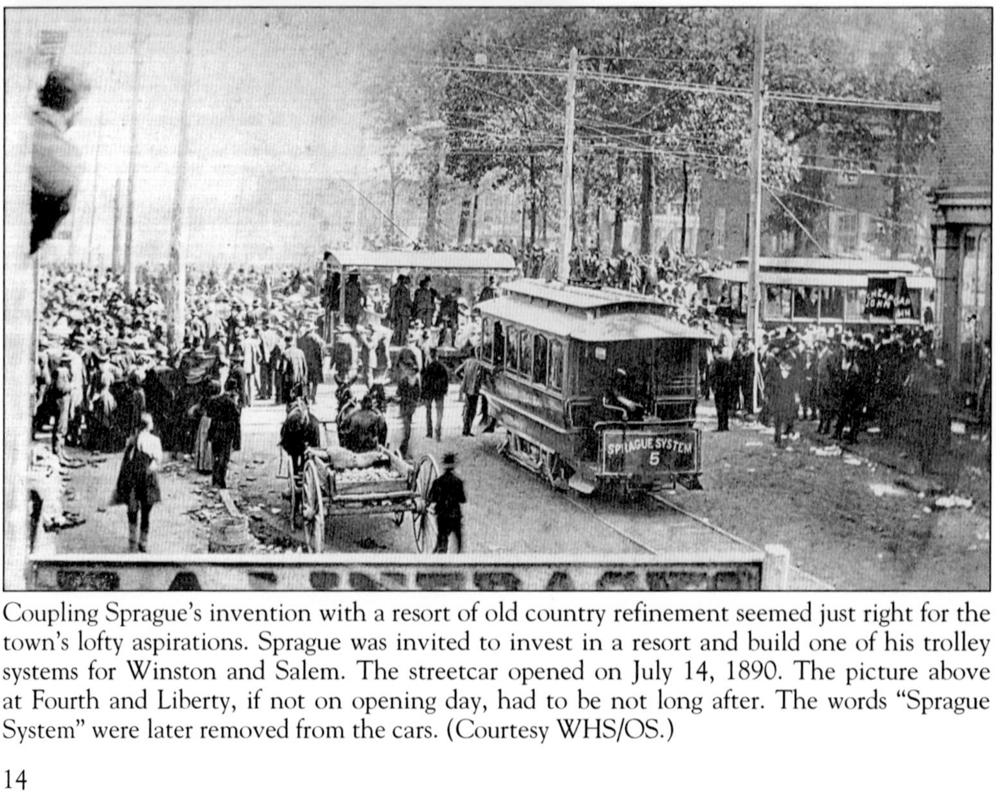

Coupling Sprague's invention with a resort of old country refinement seemed just right for the town's lofty aspirations. Sprague was invited to invest in a resort and build one of his trolley systems for Winston and Salem. The streetcar opened on July 14, 1890. The picture above at Fourth and Liberty, if not on opening day, had to be not long after. The words "Sprague System" were later removed from the cars. (Courtesy WHS/OS.)

Developers purchased 180 acres of land along Peters Creek northwest of Winston, originally the farm of J.C.W. Fries. The Fries family's fortunes increased when son Francis began woolen and cotton mills in Salem in the 1840s. The mills were the leading manufacturers in Salem by 1861. Francis's brother Henry (seated, lower left), aided by Francis's sons (also shown in this 1890 family photo), took over the mills. In 1880, they introduced electricity to Southern cotton manufacturers. (Courtesy private collection/Old Salem, Inc.)

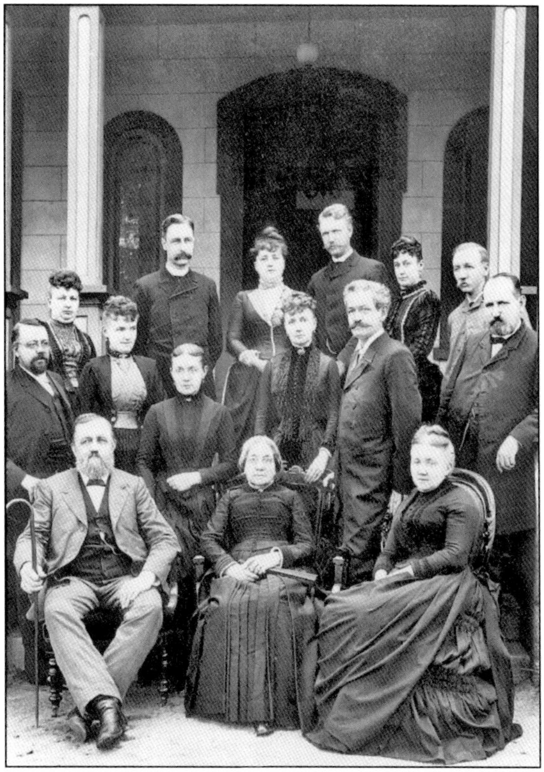

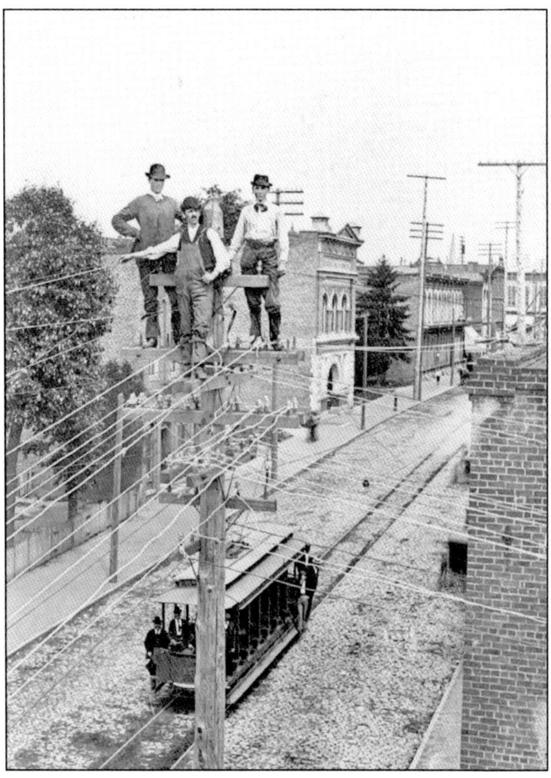

The Frieses provided Winston and Salem with their first electric streetlights in 1887. The photo here captures the daring changes to the streetscape that electricity and its inventions brought to town. On the street are the first effects of the half-million dollars that the towns spent on street improvements beginning in 1890, including granite "Belgian blocks" used to pave downtown streets. (Courtesy MA.)

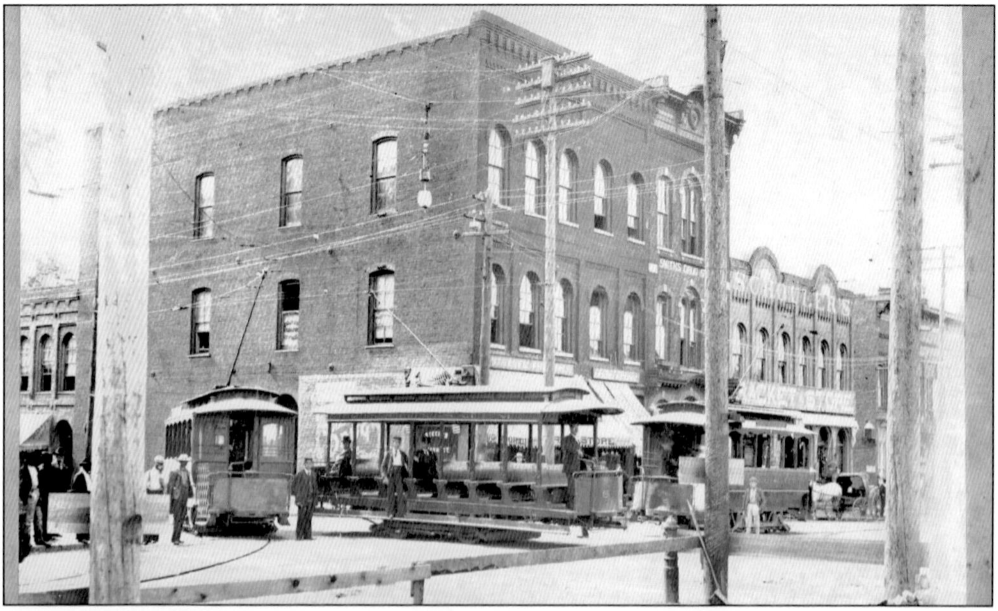

There were two kinds of trolleys: open-air and closed. West Ender Robina Mickle recalled in a family scrapbook that each had a motorman and a coachman. The latter took your parasol and packages and helped you enter the car, and then he reversed the process for you to exit. The motorman knew his riders well enough to stop and let folks dash home for a nickel if they had forgotten their fare. (Courtesy MA.)

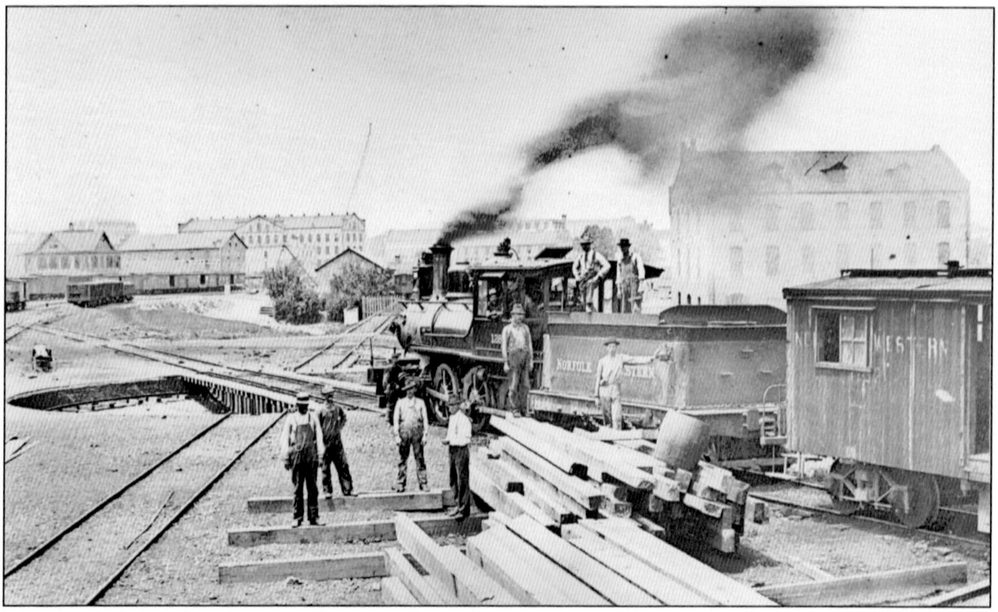

In 1885, the new board of trade (chamber of commerce) began efforts to expand railroad connections for Winston and Salem. Only the Richmond and Danville Railway linked Forsyth County to Greensboro and an outside rail network. In 1891, a spur was completed from the Norfolk and Western Railway in southwest Virginia. Some local leaders hoped promising deposits of coal and iron ore there might be shuttled to Winston for steel making as tobacco products shipped north. (Courtesy MA.)

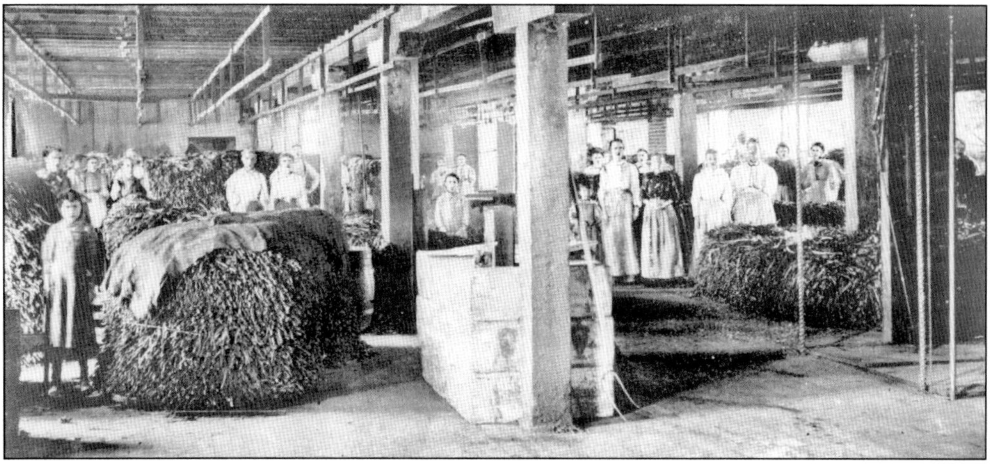

New industry, a new tourist attraction, might leaven the swings that a tobacco economy occasioned. Factories sat empty for six months of the year for lack of adequate heating and cooling. Much of the labor-intensive work—stemming, flavoring, and packing the leaf—was done by the families of freed slaves or by poor farm families who came seeking a steady seasonal payday. (Courtesy North Carolina Collection, University of North Carolina at Chapel Hill; hereafter listed as NCC/UNC.)

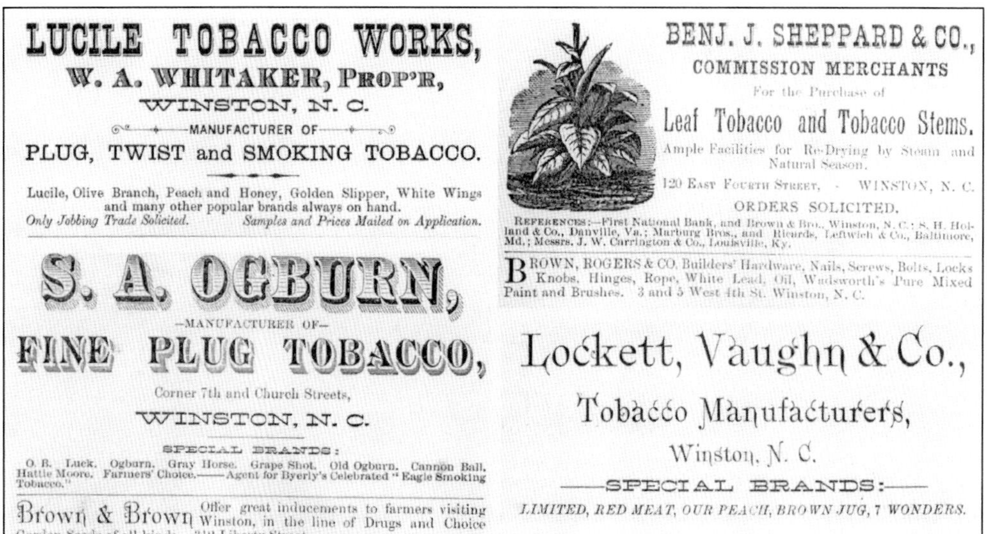

Winston's population grew from 443 in 1872 to over 8,000 by 1888; Salem's population in 1888 was at 3,000. By 1896, there would be 51 different tobacco factories in Winston and Salem. Many factory owners would be involved in the West End development as principals, investors, or landowners, including the four advertised here. (Courtesy FCPL.)

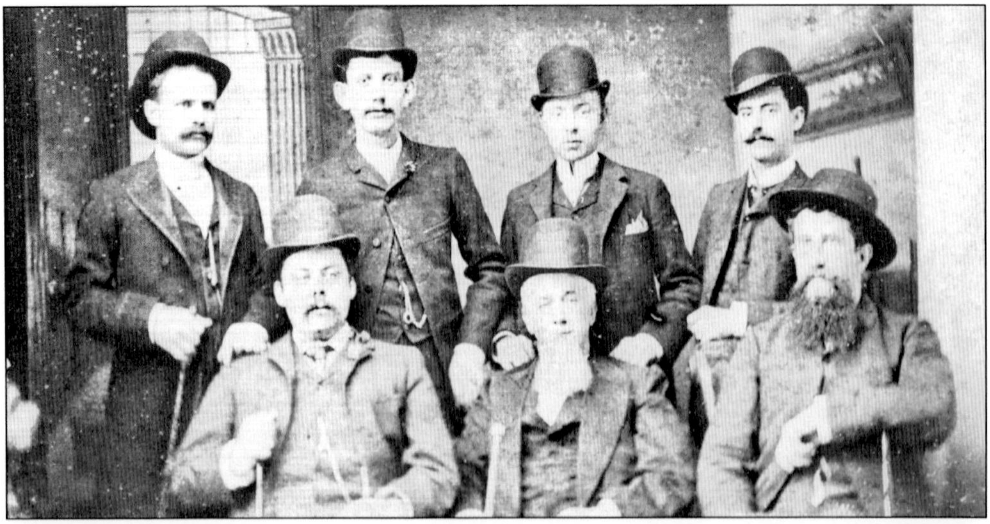

This picture shows Salem merchants in the 1890s. Although the towns of Winston and Salem would not have their official "hyphenated" merger until 1913, their post offices were joined in 1899. Their business communities often acted as "Winston-Salem" for many years before that. (Courtesy WHS/OS.)

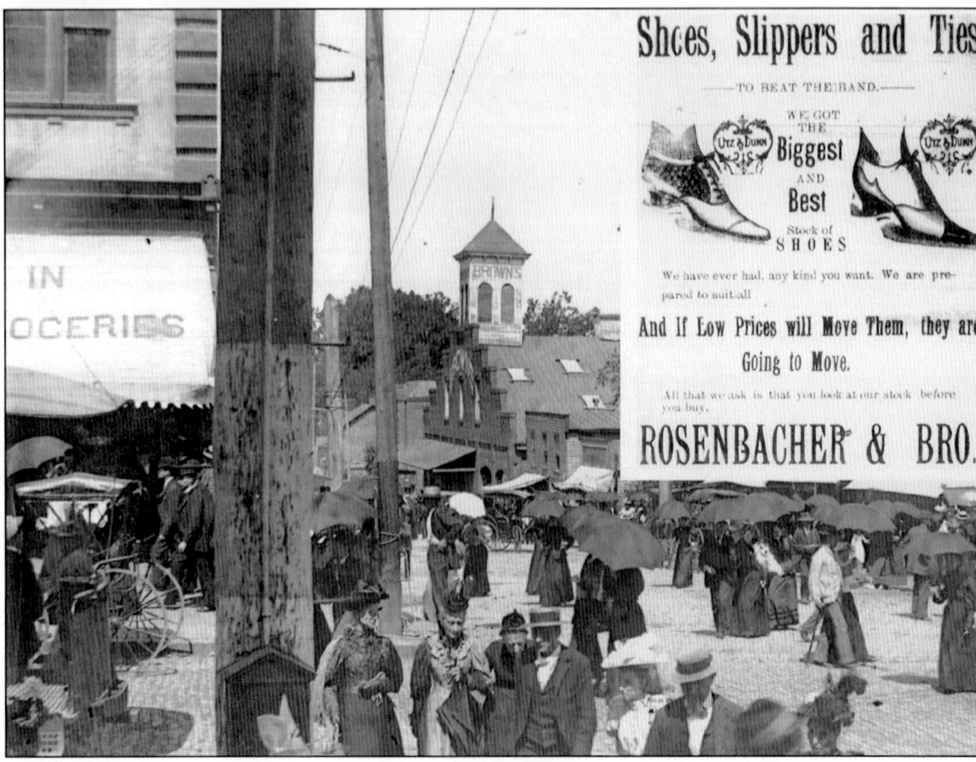

Rosenbacher's sold clothing to farmers bringing their crop for sale between Trade and Depot Streets. The store was located along the north side of the courthouse square (the building at left in this 1897 view), across Main Street from where a new city hall was built in 1895. In 1909, Rosenbacher's widow, Carrie, moved into a high-columned neoclassical mansion on West End's Fifth Street. (Courtesy FCPL and WHS/OS.)

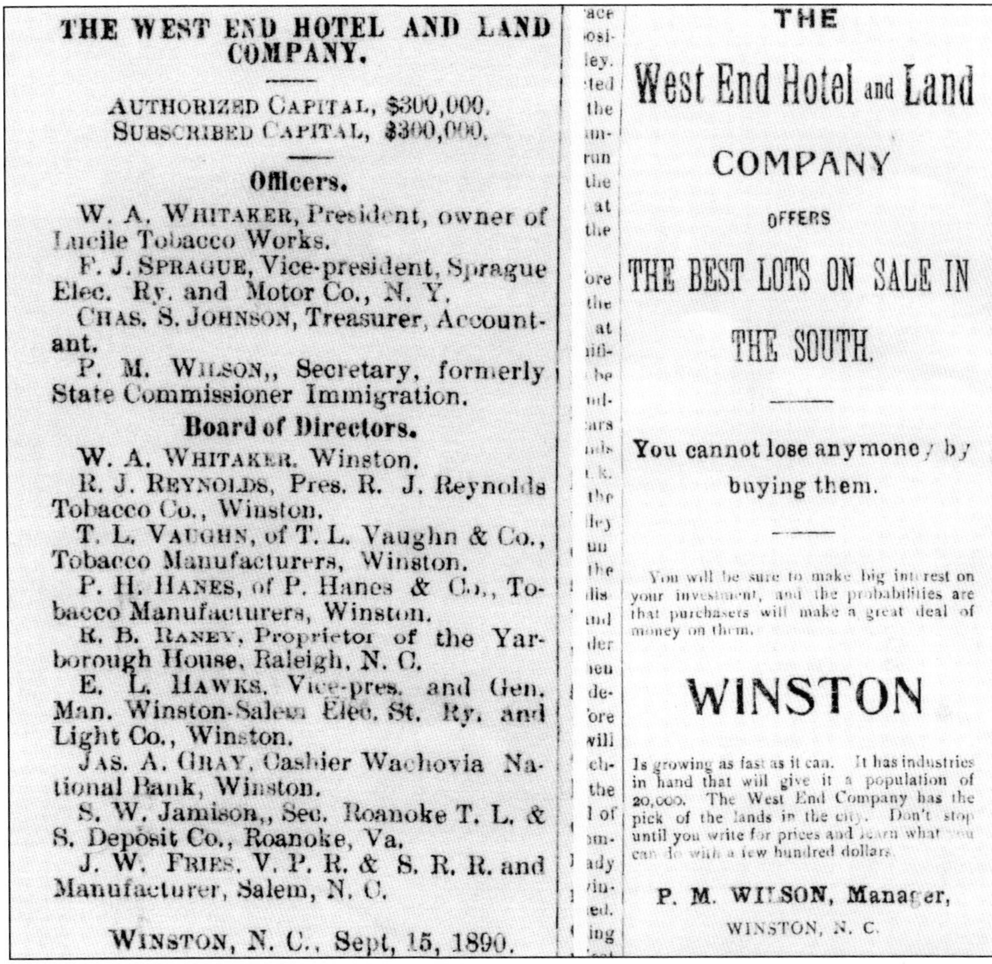

THE WEST END HOTEL AND LAND COMPANY.

AUTHORIZED CAPITAL, $300,000.
SUBSCRIBED CAPITAL, $300,000.

Officers.

W. A. WHITAKER, President, owner of Lucile Tobacco Works.
F. J. SPRAGUE, Vice-president, Sprague Elec. Ry. and Motor Co., N. Y.
CHAS. S. JOHNSON, Treasurer, Accountant.
P. M. WILSON,, Secretary, formerly State Commissioner Immigration.

Board of Directors.

W. A. WHITAKER, Winston.
R. J. REYNOLDS, Pres. R. J. Reynolds Tobacco Co., Winston.
T. L. VAUGHN, of T. L. Vaughn & Co., Tobacco Manufacturers, Winston.
P. H. HANES, of P. Hanes & Co., Tobacco Manufacturers, Winston.
R. B. RANEY, Proprietor of the Yarborough House, Raleigh, N. C.
E. L. HAWKS, Vice-pres. and Gen. Man. Winston-Salem Elec. St. Ry. and Light Co., Winston.
JAS. A. GRAY, Cashier Wachovia National Bank, Winston.
S. W. Jamison,, Sec. Roanoke T. L. & S. Deposit Co., Roanoke, Va.
J. W. FRIES, V. P. R. & S. R. R. and Manufacturer, Salem, N. C.

WINSTON, N. C., Sept, 15, 1890.

THE
West End Hotel and Land
COMPANY
OFFERS
THE BEST LOTS ON SALE IN THE SOUTH.

You cannot lose anymoney by buying them.

You will be sure to make big interest on your investment, and the probabilities are that purchasers will make a great deal of money on them.

WINSTON

Is growing as fast as it can. It has industries in hand that will give it a population of 20,000. The West End Company has the pick of the lands in the city. Don't stop until you write for prices and learn what you can do with a few hundred dollars.

P. M. WILSON, Manager,
WINSTON, N. C.

The prospectus for the resort says that properties of the West End Hotel and Land Company would be divided into 206 lots, most valued between $500 and $1,500. Terms were "one-third cash, one-third one year, one-third two years." "Winston is growing as fast as it can," the accompanying ad says. "You cannot lose any money buying them." (Courtesy NCC/UNC.)

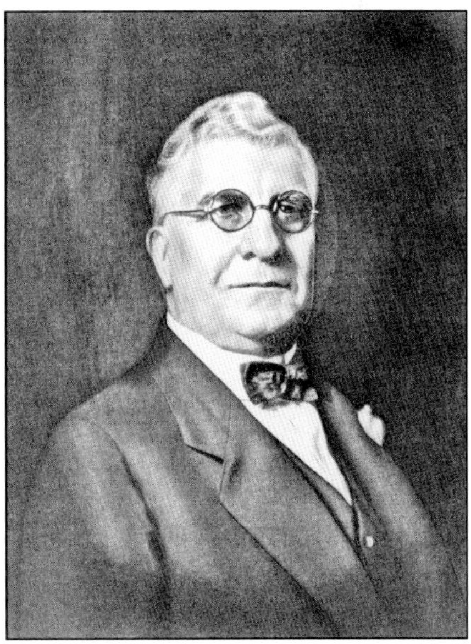

The company enlisted Col. Jacob Lott Ludlow, the city engineer shown here as head of the chamber of commerce in the 1910s, to design the streets for the new development. Ludlow followed the work of pioneer landscape architect Frederic Law Olmsted in crafting suburban streets that respected the local terrain rather than imposing a grid pattern. There is but one square block in the West End. (Courtesy FCPL.)

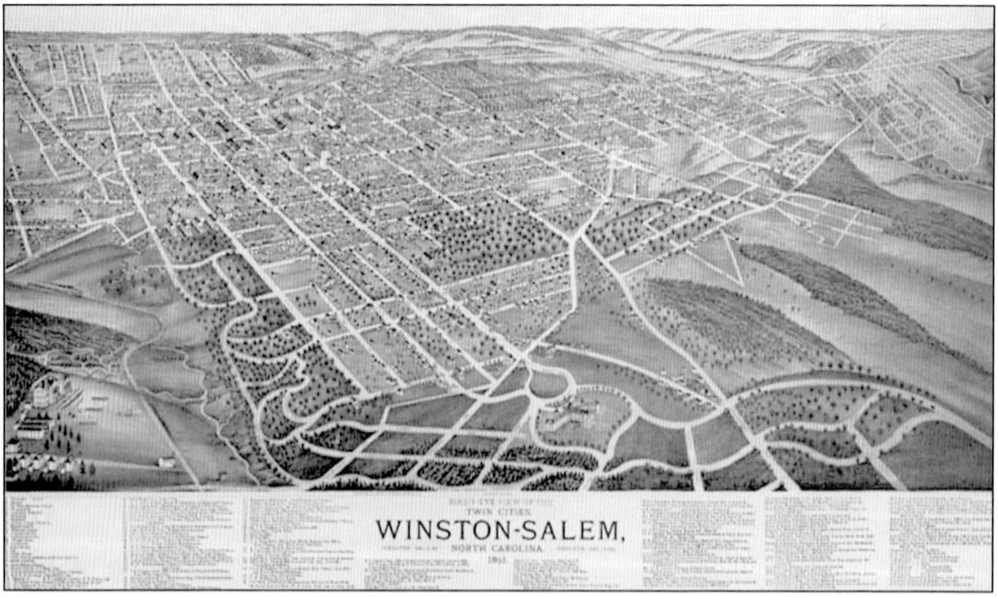

The leading entrepreneurs of the twin cities engaged the mapmakers Ruger and Stoner to do a bird's-eye view of Winston and Salem in 1891. They conveniently angled the view to highlight the most prominent real estate investment of the day, West End, with its resort hotel and serpentine surrounding streets. Anxious to market the hotel, the map shows the hotel structure as complete in 1891. In fact, it did not open for guests until May 1892. (Courtesy Library of Congress and NCSA.)

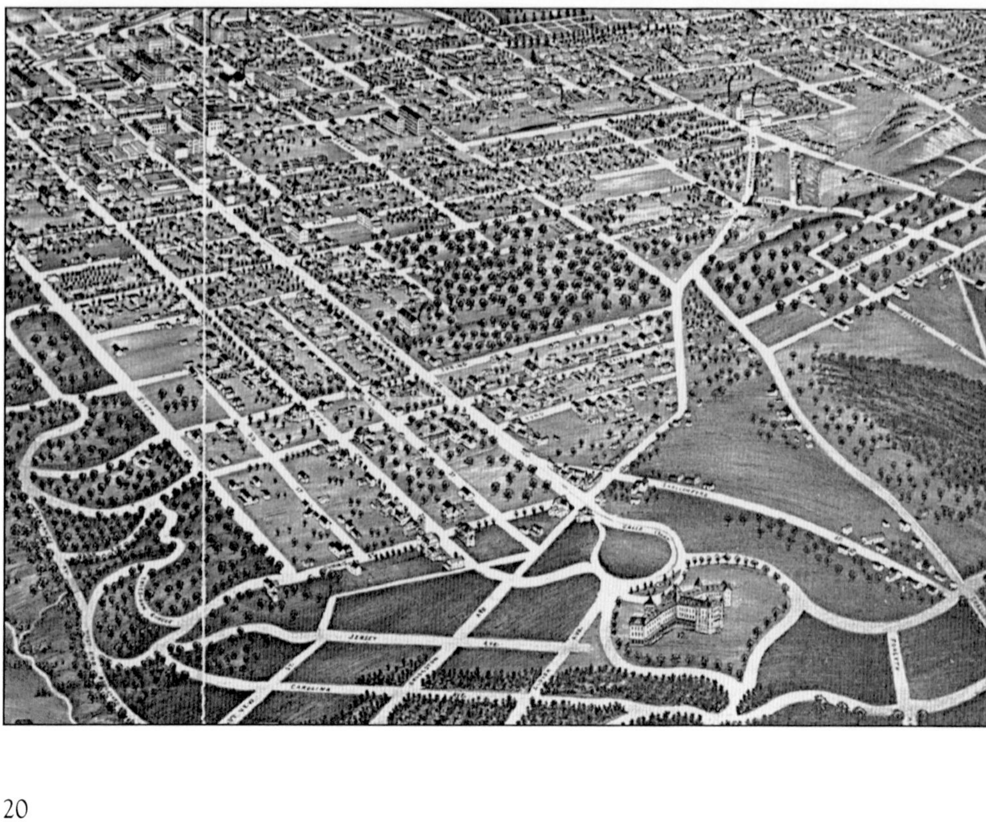

Section one of the 1891 plot map, north of Sixth Street between Spruce and Summit, included plans for two parks built around springs, Little Louise and The Springs. Terrace Heights, site of the Fries farmhouse, was reserved from the initial sale. Perhaps it would have been the location of another resort hotel had the development taken off. The lot was later split by Manly Street. Fries-Dun Circle was a road never built, while Zeb Vance Avenue became Seventh Street. (Courtesy NCC/UNC.)

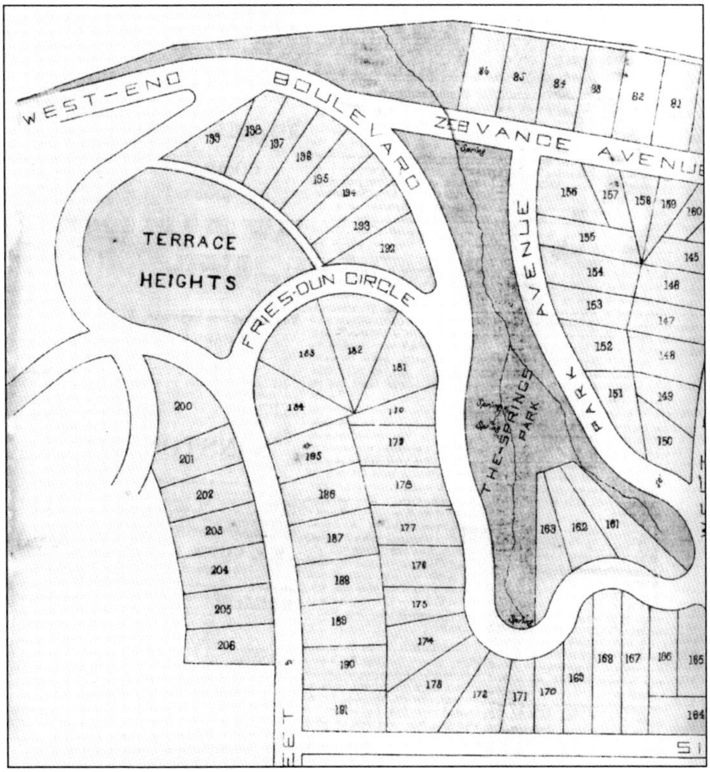

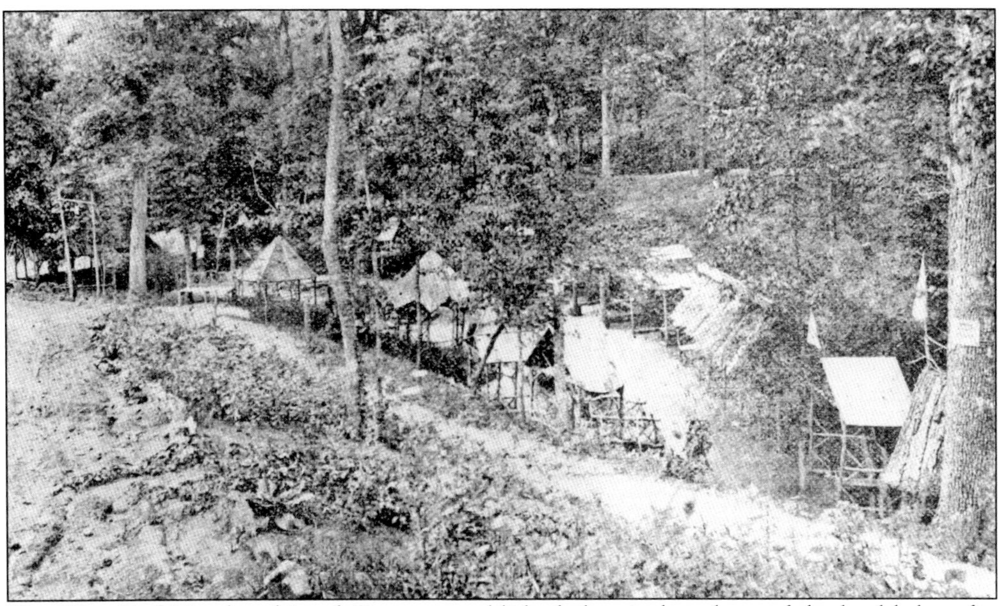

The West End Hotel and Land Company published chemical analyses of the health benefits of numerous springs in West End. Marienbad Springs, just northwest of town, is shown here in 1898. Not an elegant spa like its European namesake, Marienbad was still quite popular with locals. The Gray family history relates an undated social column describing Bess Gray and four wagons full of friends taking a hayride from downtown to Marienbad, arriving there after an hour (at hayride speed) for an evening's relaxation. (Courtesy NCC/UNC.)

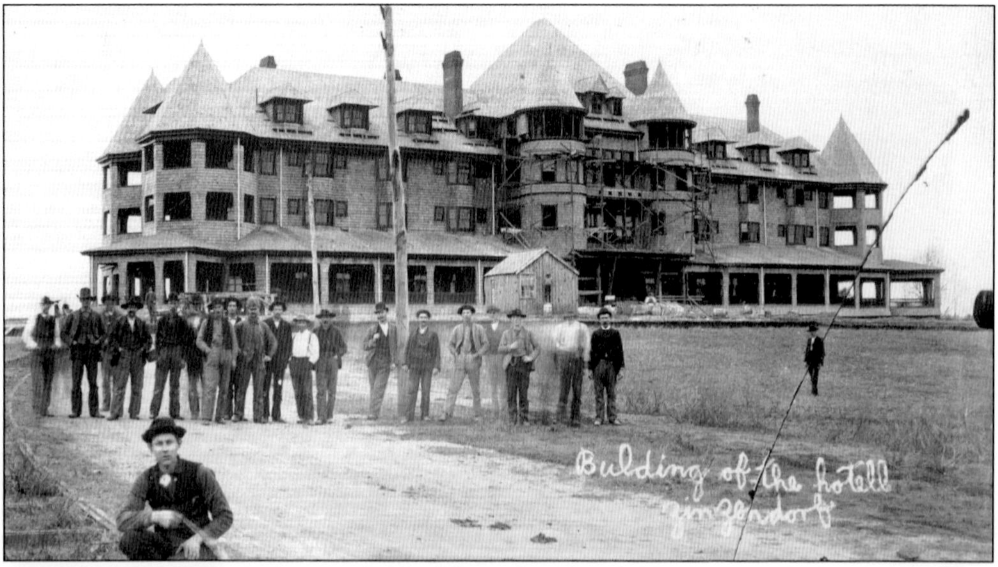

Construction workers are here in front of the resort's hotel, Hotel Zinzendorf, in late 1891 or early 1892. Count Nicholas von Zinzendorf was a wealthy landowner who in the early 1700s gave the Moravian Church refuge on his estate in Saxony. He sponsored the Moravian mission to America, which led to the founding of Moravian outposts in eastern Pennsylvania and in North Carolina's Piedmont. (Courtesy WHS/OS.)

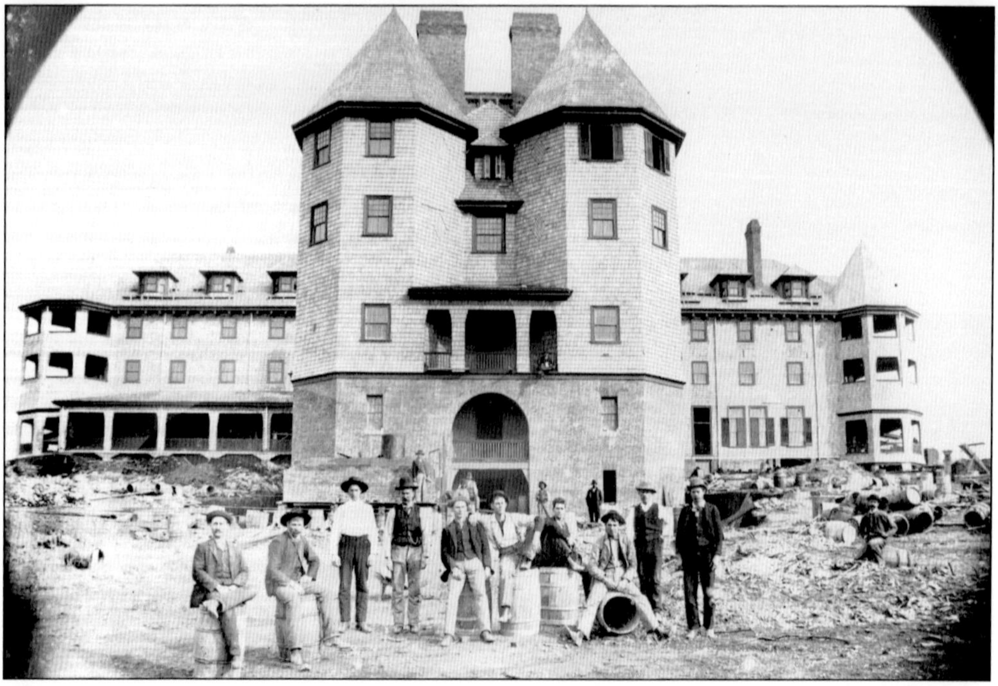

This photo of the rear of the Hotel Zinzendorf shows again the size of the hotel and its dramatic perch atop the West End ridge. Advertisements for the resort tout the view of the Blue Ridge Mountains from its rooms and the cooling breezes that waft up the hillside. "Fine quail shooting on the railroads and turnpikes leading into and out of town," it also noted. (Courtesy WHS/OS.)

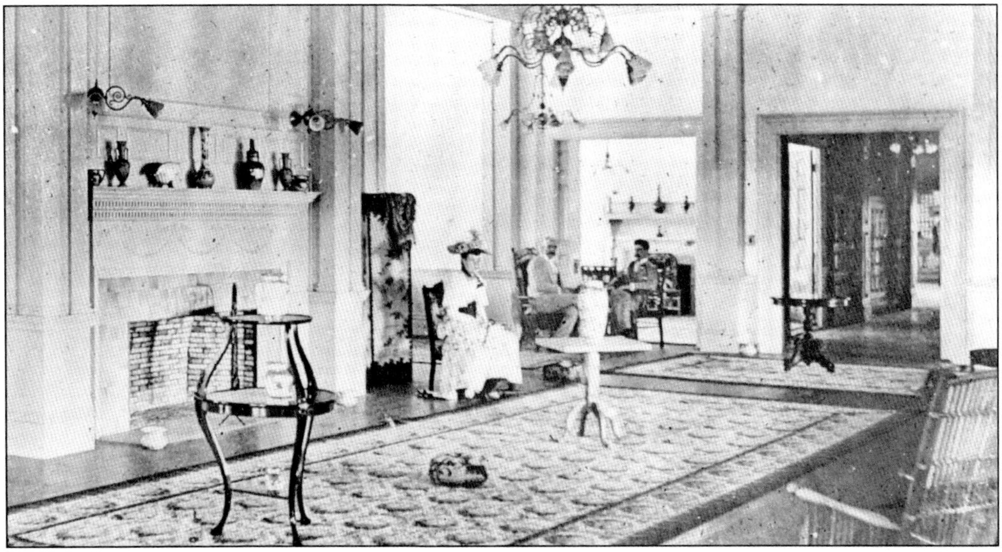

L.W. Scoville of New York City was hired to be general manager of the Zinzendorf. The hotel opened for Commencement Weekend at Salem College on May 25, 1892. For the summer season, a 12-piece orchestra played twice a day in the lobby of the hotel. Playlists included Mendelssohn and Bach, Strauss's "Blue Danube," and the North Carolina state song, "The Old North State." (Courtesy WHS/OS.)

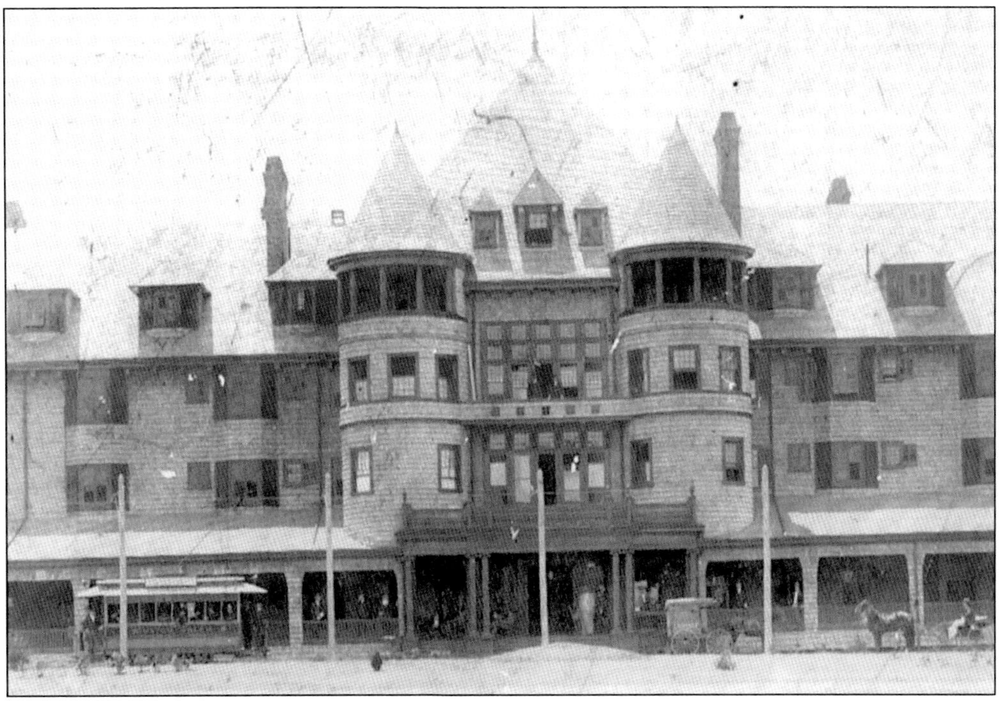

Designed by Boston architects Wheelwright and Haven, the hotel featured an 18-foot-wide front porch; some rooms were $3 a day. As this 1892 photo shows, in addition to front-door trolley service, the hotel ran its own express carriage from the town train station. Advertisements say temperatures at the hotel averaged 40 in the winter and 80 in the summer. Locals today might not vouch for those numbers. . . . (Courtesy MA.)

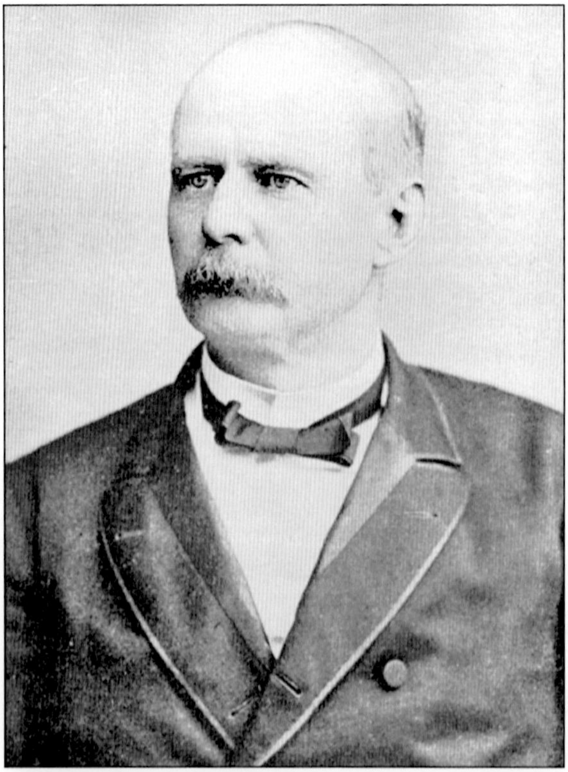

The most famous guest at the Zinzendorf arrived in September: Democratic vice presidential candidate Adlai Stevenson. Grover Cleveland tapped Stevenson, grandfather of the 1950s presidential candidate, as he sought to recapture the White House from Benjamin Harrison. Ads for his visit invited people to watch Stevenson parade from the Zinzendorf over to a town barbecue for 20,000 people. (Courtesy the author.)

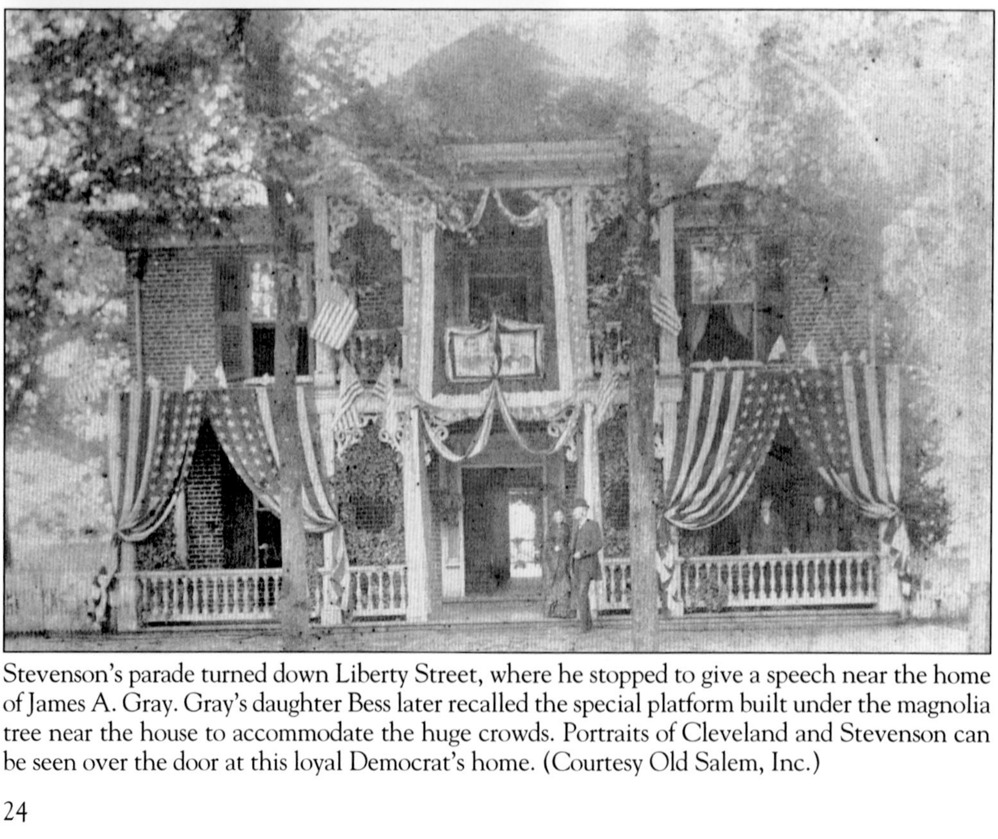

Stevenson's parade turned down Liberty Street, where he stopped to give a speech near the home of James A. Gray. Gray's daughter Bess later recalled the special platform built under the magnolia tree near the house to accommodate the huge crowds. Portraits of Cleveland and Stevenson can be seen over the door at this loyal Democrat's home. (Courtesy Old Salem, Inc.)

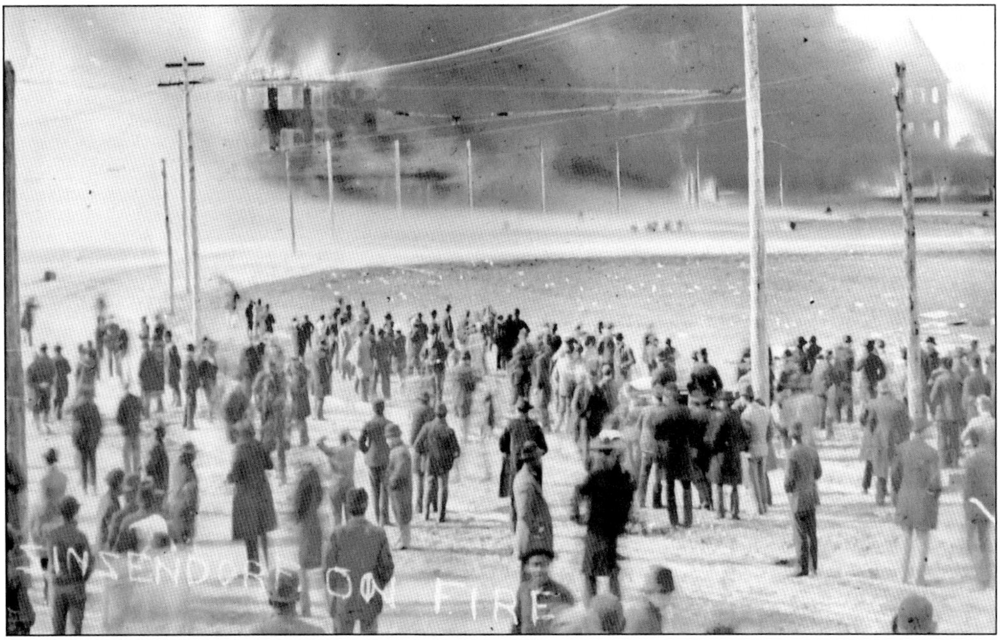

On Thanksgiving Day, November 24, 1892, as hotel guests were preparing to enjoy a noontime feast, a fire broke out near the laundry room in the Zinzendorf. Guests scrambled outside with belongings as firefighters and volunteers raced to the scene, but there was insufficient water pressure to fight the inferno that enveloped the wood and cedar-shake structure. Within two hours, the Hotel Zinzendorf was gone. (Courtesy of WCCA.)

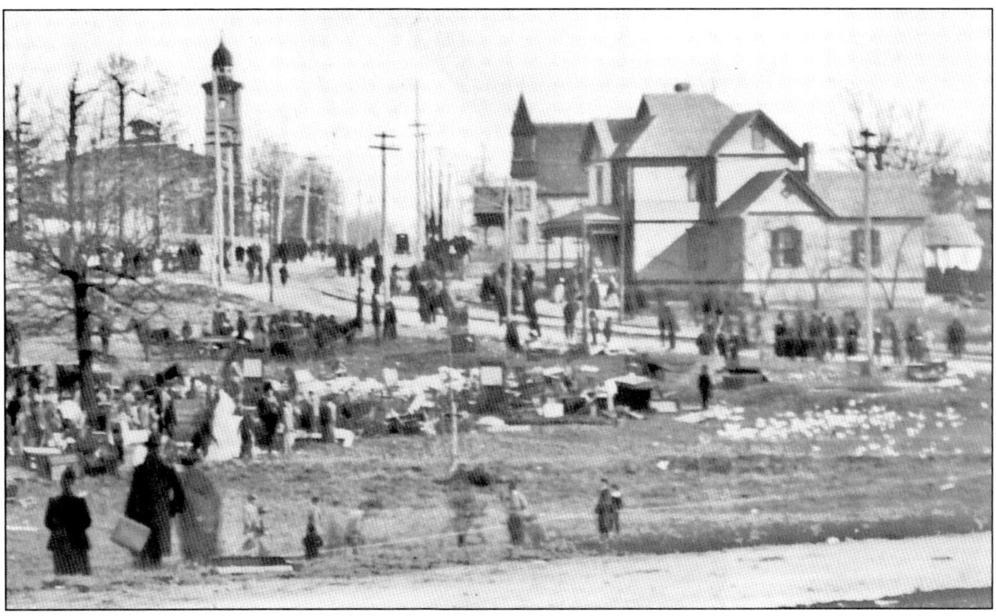

Hotel furnishings are scattered here in Grace Court directly opposite Hotel Zinzendorf. At right, along Fourth Street is a trail of returning onlookers, many of whom left midday holiday church services to race toward the fire. The tower of the former Winston Graded School, then West End Graded School, can be seen at the left along Fourth Street; the steeple of St. Leo's Catholic Church is at right. (Courtesy WCCA.)

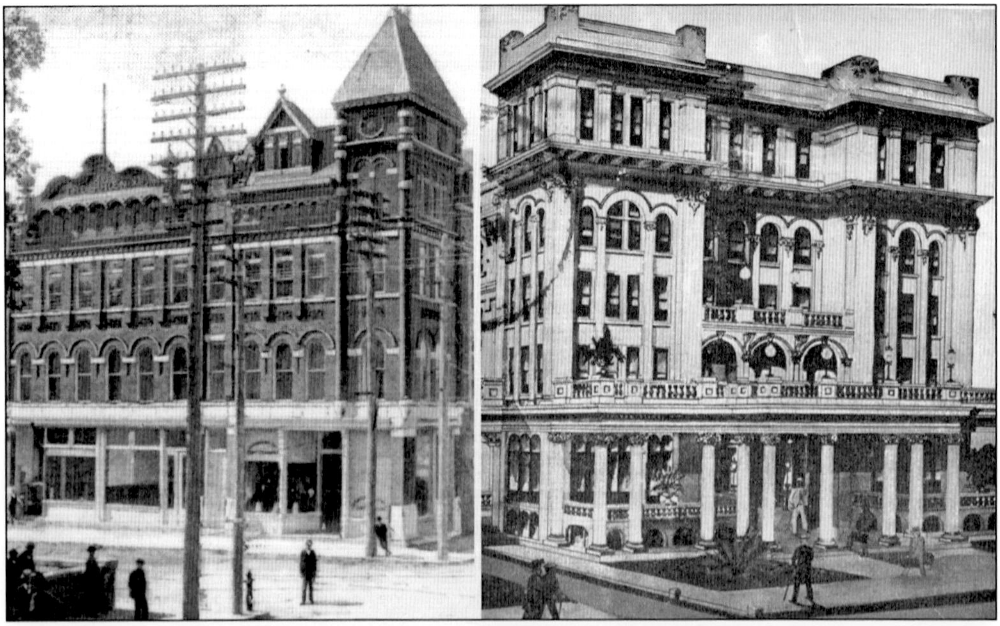

The *Union Republican* paper promised, "Hotel Zinzendorf, like the phoenix, will rise from the ashes." Tellingly, the next major hotel to open was the Hotel Phoenix in 1895 (at left), built where another fire gutted several blocks of downtown only weeks before the Zinzendorf blaze. Another Hotel Zinzendorf (right)—no spa resort—opened along Third Street in 1906 and was a part of downtown until the 1970s. (Courtesy NCC/UNC and the author.)

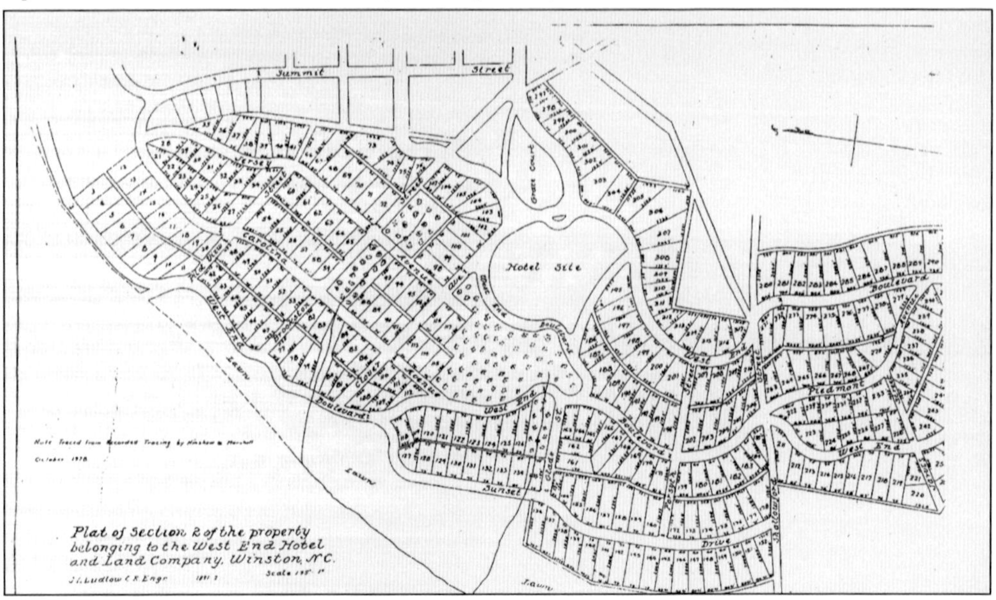

The Zinzendorf was insured for $100,000, yet losses exceeded $125,000. The Panic of 1893 limited capital available for rebuilding, and town ordinances changed to prohibit wooden hotels. Therefore, West End Hotel and Land Company officials concentrated on the sale of lots. By 1900, most sold, though there was little actual development in Section Two of company properties, save for along the part of current Fourth Street shown here as West End Boulevard. (Courtesy Forsyth County Register of Deeds Office.)

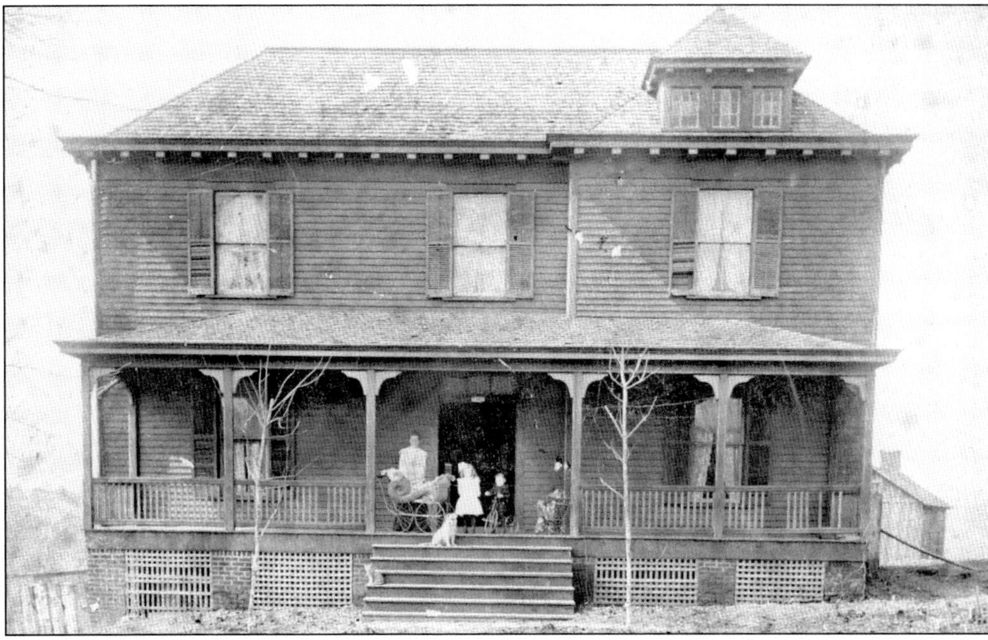

The Peter Brame house was built as an outpost at 915 West End Boulevard near Shallowford Road (later First Street) in 1895. Insurance salesman John Still purchased the house for his young family in 1902. Here on the porch is his wife, Eva, with baby Nelson, daughter Viola, and son Garland. At the time of the photo, this was the only house on the block. (Courtesy John Still.)

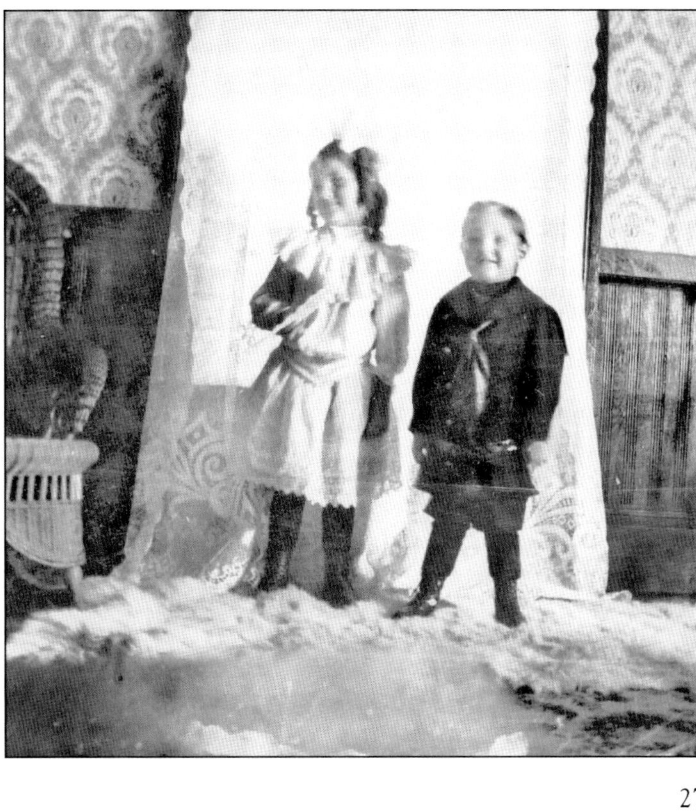

Here are the two oldest Still children, Viola and Garland, inside the home. Note the beadboard paneling and the Victorian wallpaper. The home's current owners uncovered the beadboard in a recent renovation. (Courtesy John Still.)

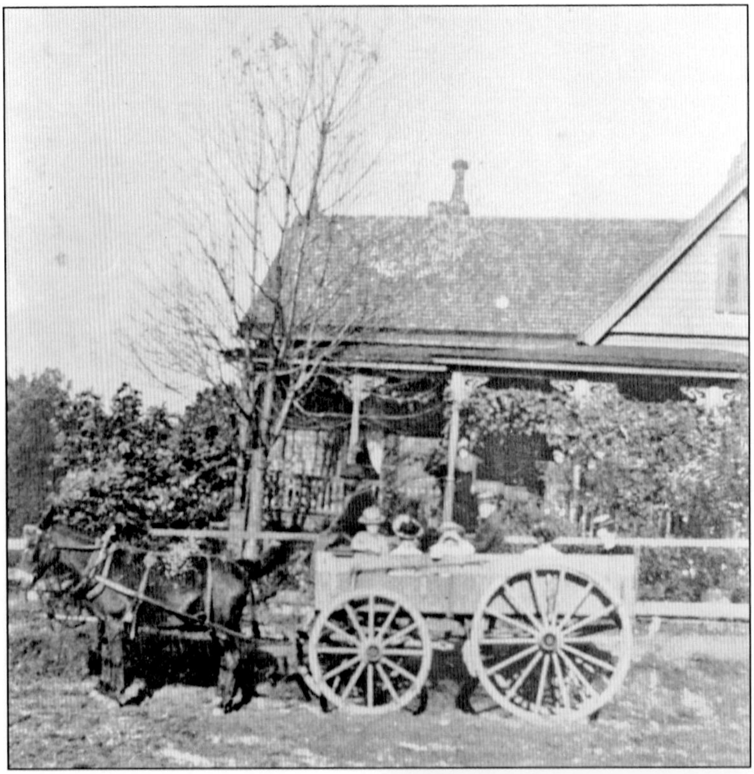

Although Col. Francis H. Fries's Wachovia Loan and Trust Company would not form as a joint-stock company until 1893, Colonel Fries hired Andrew Mickle as the company's first employee in 1891. In 1892, bookkeeper Mickle built this house at what was then the very end of Fifth Street, number 927. (Courtesy of Barbara Garrison and Donna and Andrew Mickle.)

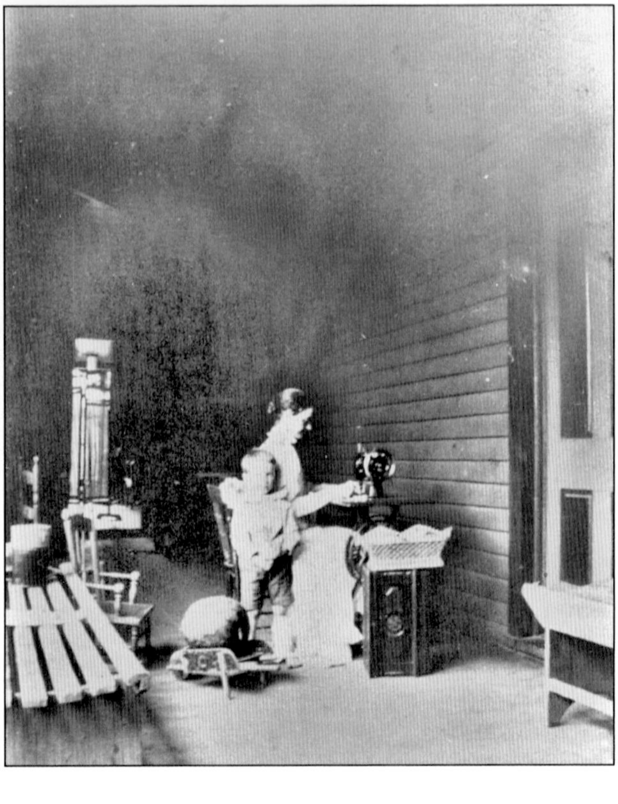

Here, Margaret Mickle works at the sewing machine in the interior of her home while her son John watches. A watermelon in his toy wheelbarrow cart lies close by. (Courtesy of Barbara Garrison and Donna and Andrew Mickle.)

Robina Mickle, Andrew's sister, walks her bicycle past next-door neighbor Ida Miller Galloway's house at 923 West Fifth. Robina was the independent-minded one in her family, a talented writer of her family's early days in West End. Around the corner on Summit Street, attorney John Buxton's daughter caused a minor scandal by riding astride her horse rather than sidesaddle, as "proper ladies" were to do. (Courtesy of Barbara Garrison and Donna and Andrew Mickle.)

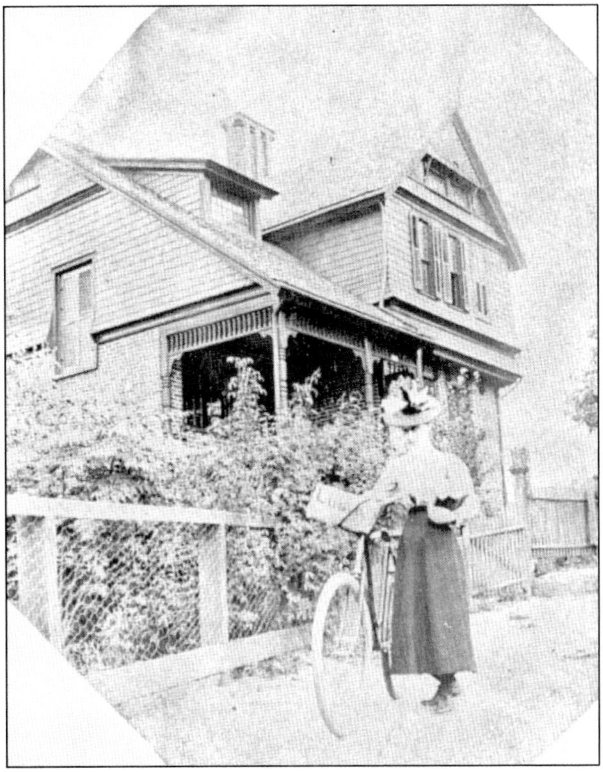

The neighborhood grocery for West Enders in those days was in an unusual, triangular-shaped building at the corner of Fourth and Shallowford (later Burke) Streets. J.W. Joyner was the proprietor of the store, shown here in 1899. In 1906, he sold the store to R.B. Crawford and stayed on as an employee. (Courtesy FCPL.)

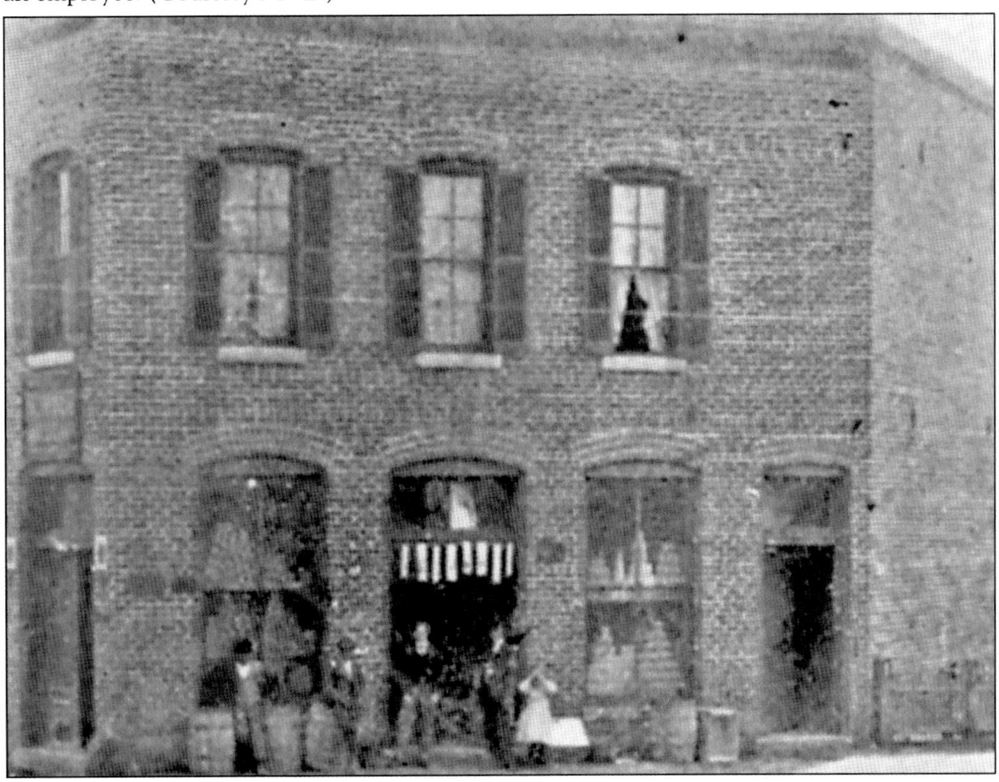

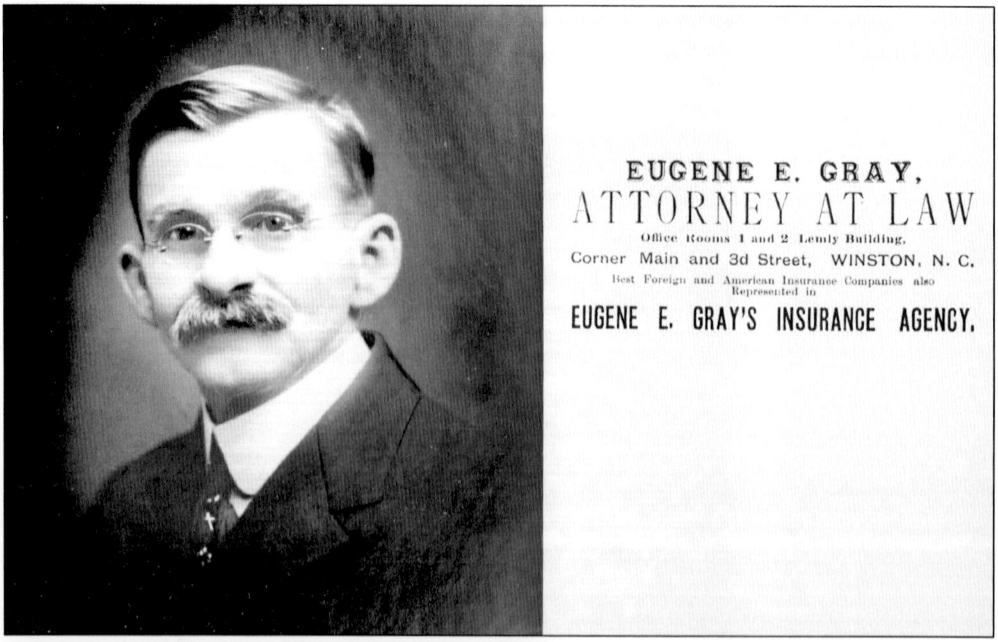

Eugene E. Gray, brother of banker James A., was an attorney and mayor of Winston in the 1890s. The Grays were literally the first family in Winston. Eugene's father, Robert, purchased the first land in town from the Moravians in 1849. Eugene's brother Dr. Robah F. Gray was said to be the first child born in Winston. Eugene Gray's home stood at the southwest corner of Fifth and Broad. (Courtesy of FCPL.)

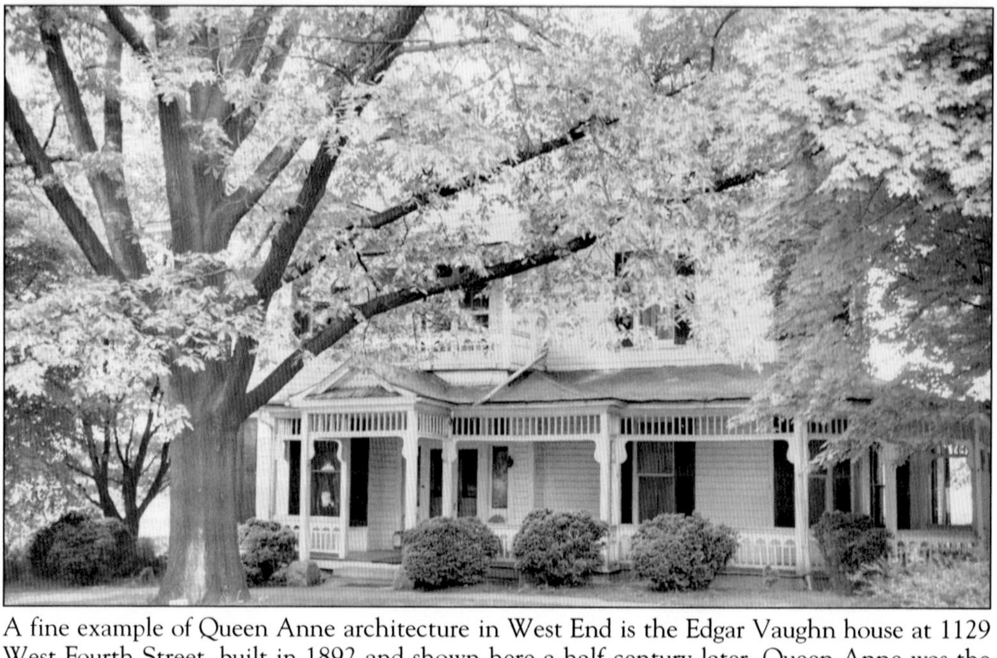

A fine example of Queen Anne architecture in West End is the Edgar Vaughn house at 1129 West Fourth Street, built in 1892 and shown here a half-century later. Queen Anne was the most popular of the Victorian house styles, eclectic and large, with great variety in window and roof detailing. Vaughn was a wholesale grocer and one of the first Winston-Salem aldermen in 1913. (Courtesy of FCPL.)

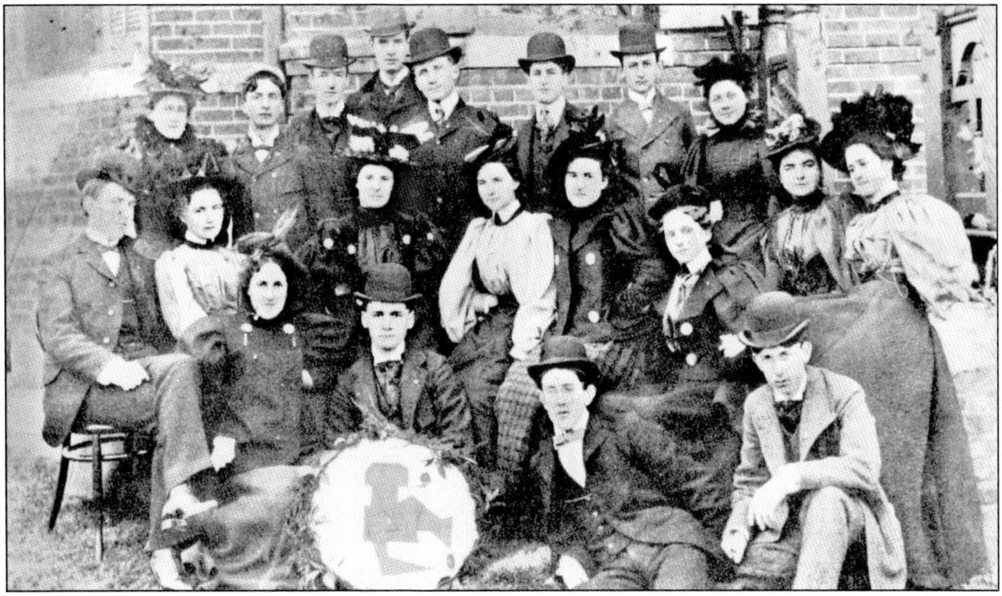

The areas along Fourth, Fifth, and Summit Streets, entering the company properties, and in Section One along "the Boulevard" (West End Boulevard) and Spring Streets, were the first properties in the historic district to be developed. Here is a gathering of the "L-cat Club," alumni of the University of North Carolina, in front of the Frank Miller home at the northwest corner of Fifth and Summit around 1905. (Courtesy FCPL.)

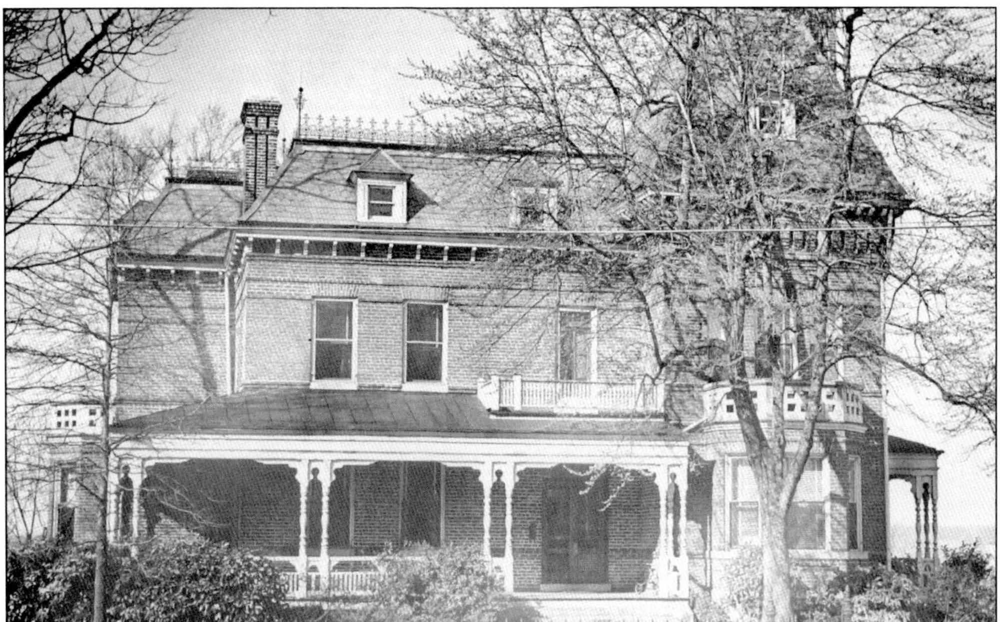

Miller's construction company, Miller Brothers, built many wooden structures in Winston and Salem in the 1880s and 1890s but went under during the Panic of 1893. Miller died not long thereafter. Most neighbors knew this as the home of A. Clint Miller, a real estate developer for whom both the town's first airport and Miller Park were named. Only the carriage house in the rear of the home survives from the construction. (Courtesy FCPL.)

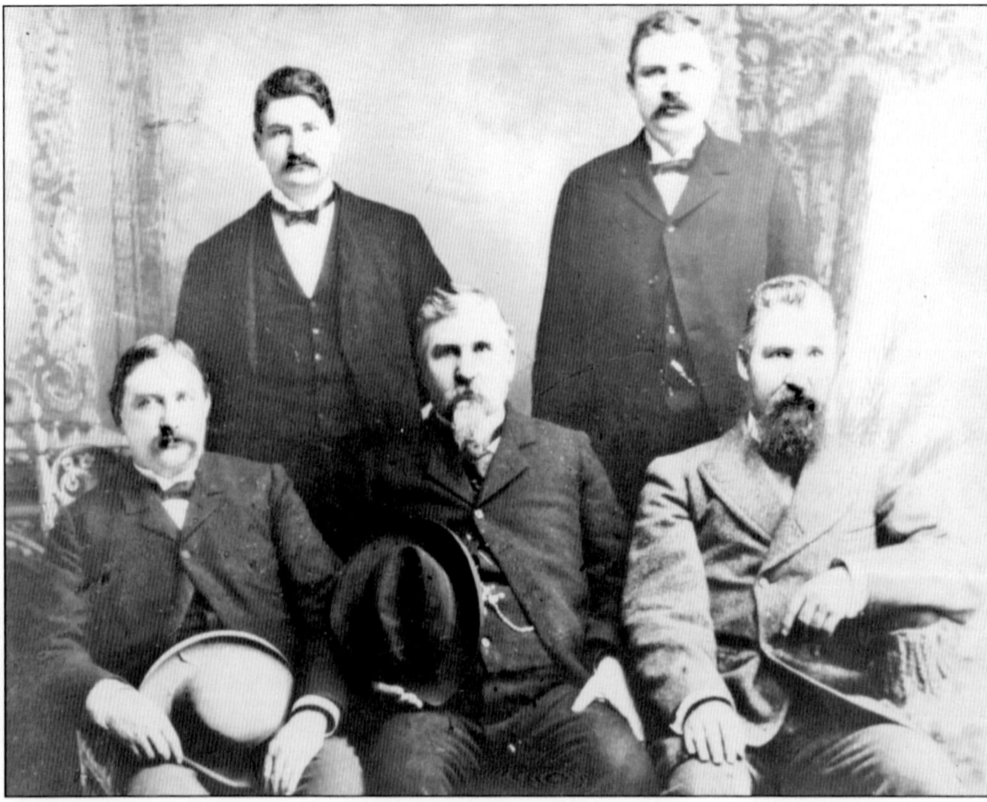

Pictured from left to right are the Reynolds brothers, tobacco entrepreneurs who had moved from Virginia as the Winston trade boomed: (seated) Hiram, Abram, and Richard Joshua; (standing) Walter and Will. The industry grew despite difficult economic times in the 1890s, but dramatic changes came at decade's end with Buck Duke's acquisition of rivals to his American Tobacco Company in Durham. Many local independent tobacco men were either forced out or bought out by R.J. Reynolds, whose firm was aligned with the Duke trust but who had secured the independence of his plug, fancy, and twist tobacco brands. (Above, courtesy Kate Bitting Reynolds Trust Photo Archive, hereafter listed as KBRT; below, courtesy NCSA.)

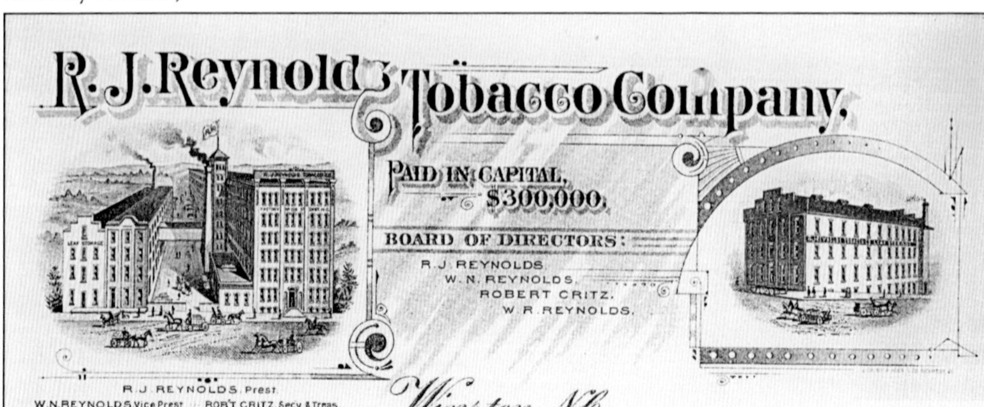

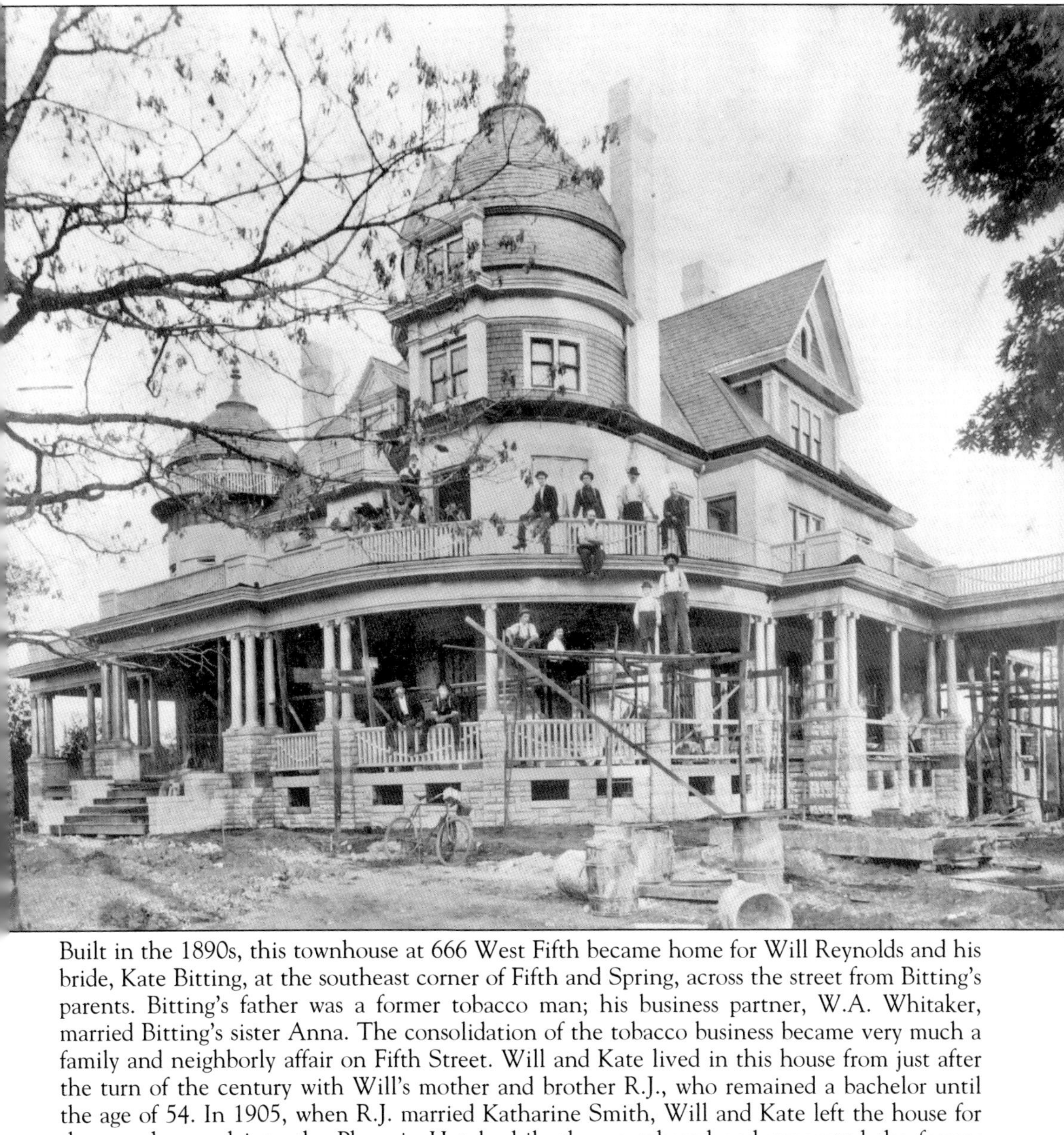

Built in the 1890s, this townhouse at 666 West Fifth became home for Will Reynolds and his bride, Kate Bitting, at the southeast corner of Fifth and Spring, across the street from Bitting's parents. Bitting's father was a former tobacco man; his business partner, W.A. Whitaker, married Bitting's sister Anna. The consolidation of the tobacco business became very much a family and neighborly affair on Fifth Street. Will and Kate lived in this house from just after the turn of the century with Will's mother and brother R.J., who remained a bachelor until the age of 54. In 1905, when R.J. married Katharine Smith, Will and Kate left the house for them and moved into the Phoenix Hotel while they purchased and renovated the former M.N. Williamson property next door. (Courtesy Reynolda House, Museum of American Art; hereafter listed as RH/MAA.)

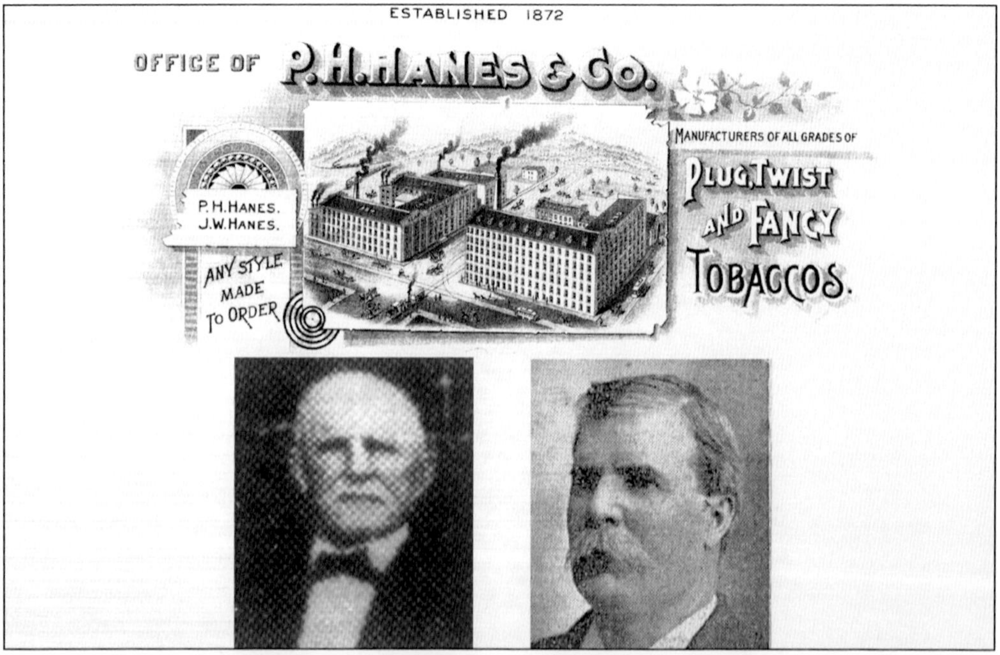

The largest tobacco manufacturer through the 1890s was not R.J. Reynolds, however, but P.H. Hanes Tobacco, run by brothers Pleasant Henderson Hanes and John W. Hanes. At century's end, Reynolds bought out the Hanes company for more than $750,000. Rather than retire contentedly, the brothers founded two new industries that diversified and nationalized the Winston reputation for manufacture. (Courtesy NCSA; The Children's Home of North Carolina, hereafter listed as CH; and FCPL.)

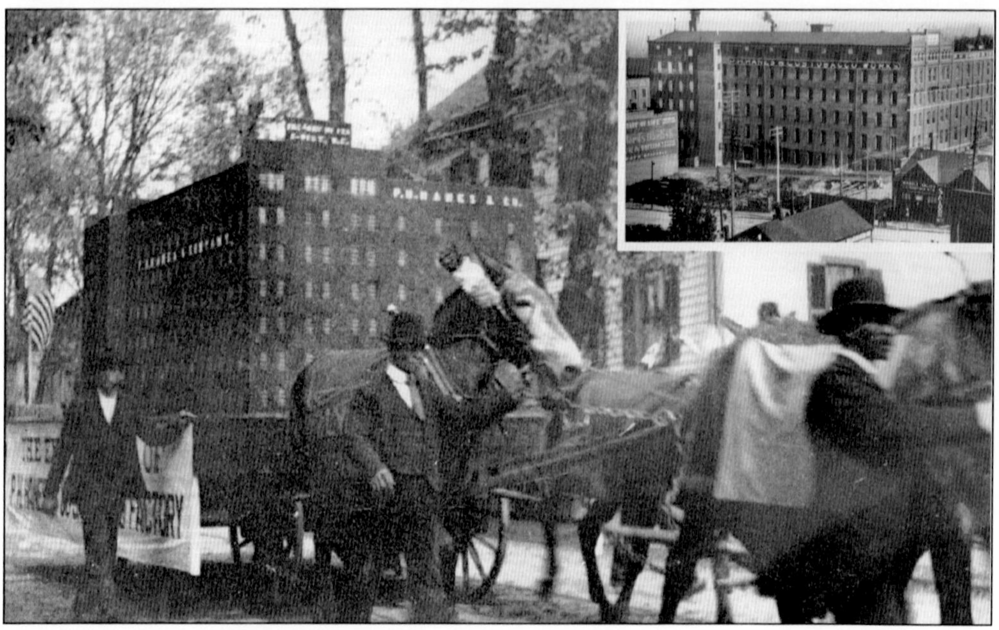

This picture of a parade float, likely taken during the Annual Tobacco Fair in either 1897 or 1898, shows the new six-story P.H. Hanes factory. A photo of the actual building is shown in the inset. (Courtesy WHS/OS and NCSA.)

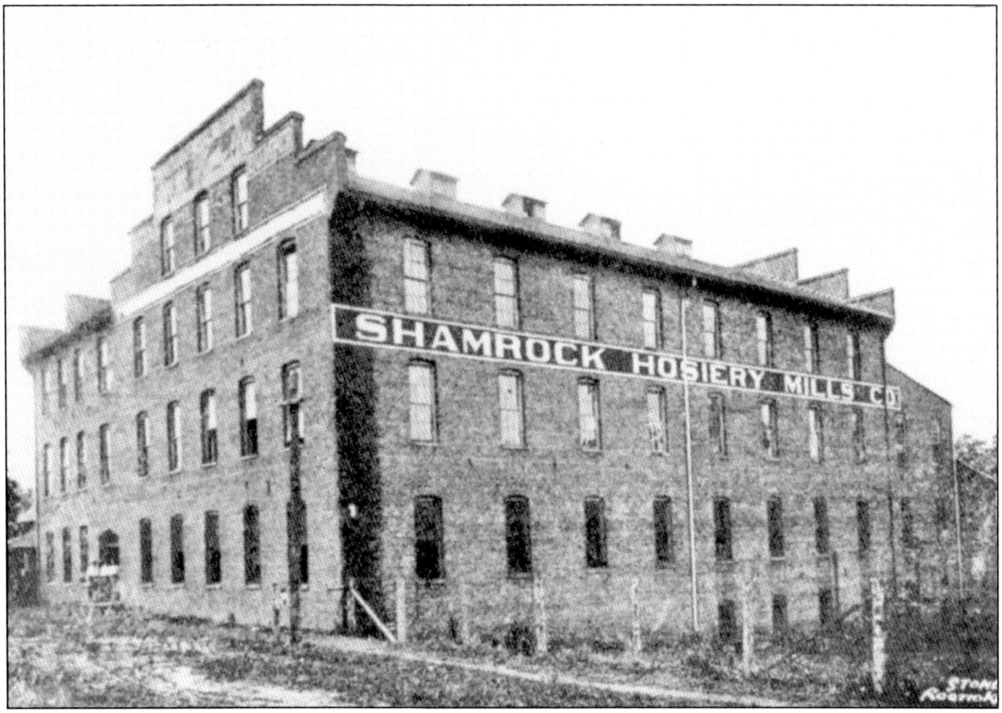

John W. Hanes took his share of sale proceeds and by 1902 had founded the Shamrock Hosiery Mills, initially manufacturing men's and children's socks. In 1911, this facility was replaced by the Sawtooth Building, familiar to local residents along Marshall Street at Second. (Courtesy FCPL.)

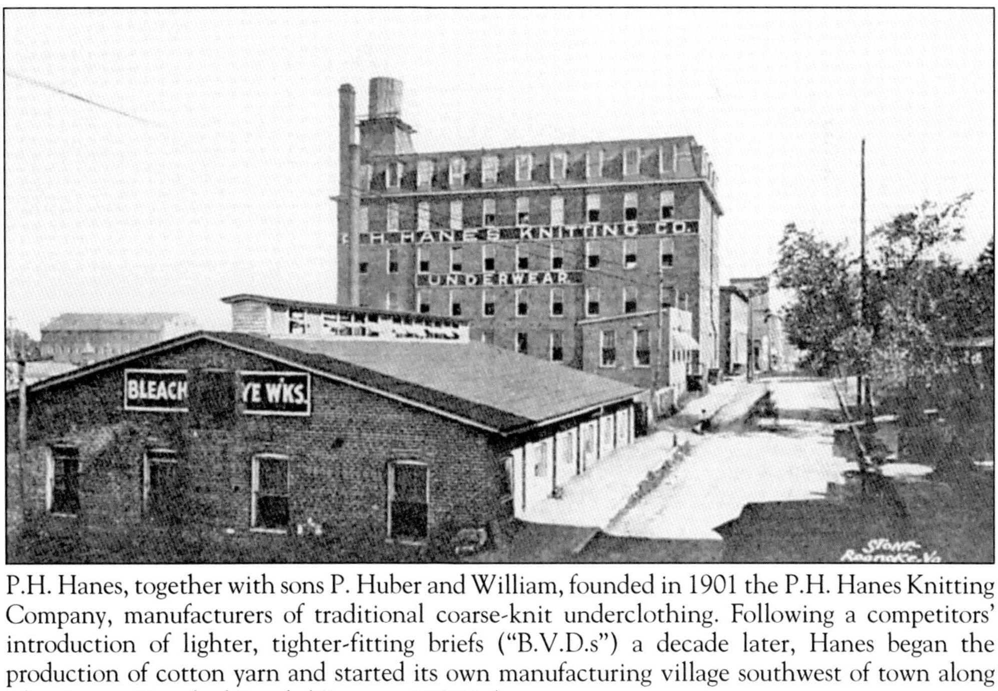

P.H. Hanes, together with sons P. Huber and William, founded in 1901 the P.H. Hanes Knitting Company, manufacturers of traditional coarse-knit underclothing. Following a competitors' introduction of lighter, tighter-fitting briefs ("B.V.D.s") a decade later, Hanes began the production of cotton yarn and started its own manufacturing village southwest of town along what is now Stratford Road. (Courtesy NCSA.)

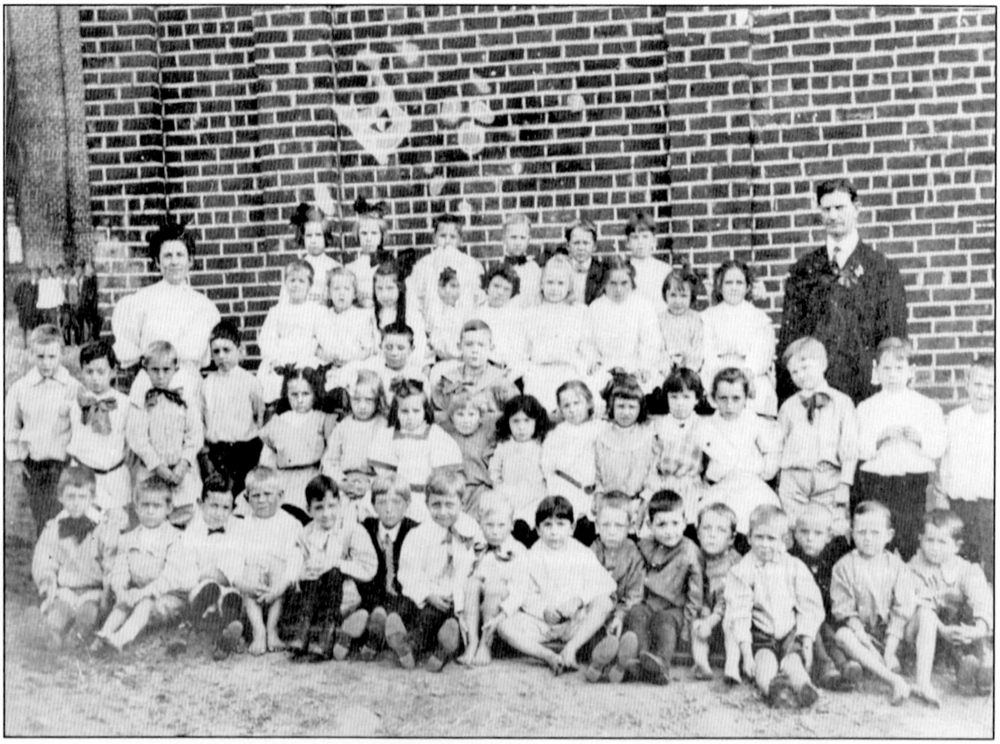

This class photo of third graders at West End Graded School, 1900–1901, shows that shoes were not yet a required item for students. (Courtesy FCPL.)

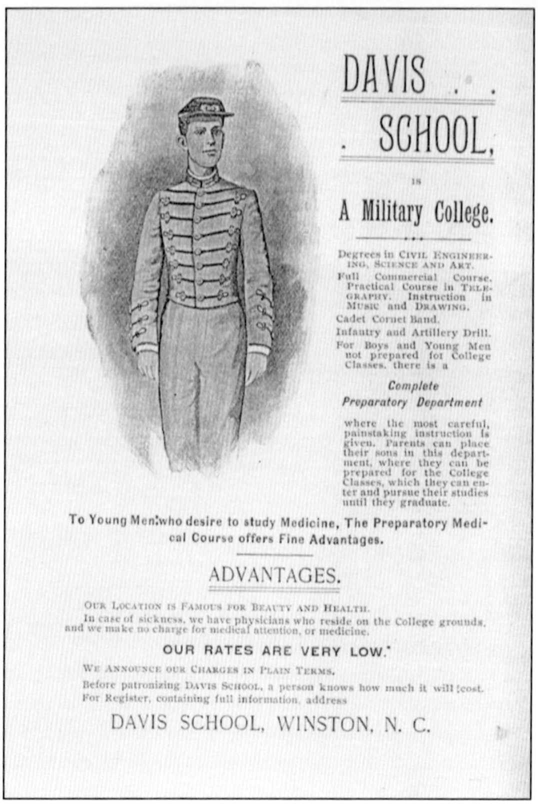

Davis School was a military school popular with local families. It had relocated from Lenoir County to a campus just west of West End in 1890. Davis cadets rushed in vain to help put out Zinzendorf's fire in 1892. The school's recurrent financial difficulties in the 1890s caused Davis's closure on more than one occasion. Finally, a major campus fire in 1904 destroyed all but a handful of its buildings, and the facility closed. (Courtesy FCPL.)

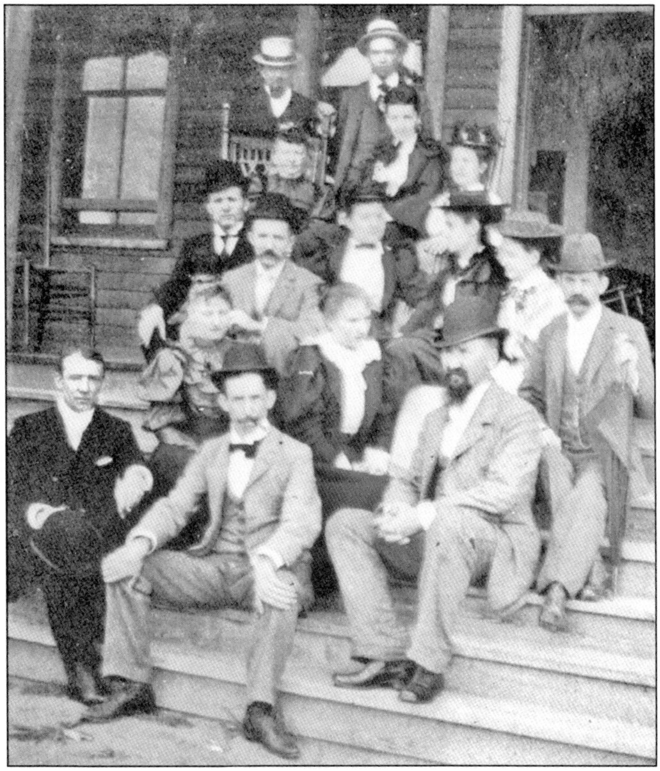

A summer tradition for many West Enders was a visit to Roaring Gap resort in Alleghany County. Begun in 1893 by manufacturer Hugh Chatham of Elkin with help from Winston-Salem banks, the 30-room Roaring Gap Hotel hosted frequent traveling parties until a fire in 1913. The area remains a popular retreat for Winston families. Among those pictured here are R.J. Reynolds at lower right, John W. Fries at back left, and W.A. Blair at center right. (Courtesy KBRT.)

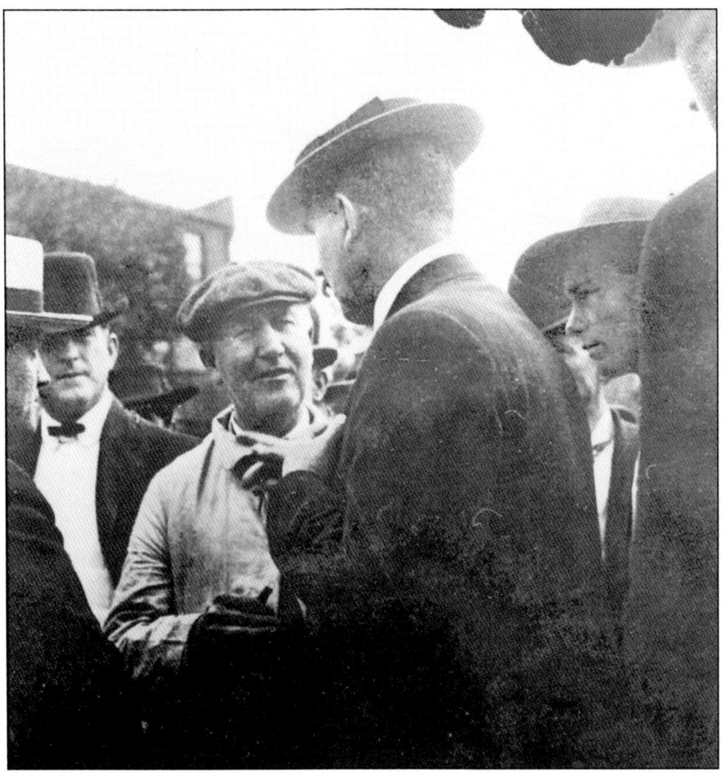

The local paper records this visitor in the newsboy cap in May 1906. Thomas Edison, attired in a motoring jacket, stopped to see the town and trolley for the afternoon on his way to Charlotte for business. The surprise visit of the man who had revolutionized modern life was literally front-page news the next day. (Courtesy FCPL.)

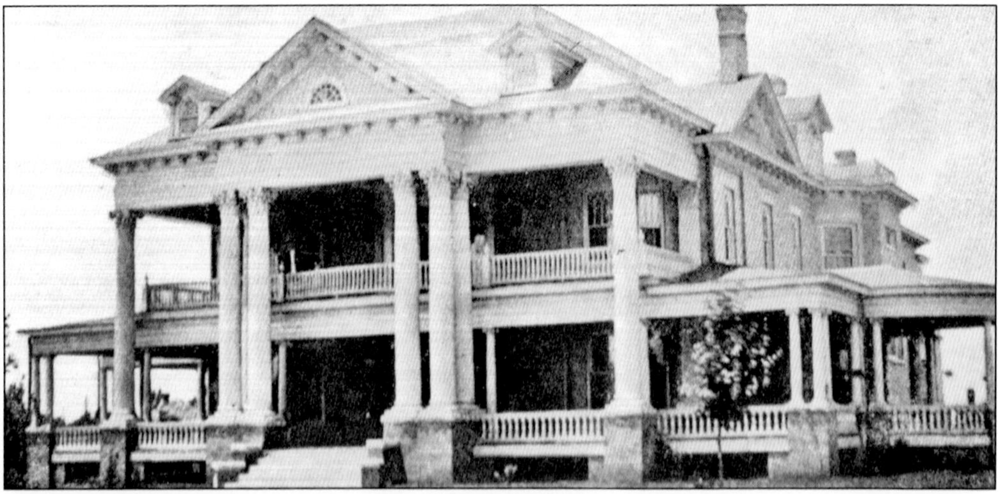

Adjacent to the site of the former Hotel Zinzendorf, John W. Hanes began work in 1900 on the new family home, Westerleigh. For over a half-century, the house dominated the vista looking west out Fourth Street. Shamrock Street today runs from Fourth to the alley behind the former Hanes property as a reminder of the owner and his mill. Hanes died at 54 in 1903, leaving it to "Mother Hanes," Anna Hodgin Hanes, to raise the couple's eight children. (Courtesy RH/MAA.)

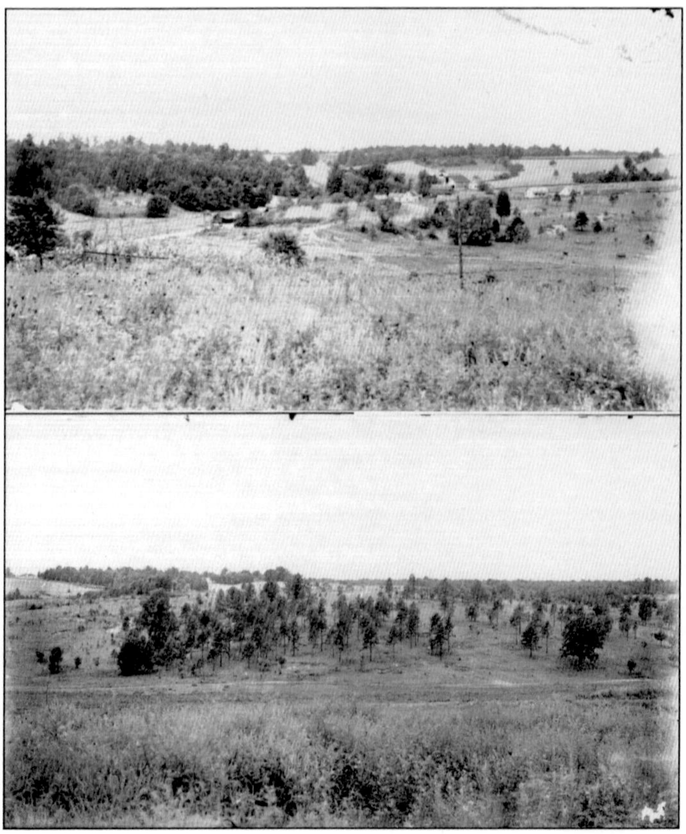

P.H. Hanes opened the West End Dairy just west of the West End Hotel and Land Company lands around 1906. His Holstein-Friesian cattle provided milk to much of the city for a time. The dairy barn can be seen at center right in the top picture, which was near the present corner of Cloverdale and First Streets. What was the "lawn" in the original West End development (later Hanes Park) can be seen in the bottom photograph, taken just to the right of the first. (Courtesy FCPL.)

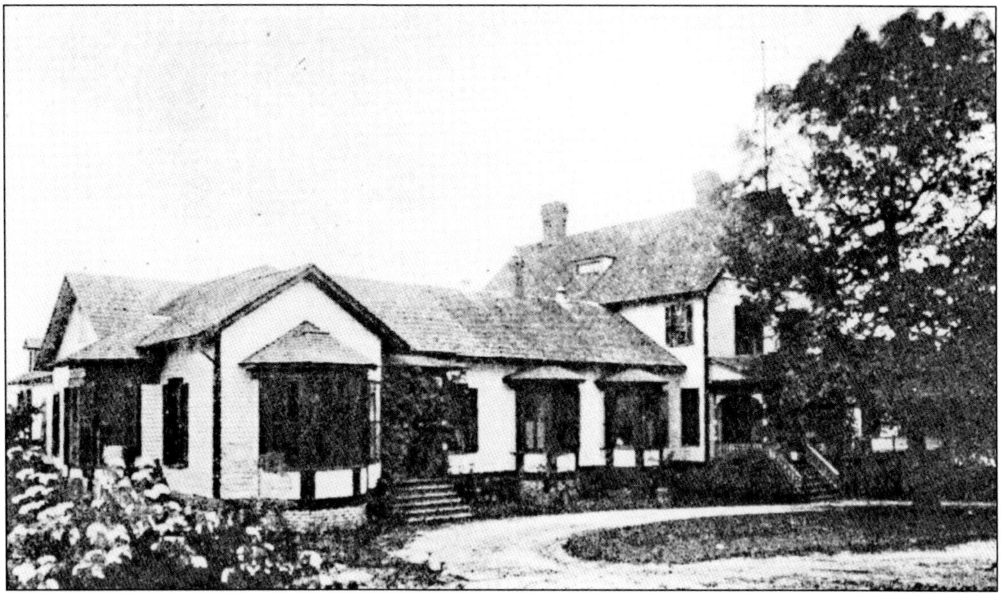

In 1895, Anna Hodgin Hanes and Kate Bitting Reynolds were two of a number of contributors who helped build the town's first hospital, Twin City Hospital, along Brookstown Avenue near Shallowford (First Street). (Courtesy FCPL.)

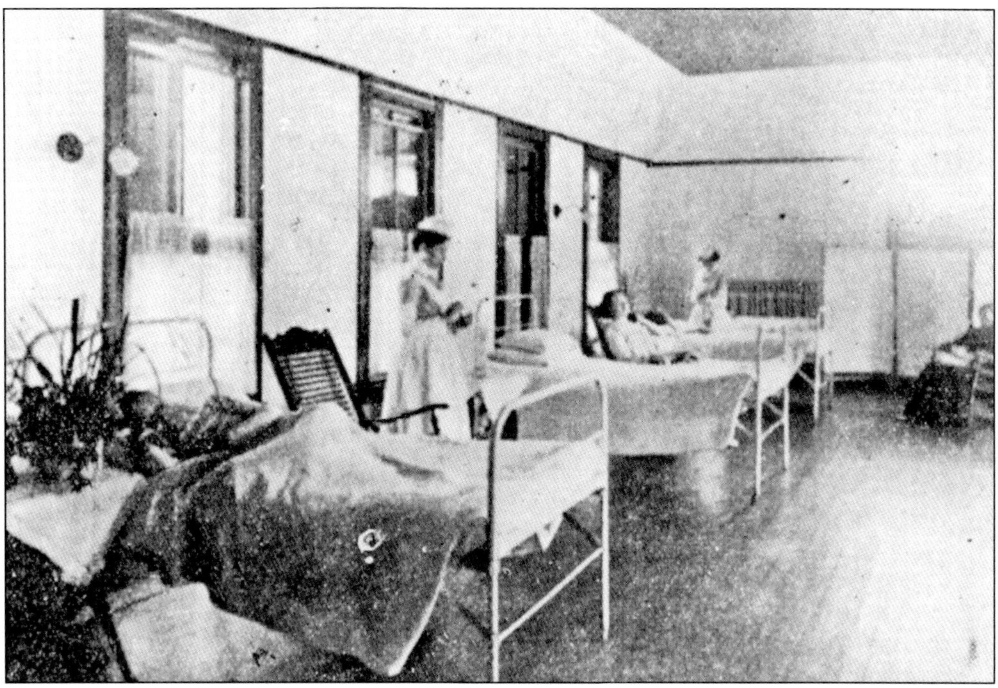

This picture from 1905 shows a ward inside Twin City Hospital and was part of an effort to recruit more funding for the hospital. A new city hospital was built in 1913, and Twin City closed. (Courtesy FCPL.)

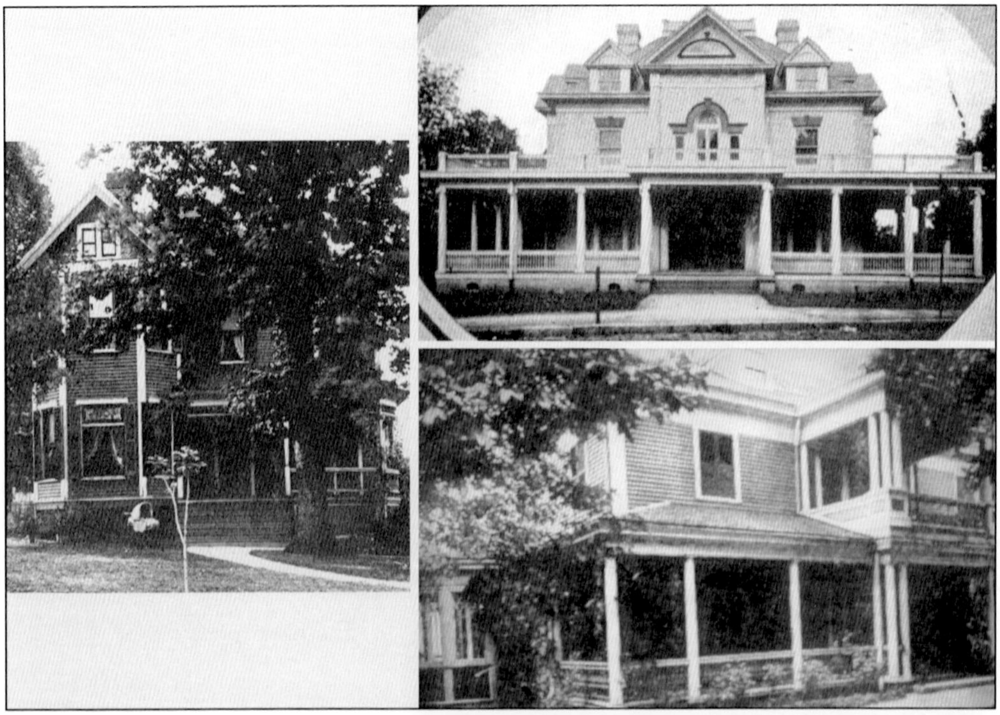

In 1905, the booklet "Winston-Salem: The Natural Geographic Gateway" advertised Winston-Salem industry and architecture. West End residents' factories, shops, and homes figured prominently. Above left is the A.B. Dangerfield house along Fifth Street; the John C. Coleman house at Sixth and Summit is at top right; and Mayor J.C. Buxton's home on Summit at Pilot View is in the lower right. Only the Coleman home still stands. (First two courtesy RH/MAA; third, St. Paul's Episcopal Church, hereafter listed as StP.)

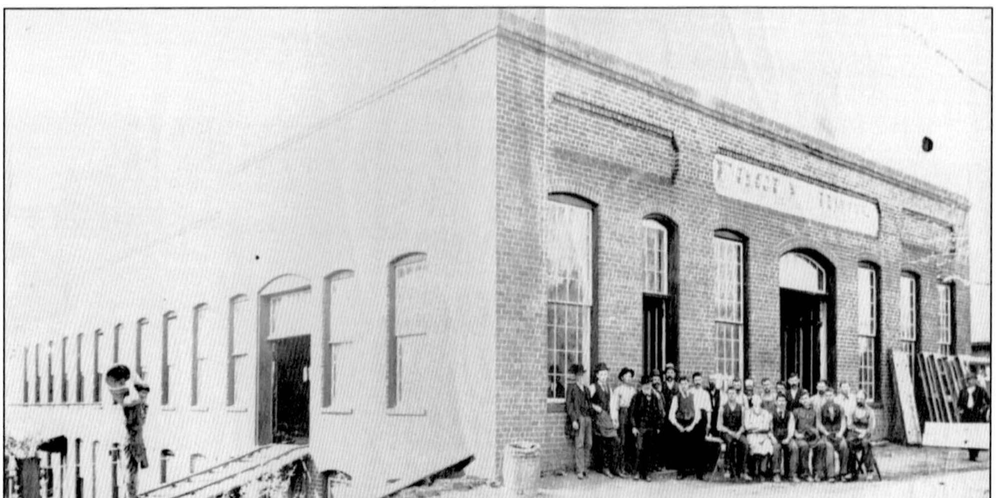

Fogle Brothers was a principal builder on many of West End's houses and for much of Winston-Salem construction from the 1890s onward. This 1890 photo shows the shop for the firm, located along Belews Creek Road near the present interchange of Business 40 and U.S. 52. (Courtesy WHS/OS.)

Clement Manly lived next to the Buxton home on Summit Street. He succeeded J.B. Watson as Robert Glenn's law partner in the early 1890s. Although he made a sizeable income representing insurance companies in the 1880s, in the aftermath of the Zinzendorf fire, Colonel Manly (as he was always known locally) represented the company in its claims against its insurers. (Courtesy St. Leo's Catholic Church.)

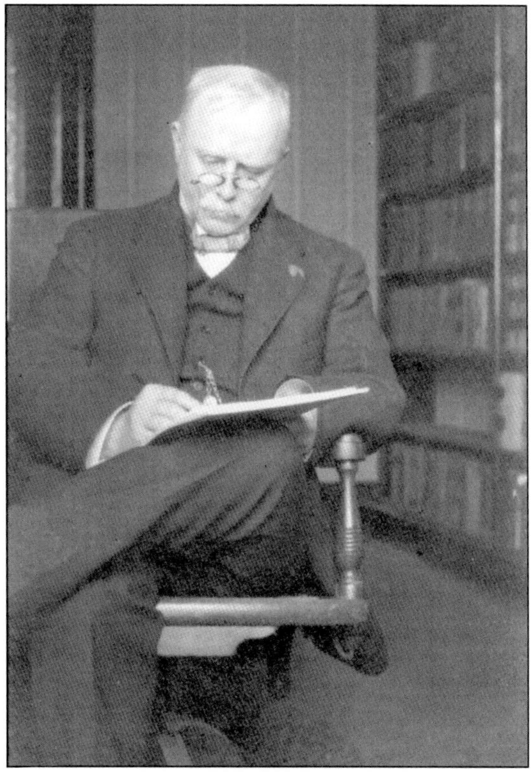

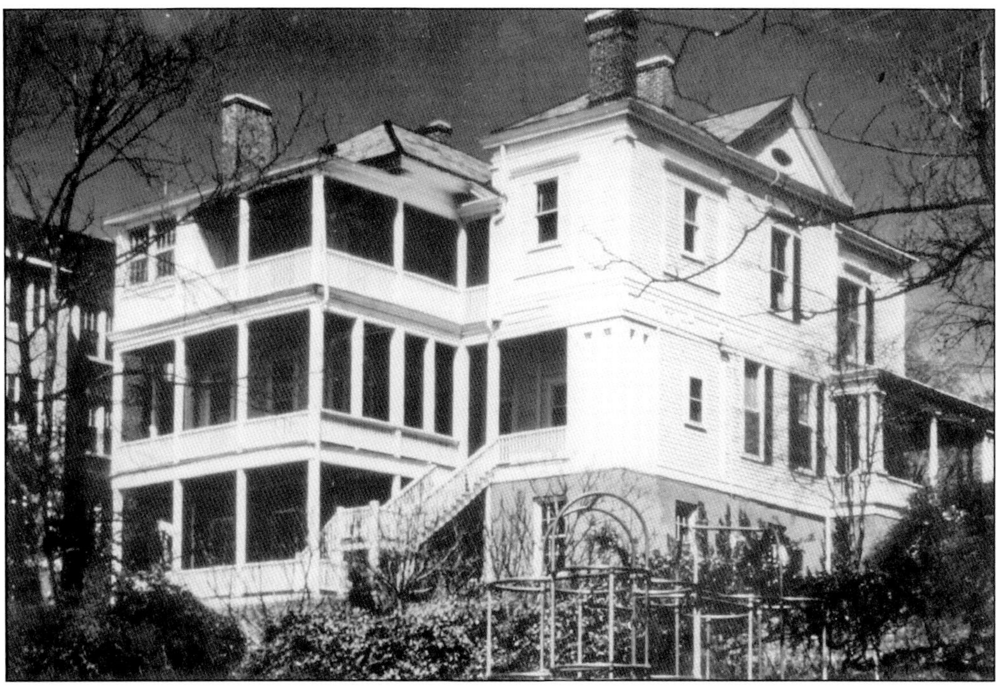

This is a view of the rear of Manly's Summit Street home about 1950. Homes at the crest of Summit Street faced a severe drop-off along either side of the street. The Manly home's three levels of back porch could be seen from quite a distance. (Courtesy StP.)

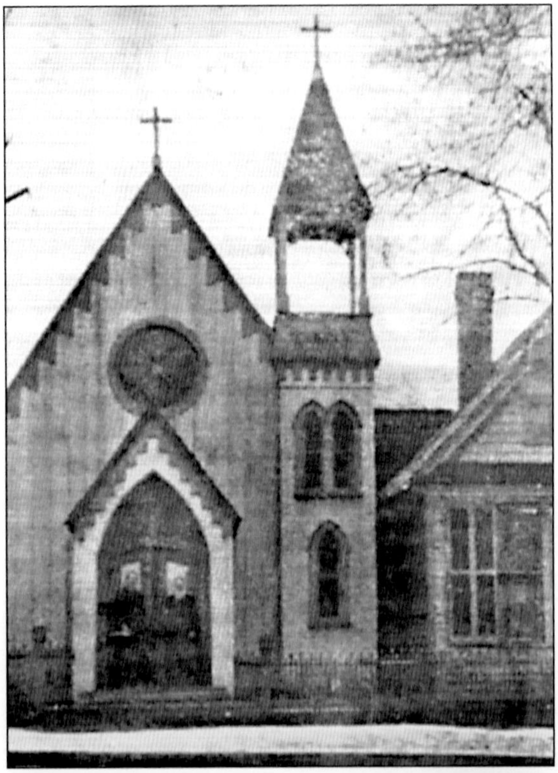

Manly was an early supporter of St. Leo's, the small Catholic church on the southeast corner of Fourth and Brookstown, where mass was first offered in 1891. The first church in West End, St. Leo's expanded in 1903 and a rectory was added next door. Manly's influence helped bring in citywide donations in the 1920s for construction of a larger church for the congregation on Angelo Street. (Courtesy St. Leo's Catholic Church.)

In 1877, Rev. H.A. Brown came to help Baptists in Winston-Salem. He established the missionary Broad Street Baptist Church just south of the intersection of Fourth and Broad. In 1911, a new congregation named in honor of his many years of service, Brown Memorial Church, opened at the southwest corner of Spring and Fourth. Below, Reverend Brown addresses a celebration honoring his 22nd year in Winston-Salem. (Courtesy First Baptist Church.)

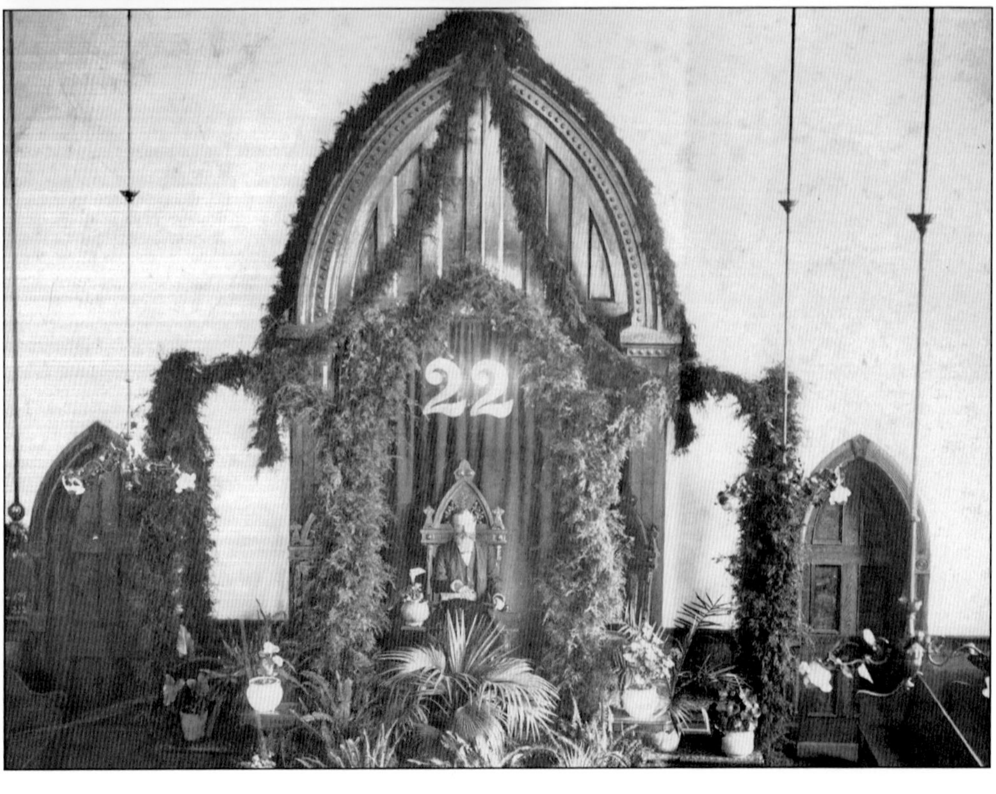

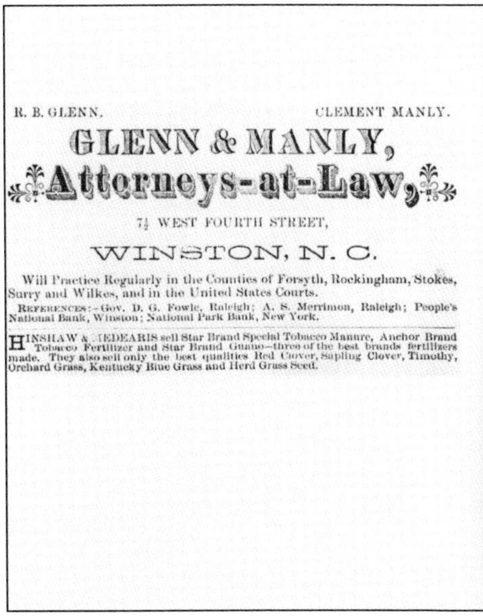

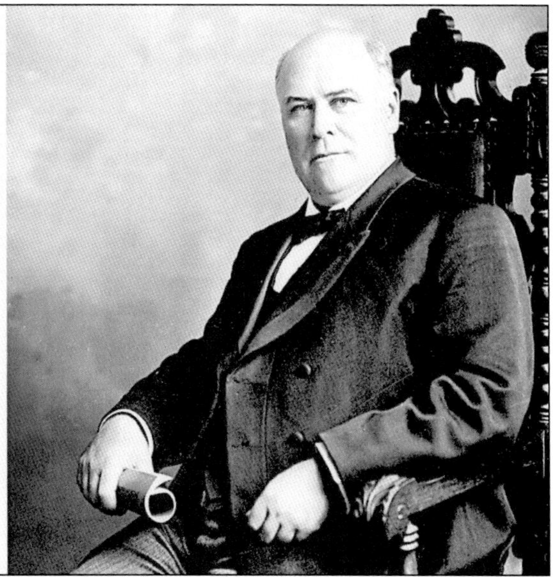

In 1906, Robert Glenn was elected governor of North Carolina, the only Forsyth County resident to serve as such. Glenn championed Prohibition, and after his term in office, he decided not to return to his law practice. Instead, he became a regular on the Chautauqua circuit, preaching the evils of intemperance. After Glenn's death in 1920, his widow, Nina, moved from opposite West End School on Fourth to 814 Carolina Avenue in the West End. (Courtesy NCSA.)

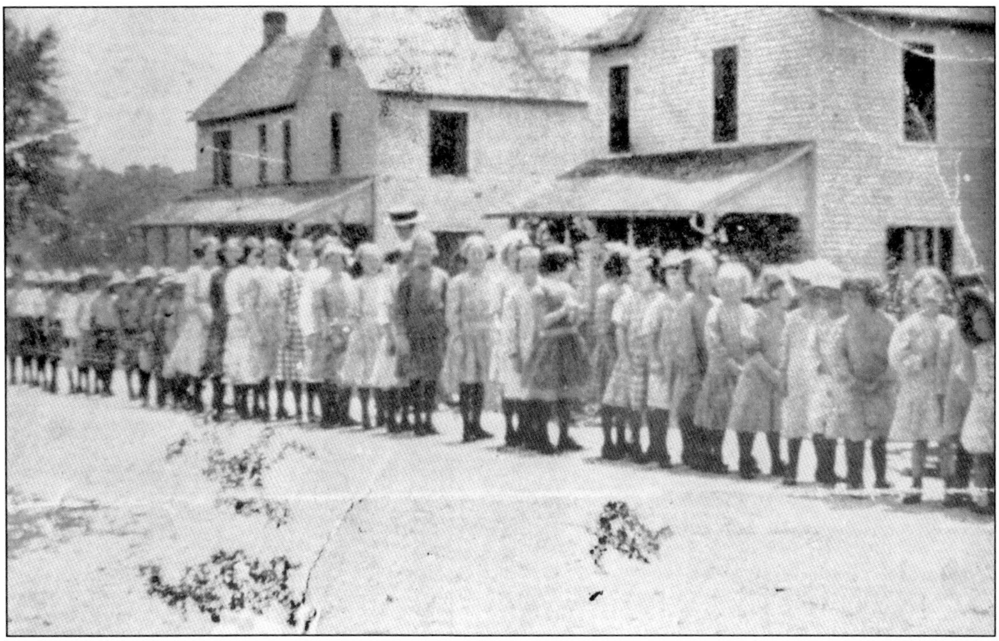

In 1909, Western North Carolina Methodists began an orphanage at the site of the Davis School. West End Methodists began their own congregation separate from downtown Centenary Church in 1909 and were ready supporters of the children. Children's Home kids line up here in front of the former Davis School buildings. On Sundays, they would parade up the hill for church services in West End School with the local Methodists. (Courtesy CH.)

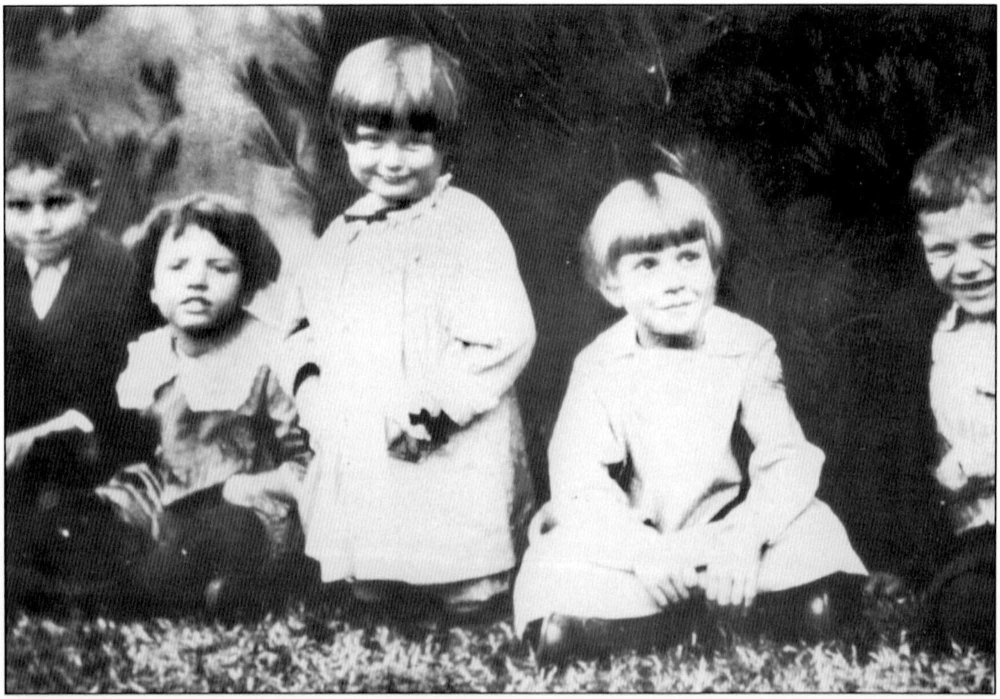

There were bright hopes for these Children's Home kids and a young neighborhood in 1909. Assembled below on the lawn of the Children's Home is its board of trustees. Among the prominent West Enders are P.H. Hanes (second from right, seated) and Mrs. Anna Hodgin Hanes (standing, third row, first woman from the left). In 1909, the West End Hotel and Land Company formally dissolved. The dream of the "spa on the ridge" was over; however, for the neighborhood, much good was yet to come. (Both courtesy CH.)

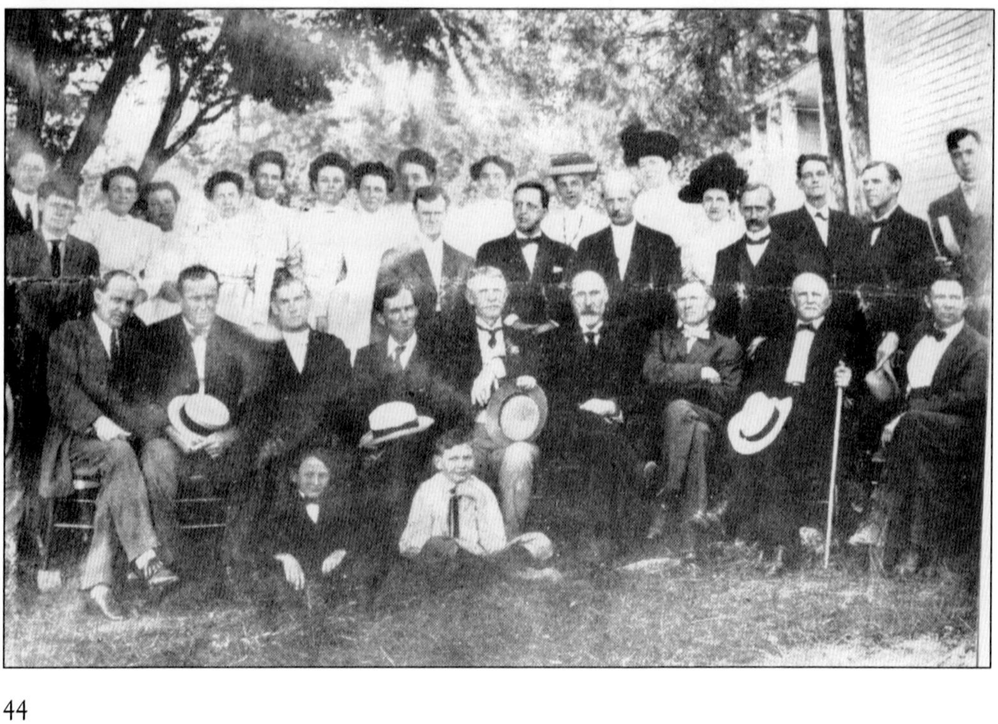

Two

WEST END IN THE DRIVER'S SEAT *1910–1929*

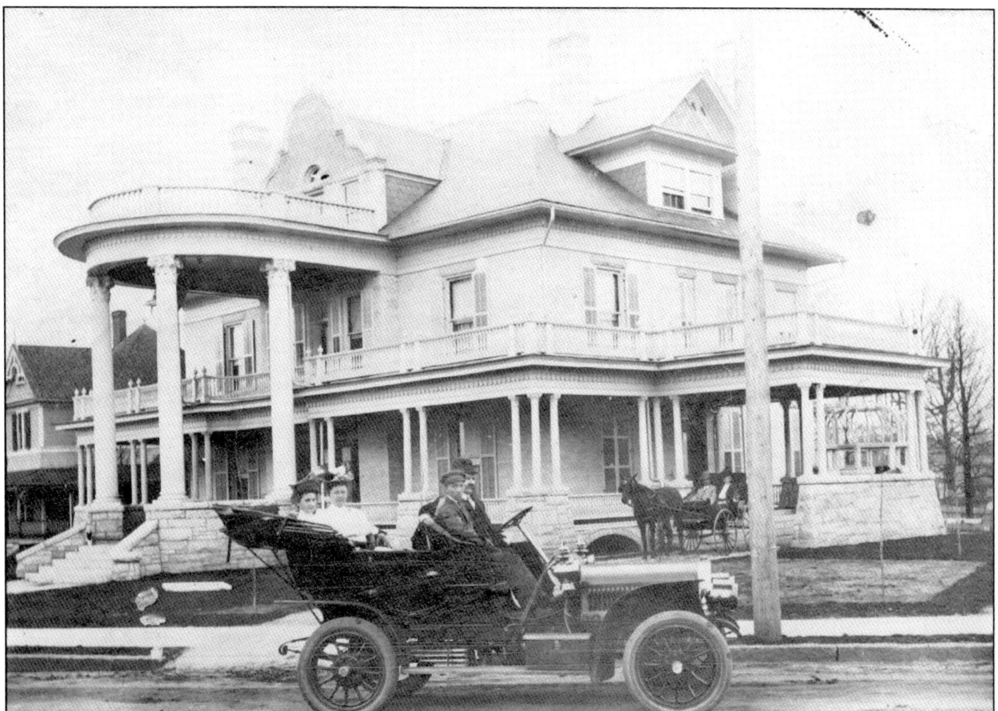

Real estate developer Cisero Tise built this large neoclassical mansion in 1906 across from the Mrs. John W. Hanes home. In the 1910s in Winston-Salem, Prince Albert was definitely "in the can," "the Camels were coming," and Hanes was well on its way to being "your way." For a time in the 1920s, consumer successes made Winston-Salem the leading industrial city south of Baltimore. West Enders were in the driver's seat. (Courtesy FCPL.)

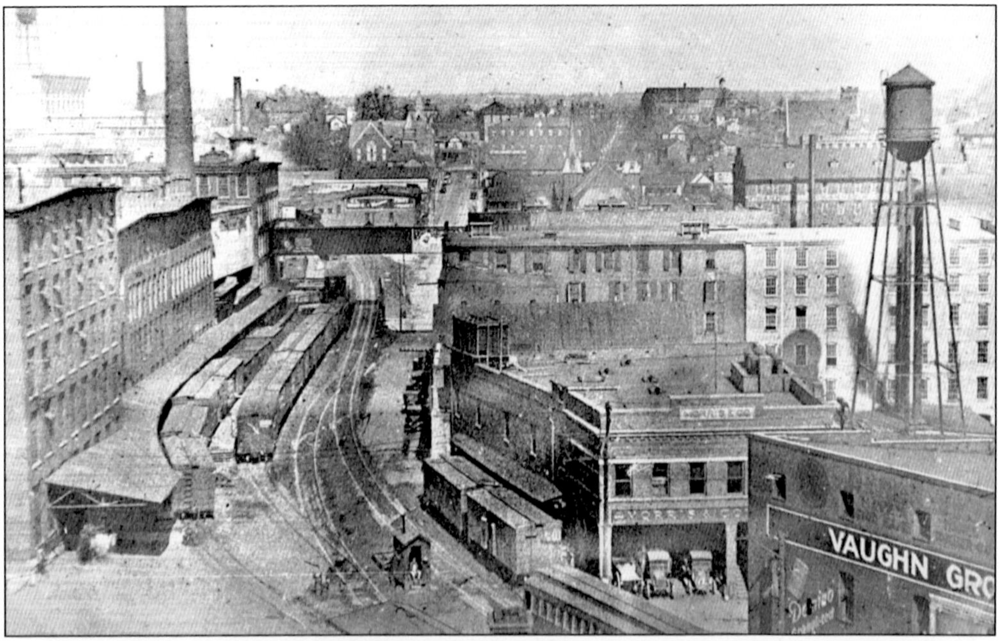

By 1900, 10,000 people lived in Winston. Ten years later, the population had grown to close to 18,000. From a single spur line in the 1880s a generation earlier, railways were completed in 1910 in all four directions through Winston-Salem. Here is a view of the busy Winston rail yard at that time; Edgar Vaughn's grocery warehouse can be seen at lower right. In 1913, Winston's town government formally joined that of Salem to form the united Winston-Salem. (Courtesy WHS/OS.)

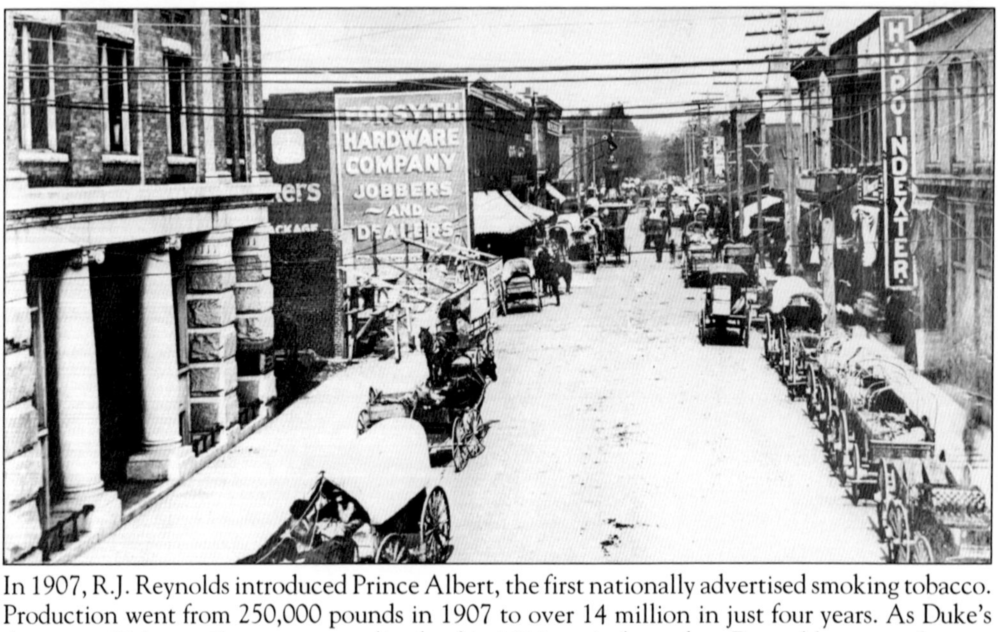

In 1907, R.J. Reynolds introduced Prince Albert, the first nationally advertised smoking tobacco. Production went from 250,000 pounds in 1907 to over 14 million in just four years. As Duke's American Tobacco Company trust dissolved in 1911, an independent Reynolds prepared a new field for his firm—cigarettes. Growth in tobacco sales insured that locally-made Nissen wagons, used to haul tobacco to market, would not soon be obsolete. (Courtesy NCSA.)

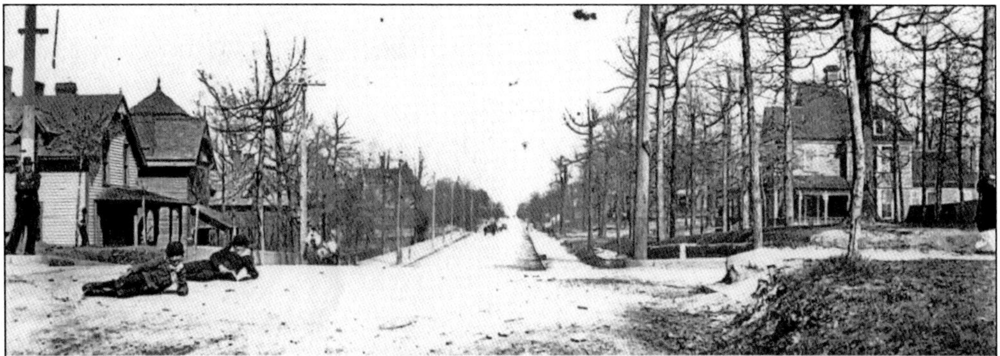

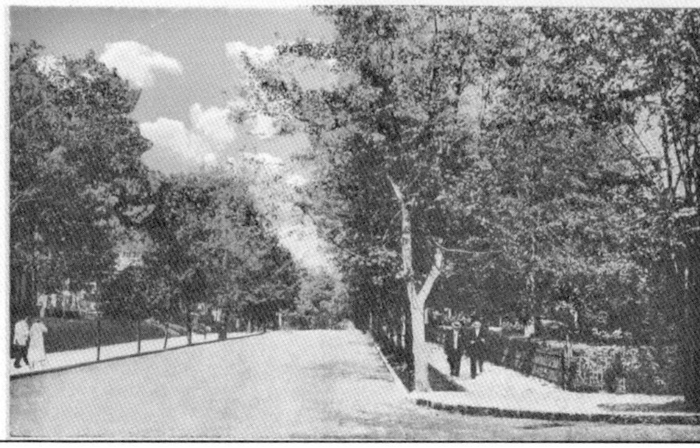

Looking into town along Fifth from Summit Street in 1894, the scattered construction of large frame homes is visible. The paved street ends at Summit, as do sidewalks. Twenty years later, the biggest transformation seems the growth of a forest of trees encircling the homes. Yet, Fifth Street and its mansions became known as "Millionaires' Row" for the homes of business leaders, professionals, and upper management that lined its way. (Courtesy WHS/OS and MA.)

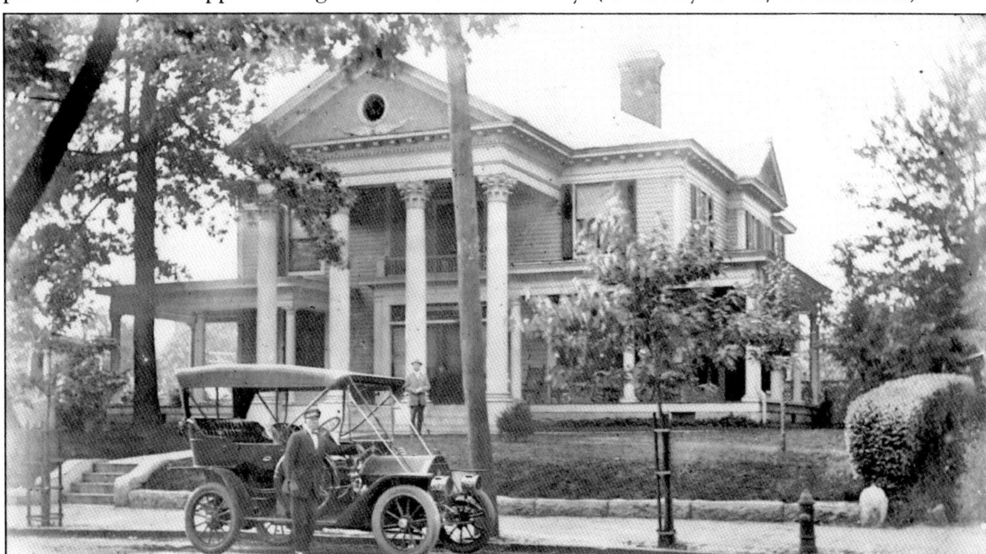

The home of George C. Coan, secretary of Reynolds Tobacco Company, was located at 651 West Fifth Street in 1910. Coan's son George Jr. served as mayor of Winston-Salem in the early 1930s. (Courtesy FCPL.)

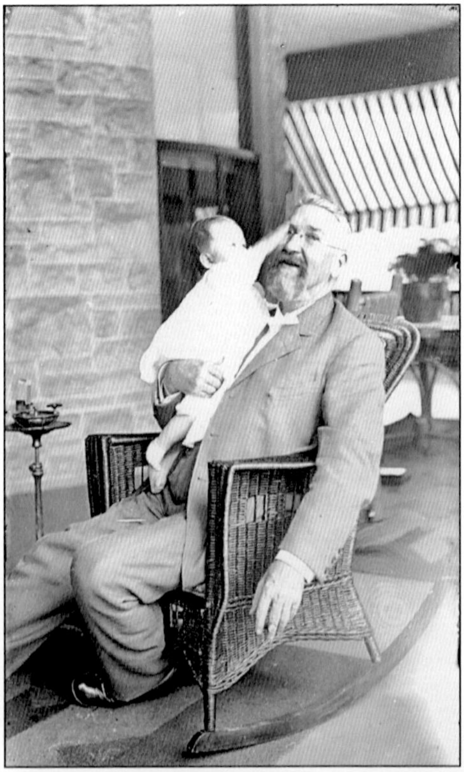

The "biggest blood" in Winston, R.J. Reynolds, is shown here with his youngest son, Zachary Smith, around 1912. Located diagonally across from the Coan property, Reynolds's Fifth Street townhouse took up three lots along the southern side of Fifth at its intersection with Spring Street. (Courtesy NCSA.)

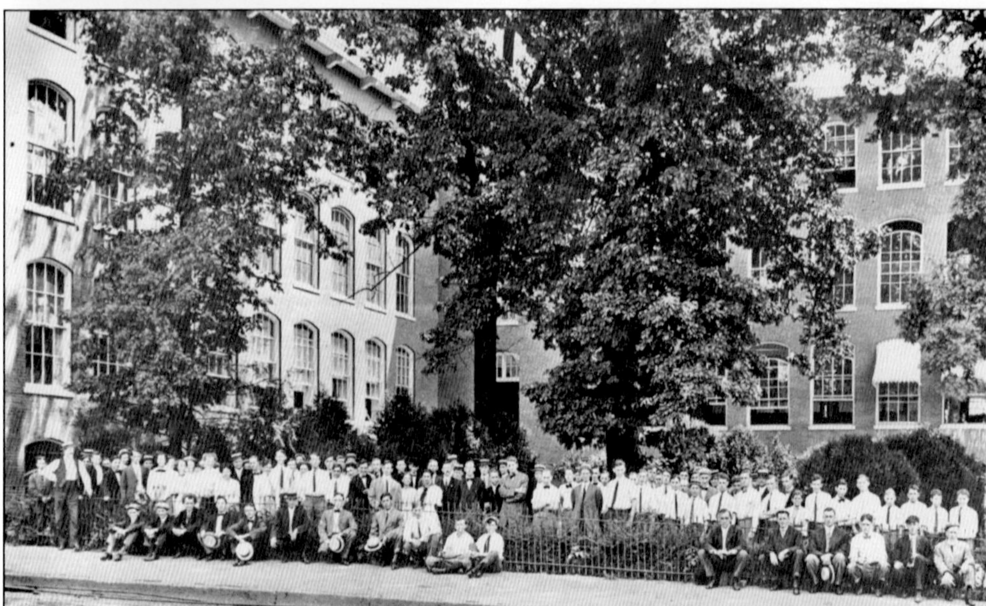

In 1913, Reynolds introduced Camel cigarettes. A half billion Camels were sold by 1914; by 1917, 12.3 billion were sold—35 percent of all cigarettes in the nation. In 1921, half the cigarettes smoked in the United States were Camels. The prosperity from such a dominant market share shaped not just the fortunes of Reynolds and workers pictured here, but also the architectural legacy of West End and the fiscal capacity of Winston-Salem. (Courtesy NCSA.)

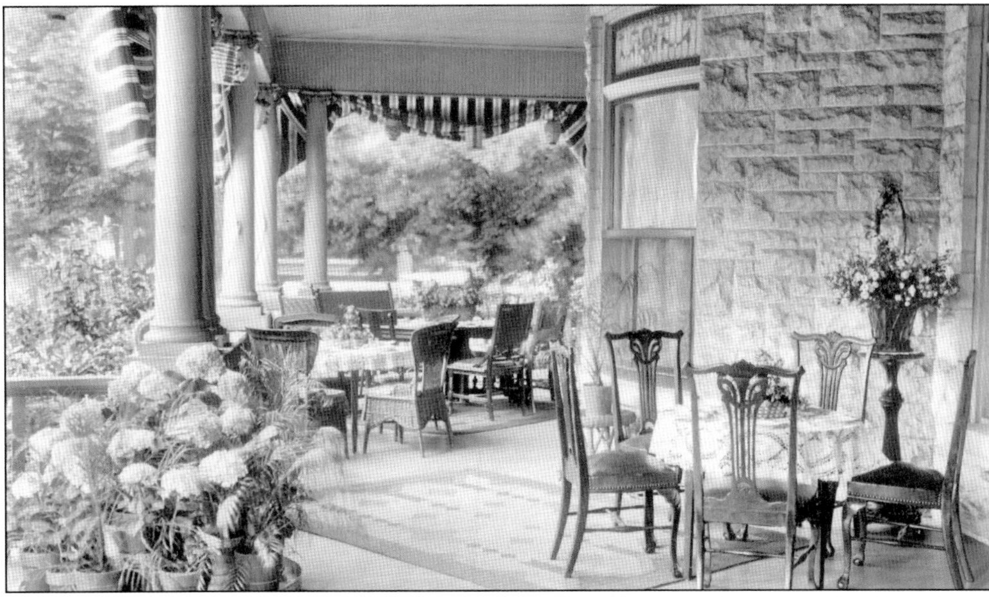

If West End is today a community of "front porches," no front porch was grander than that of R.J. Reynolds, where guests were entertained and business decisions made in consultation with the Reynolds management who lived in neighboring homes. The porch wrapped around two sides of the house; here, just one corner is visible. (Courtesy RH/MAA.)

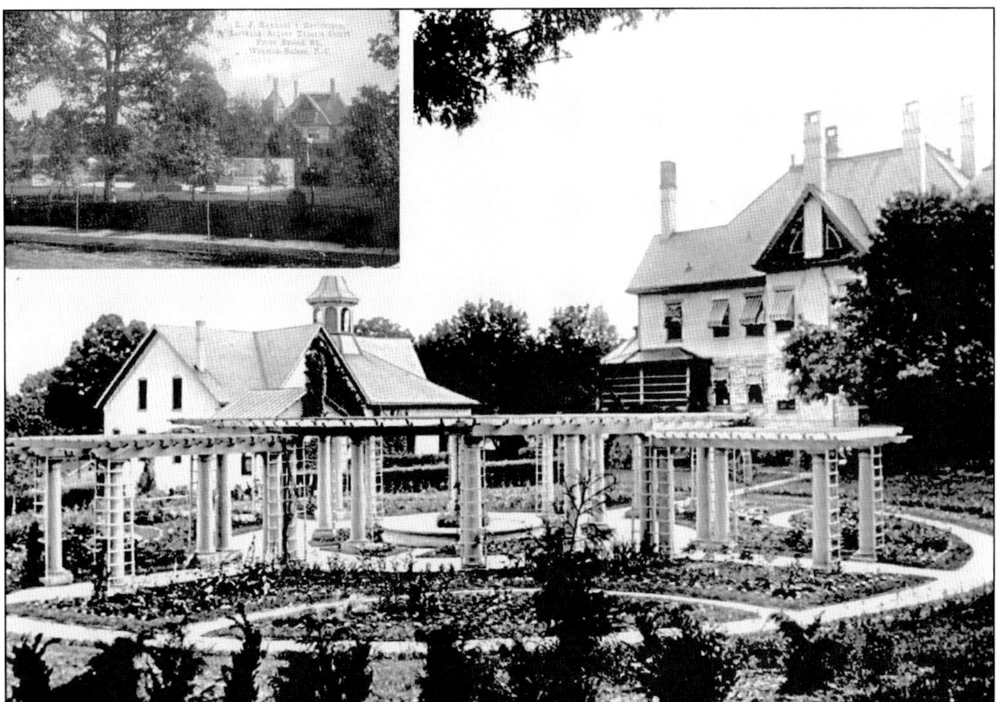

To the east of the house at 666 West Fifth was an elaborate arbored garden. On the west side (inset), the entire block between Spring and Broad Streets contained tennis courts built for the family. (Courtesy NCSA and RH/MAA.)

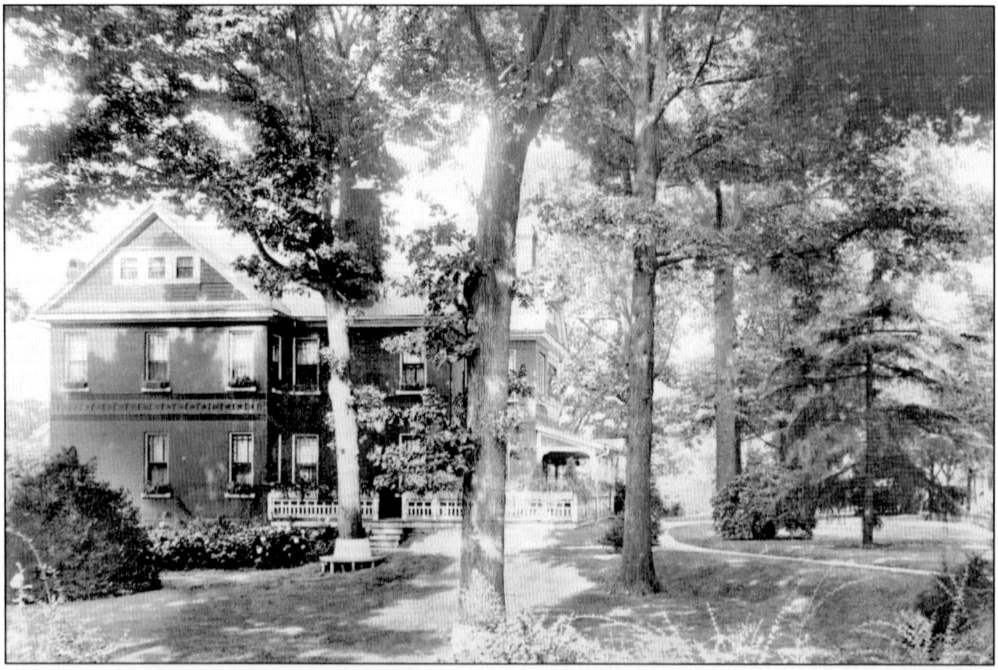

Moving into the house just east of his brother, Will Reynolds renovated and expanded the charms of the former M.N. Williamson home at 648 West Fifth (the distinctive front railing seen on page 13 is still visible here). This rare view of the house is kept on the boardroom wall at the offices of the Kate B. Reynolds Trust. (Courtesy KBRT.)

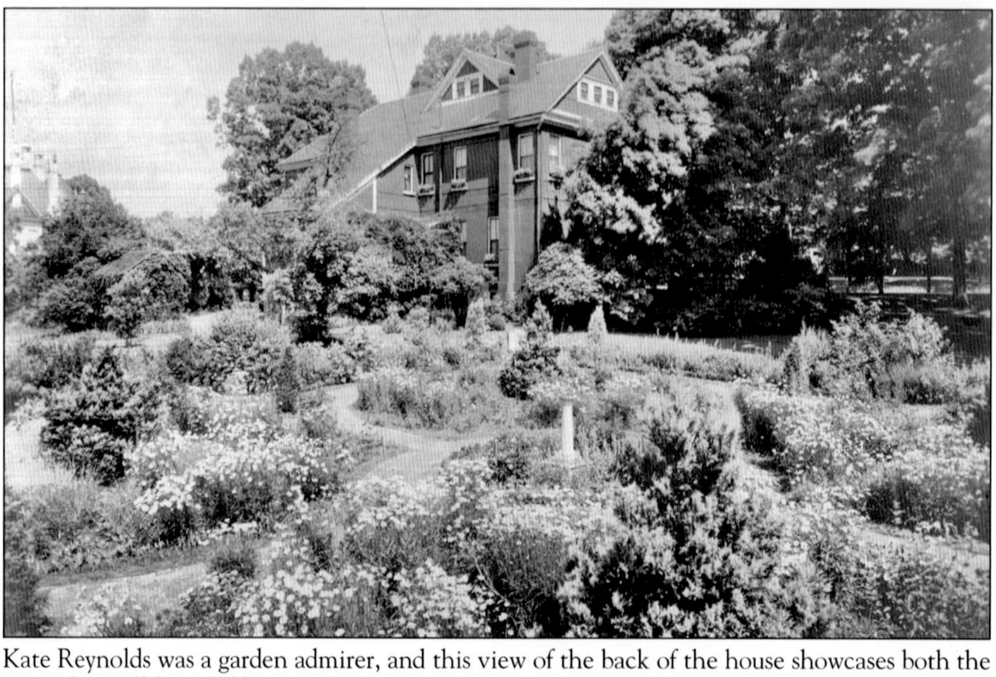

Kate Reynolds was a garden admirer, and this view of the back of the house showcases both the steep drop-off from Fifth to 4 1/2 Street and Mrs. Will Reynolds's passion for perennials. Hers was a shared neighborhood enthusiasm then and now: for nearly half a century, commercial greenhouses stood at the corner of West End Boulevard and Glade Streets. (Courtesy KBRT.)

Bowman Gray Sr., banker James A.'s son, became president of Reynolds Tobacco Company in 1924 after a 30-year career as a salesman and sales manager. His family lived in a "bungalow" at 630 West Fifth, just to the east of Will Reynolds. The powerful Reynolds block between Poplar and Spring Streets on Fifth mirrored a cluster of Hanes family homes near the old Zinzendorf site along Fourth, Fifth, and Glade. By 1940, 60 percent of the town's workforce worked directly for either Reynolds or the Hanes companies. (Courtesy Bowman Gray family, from Jo White Linn's Gray family history.)

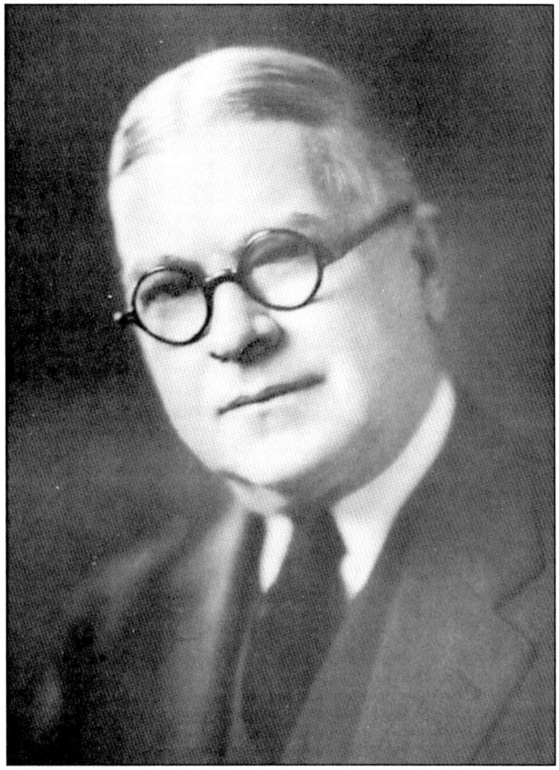

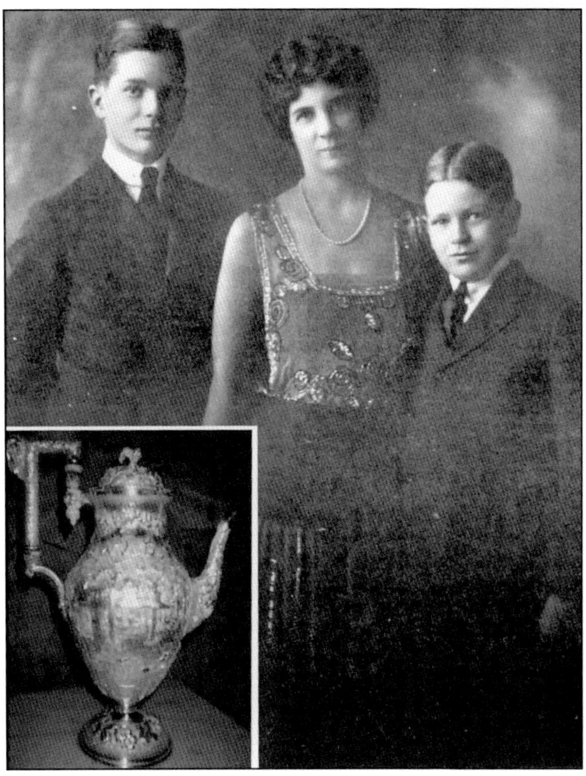

Bowman Gray's wife, Nathalie, stands with their sons, Bowman Jr. (left) and Gordon. The one picture of the Gray Fifth Street home known to the family is preserved on this silver service at their Graylyn estate (inset), crafted after they left the home in the 1920s. The front of the home is on one side of the service; the pool that was located at the back of the home is on the other side. (Courtesy Bowman Gray family, from Jo White Linn's Gray family history; and Graylyn International Conference Center of Wake Forest University.)

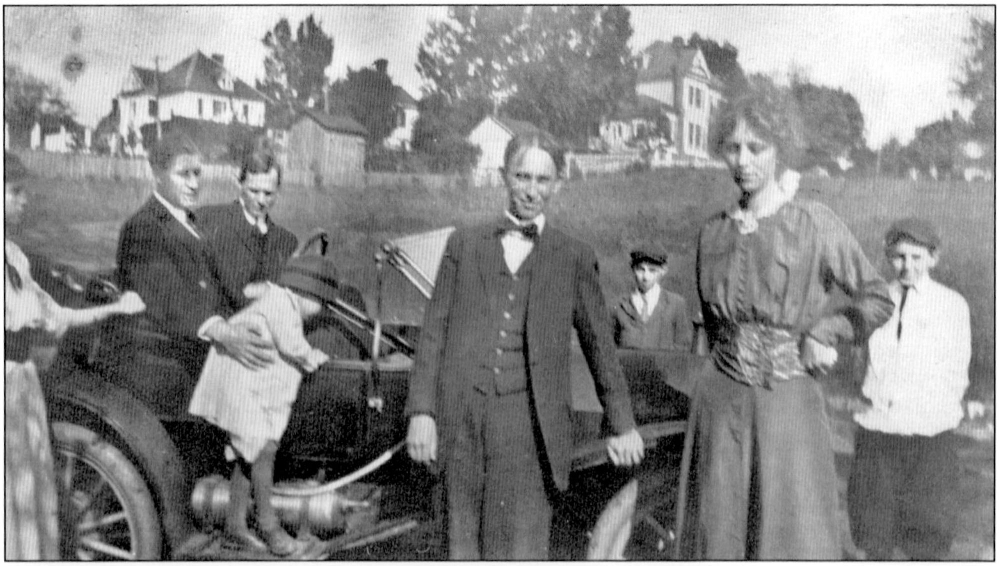

In this 1912 picture, across the street from the Still family home on West End Boulevard (see page 27), father John Still is holding his son Rom, and sons Nelson and Garland are pictured at right. Note that there are no buildings on the block between the Still home and the back of the E.D. Vaughn house (see page 30), pictured at top center on West Fourth Street. The Vaughn-Fletcher House at 1123 West Fourth is upper left. (Courtesy John Still.)

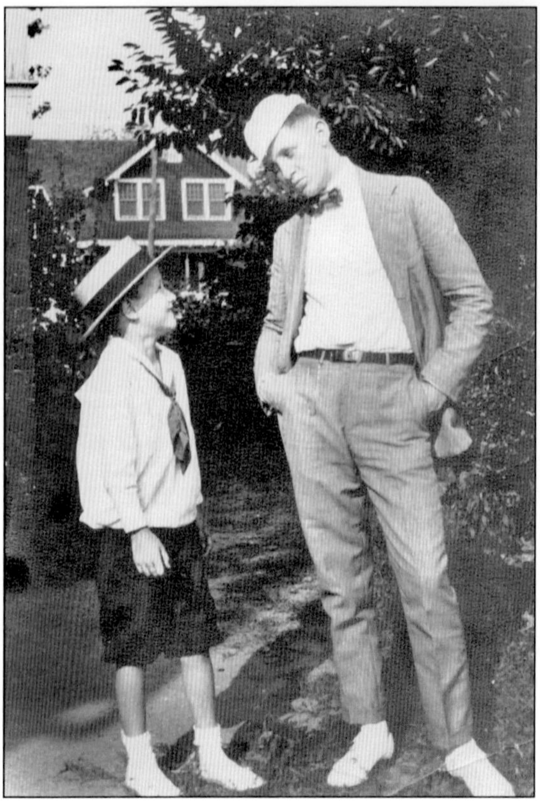

Ten years later, as Rom and his older brother Garland joked in the side yard, exchanging hats, the block has been filled in with homes. The Frank P. Davis home at 922 West End can be seen in the rear of the picture. (Courtesy John Still.)

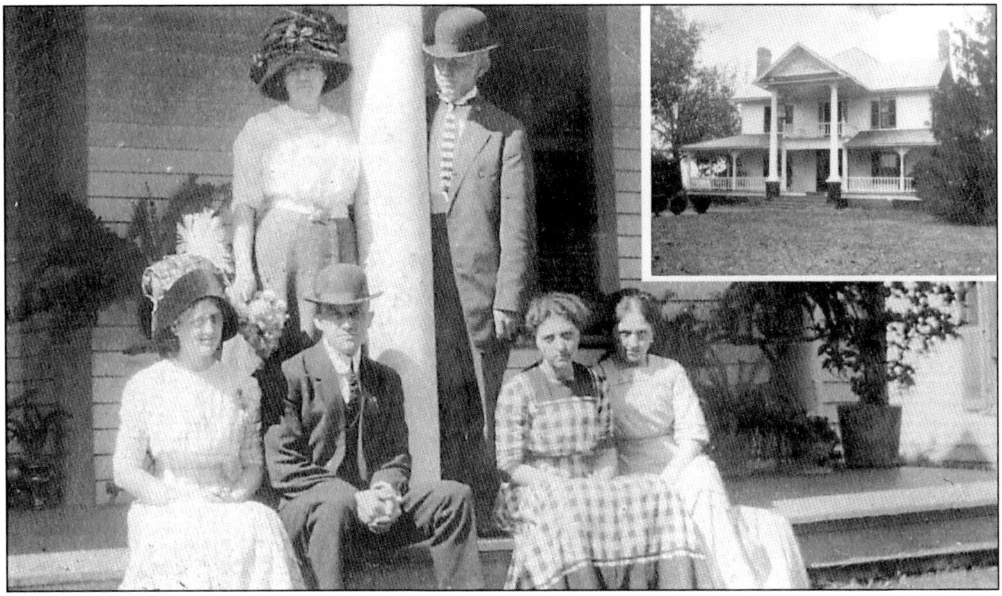

Egbert L. Davis grew up on a farm in Forbush, Yadkin County (inset). In 1908, his dad, Eli, built this house at 660 North Spring Street so his children could find work and education in the city. After a career with Reynolds Tobacco, in 1925, Egbert and family members formed Atlas Supply Company, a plumbing and heating supply dealer, and in 1931, Davis Department store. Egbert was also president of Security Life and Trust Company. (Courtesy Linwood Davis.)

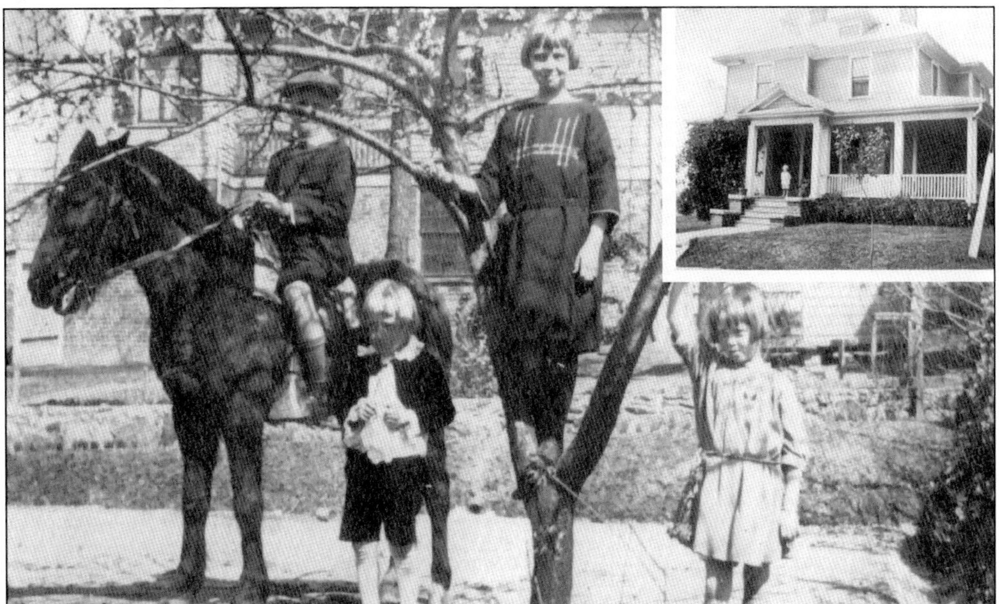

Egbert moved to a house at 1219 Forsyth Street in 1915 (inset) and in 1918 returned to 660 North Spring. Here in 1923, Egbert Jr., later head of Atlas Supply, is on his pony Coley next to sisters Julia Caroline and Annie Pauline. In front of the pony is brother Thomas Henry, who founded Piedmont Airlines, one of the nation's largest regional airlines in the 1980s. (Courtesy Linwood Davis.)

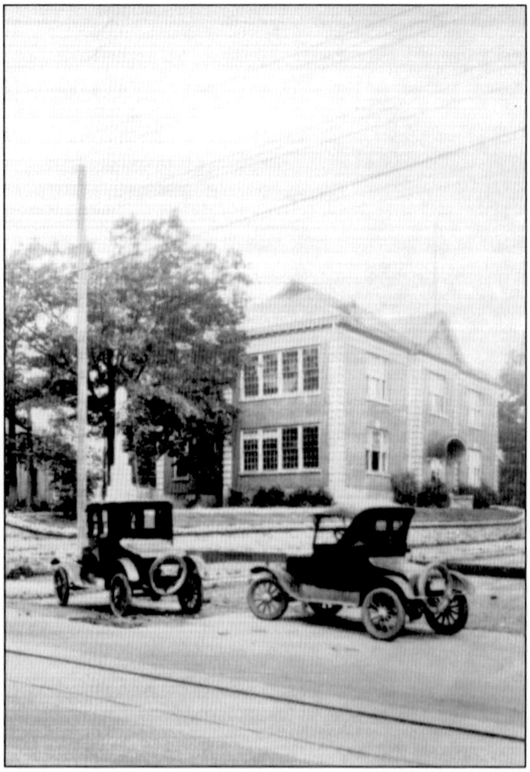

West End Primary School opened in 1911 along Broad Street on the property of the West End Graded School. A free-standing Winston High School had opened in 1909 along Cherry Street in town. With the primary school built, the old graded school became headquarters for an expanding school administration. (Courtesy FCPL.)

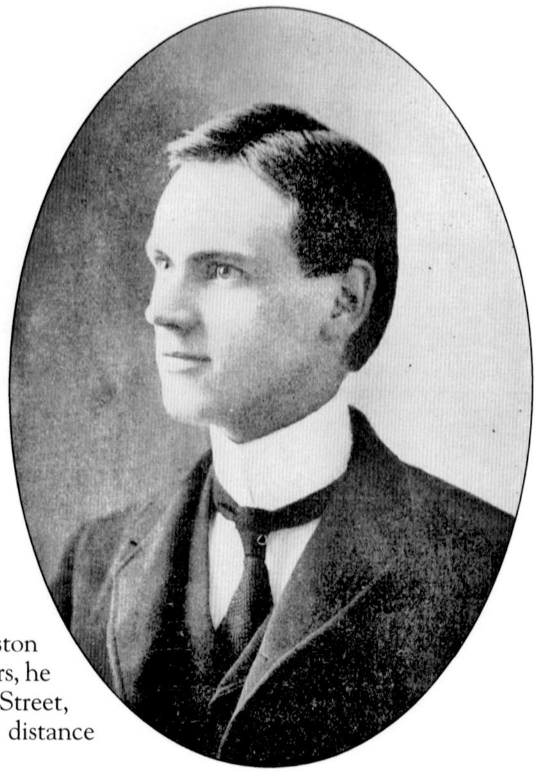

Superintendent R.H. Latham ably ran Winston schools from 1910 to 1935. During those years, he lived with his wife, Mamie, at 735 Summit Street, as with many West Enders, within walking distance of work. (Courtesy FCPL.)

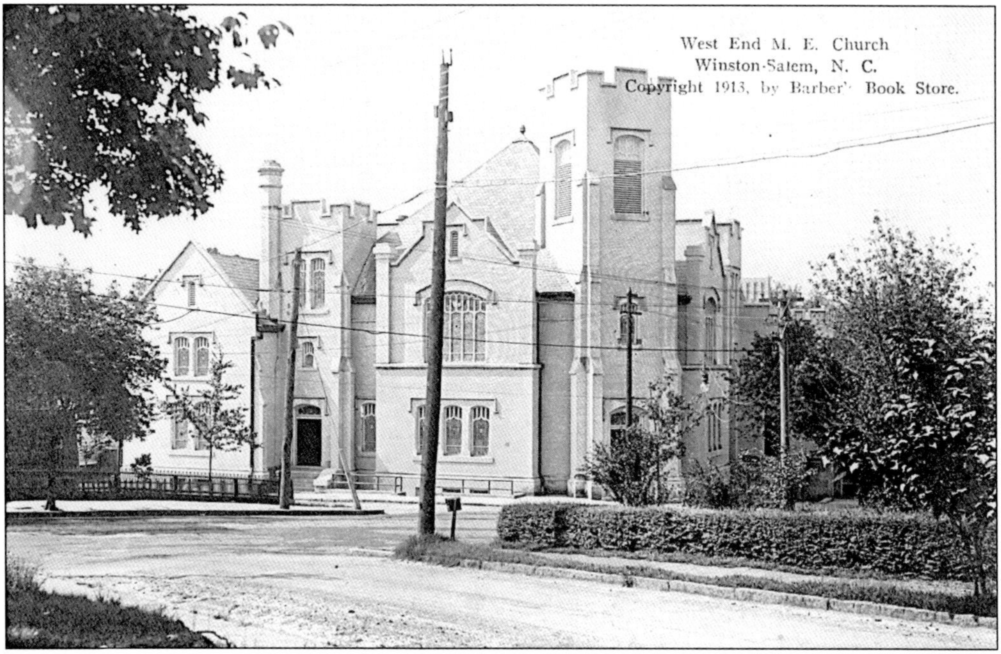

West End Methodists opened the doors of a new church building in 1913 at the southwest corner of Brookstown Avenue and West Fourth Street. Originally a satellite congregation of Centenary Methodist on Sixth Street, the congregation grew to 1,100 members, and it was the larger of the two churches when the congregations reunited in 1927. (Courtesy FCPL.)

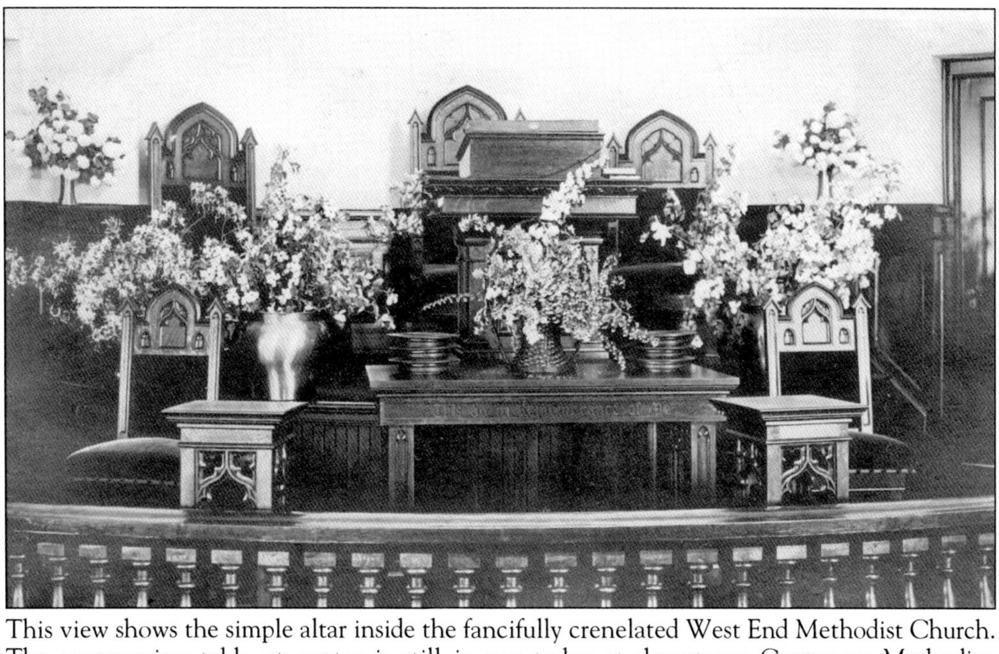

This view shows the simple altar inside the fancifully crenelated West End Methodist Church. The communion table at center is still in use today at downtown Centenary Methodist. (Courtesy Jule Spach.)

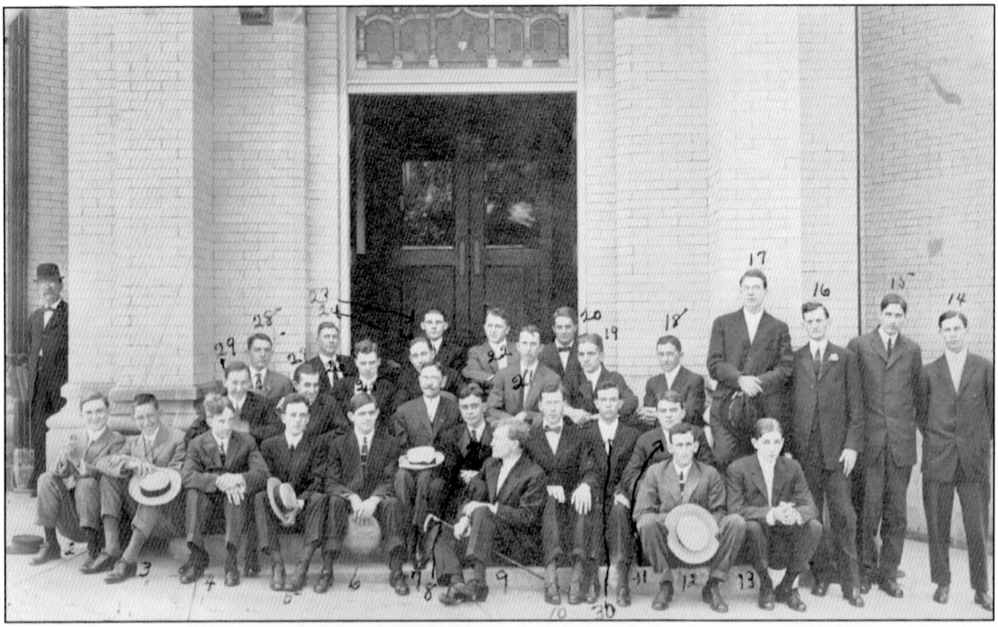

This photo shows West End Methodist's Baraca Sunday School class with class leader and prominent retailer M.D. Stockton at center with a hat on his lap. Prosperous West Enders paid off the note on their church within four years. With St. Leo's across the street, Brookstown and Fourth gave a religious center to the neighborhood. (Courtesy Archives and History Committee, Centenary United Methodist Church; hereafter listed as CUMC.)

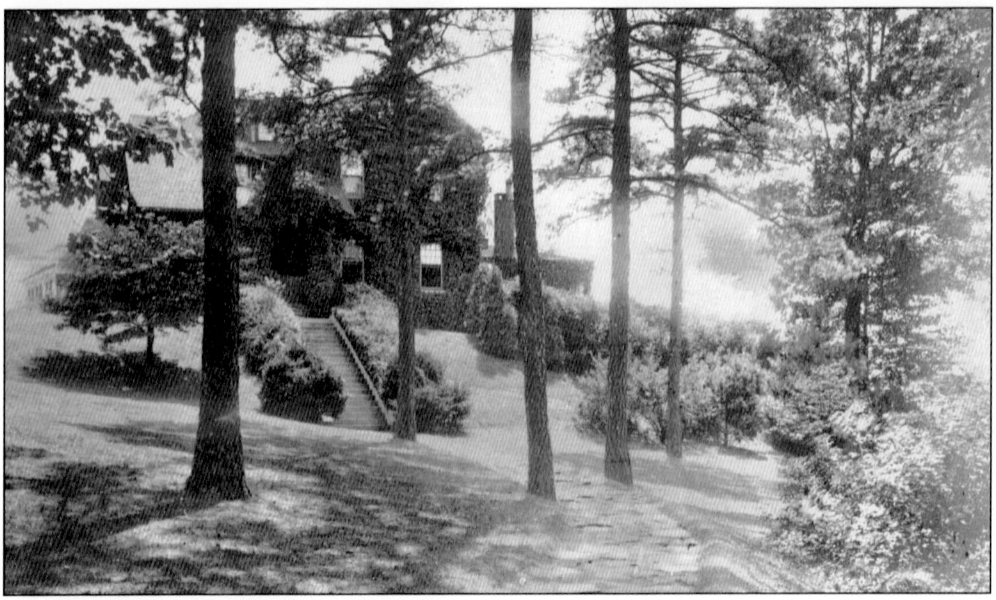

This Dr. Thomas W. Davis home was built in 1911 along West End Boulevard near Glade Street, the site of the present Colonial Arms Apartments. Davis was an ear, nose, and throat specialist, a chamber of commerce president, and an early member of Winston-Salem Rotary. The interconnectedness of the civic life of Winston-Salem leaders, coupled with the physical proximity of their West End homes, was a distinct feature of the community at the time. (Courtesy Tom Davis.)

One of Winston-Salem's first skyscrapers, the O'Hanlon Building, is shown here under construction around 1915. Dr. Davis had his office in this building. Not long after its opening, daredevil George Gibson Polley, who advertised himself as a "human fly," attempted to scale the eight-story building. His courage failed going up, and Davis had to haul him him to safety through his office window. Polley later succeeded in his task. (Courtesy MA.)

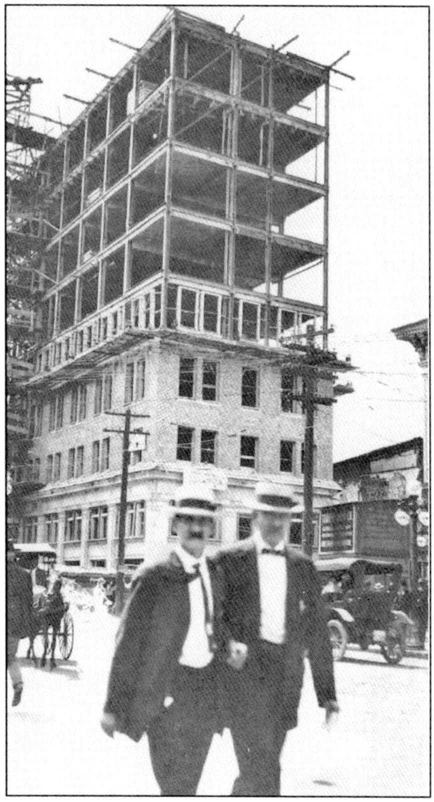

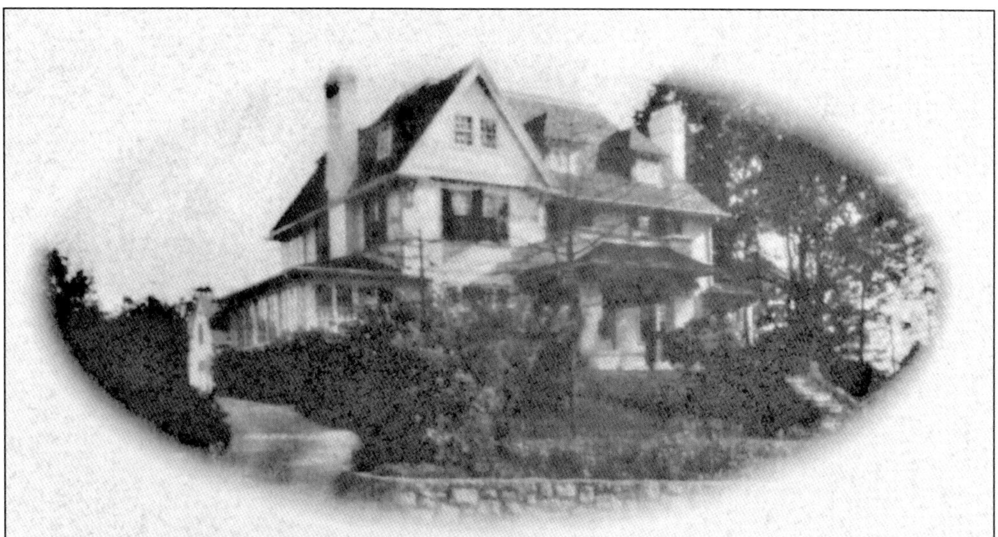

P. Huber Hanes built this home at 1200 Glade in 1915. After the Reynolds buyout, Huber's father, Pleas, never left the family home on Cherry Street, the old neighborhood of so many early Winston leaders. Huber, though, built behind his aunt's newer house. His cousin James G., who as head of his uncle's company steered production to women's hosiery in 1919, built across the street. (Courtesy Kilpatrick Stockton LLP.)

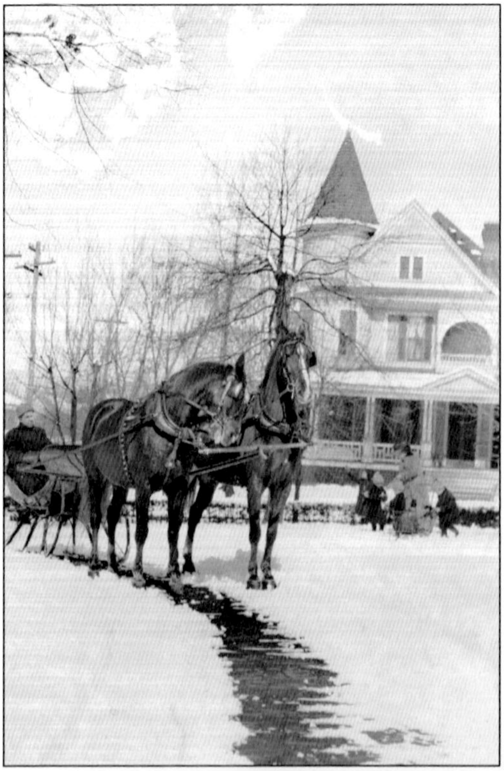

The Reynolds children enjoy the snow in West End with the family's sleigh pulled by horses Prince and Albert. The success of Prince Albert enabled Reynolds and his wife to envision a bigger country estate for his family away from town living. In 1909, work began on "Reynolda" on 1,100 acres west of town. (Courtesy RH/MAA.)

By 1917, Reynolda became the primary home for the Reynolds family, though they still kept the Fifth Street townhouse. Reynolda House is here pictured in the center, with Lake Katharine, named for Mrs. Reynolds, at the top. The estate's barn and outbuildings, now the shops at Reynolda Village, are at upper left. (Courtesy RH/MAA.)

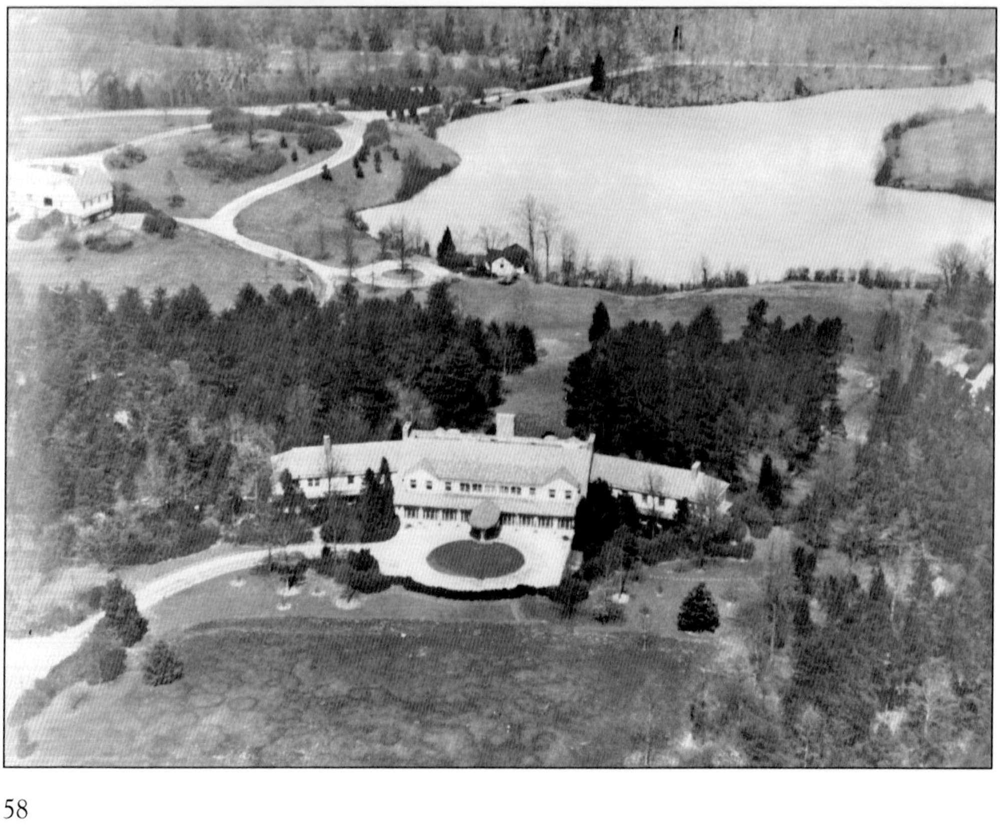

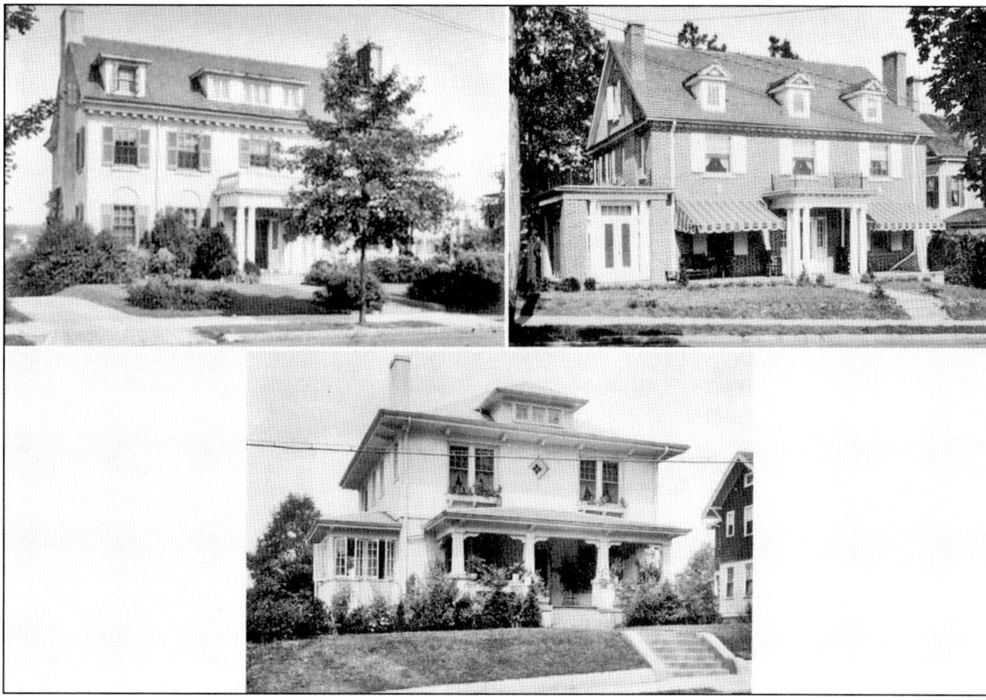

In *Art Work of Piedmont Section of North Carolina*, a 1924 photo book tour of better neighborhoods in the largest Piedmont cities, West End homes featured prominently. Here are, clockwise from lower center, the West End Boulevard homes of Alphon Nash, a realtor and insurance agent, and Robert Galloway, a lumber company president; and the Summit Street home of John Thomas, a local coal and ice dealer. (Courtesy FCPL.)

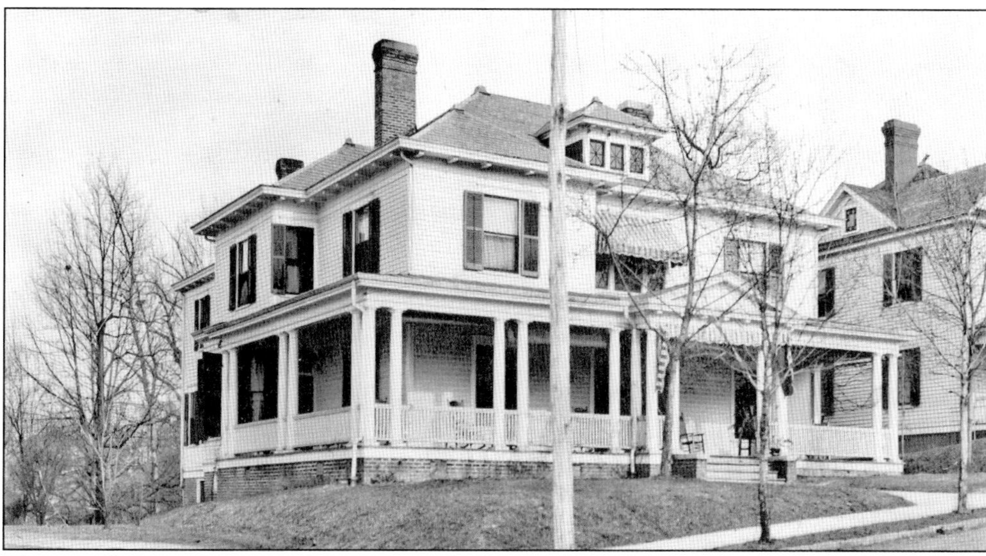

The 1911 home of James Dodson, a Reynolds employee, at 633 Summit Street is typical of the Colonial Revival house style found often in West End through the 1920s. Inspired by Georgian Colonial architecture of the 1700s, homes have symmetrical façades and often triangular pediments. The heat of Southern summers made awnings a not uncommon West End house accessory. (Courtesy Helen and Mo Waite.)

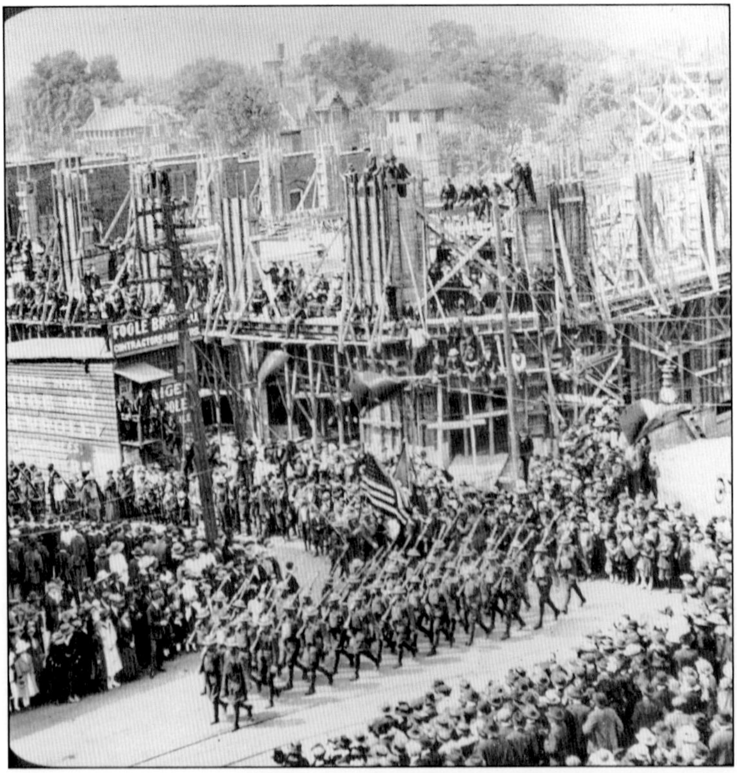

In 1919, Winston-Salem celebrated the end to World War I, and soldiers are here turning the corner of the parade route. An ad at the rear of the picture touts Fogle Brothers, the construction mainstay for years. In 1920, the population of Winston-Salem topped 48,000. It was the largest town in the state and the largest in the South between Richmond and Atlanta. (Courtesy WHS/OS.)

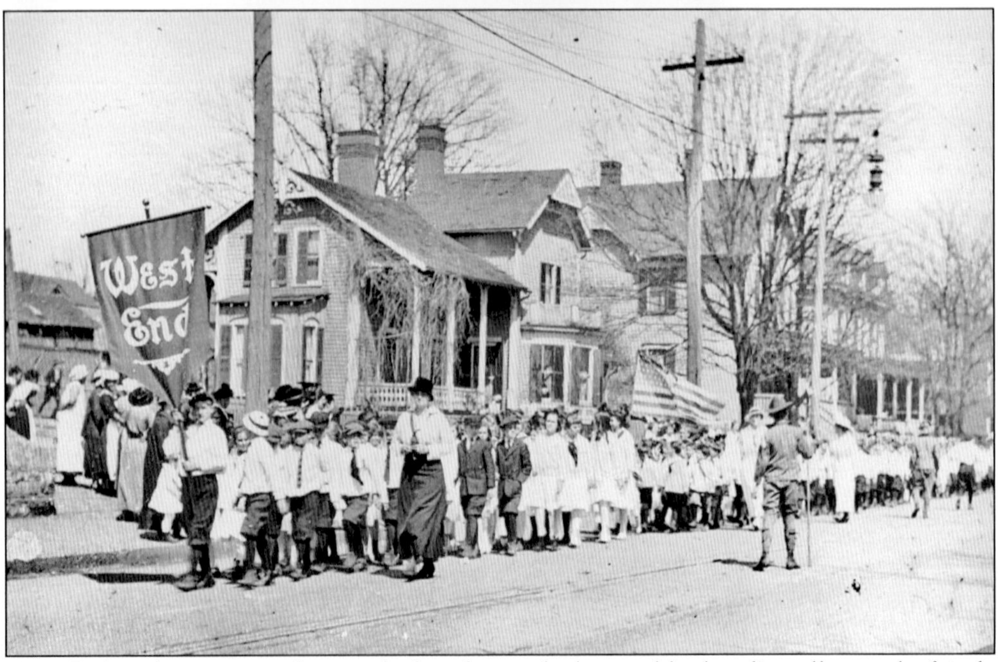

West End students are on the march that day, with the neighborhood's trolley tracks faintly visible at their feet. Fourth Street developed as a commercial and institutional district westward from Spruce and Poplar in the 1910s and 1920s, as Fifth Street strengthened its residential character. (Courtesy WHS/OS.)

Anna Hodgin Hanes's son Robert was a colonel in World War I, here writing to his wife on "the greatest day in history"—the end of the war on November 11, 1918. After the war, Hanes returned to Winston-Salem, living at 1219 Forsyth Street, the former Egbert Davis home, not far from other Hanes family members on the end of the ridge between Fourth, Glade, and West End. (Courtesy NCC/UNC.)

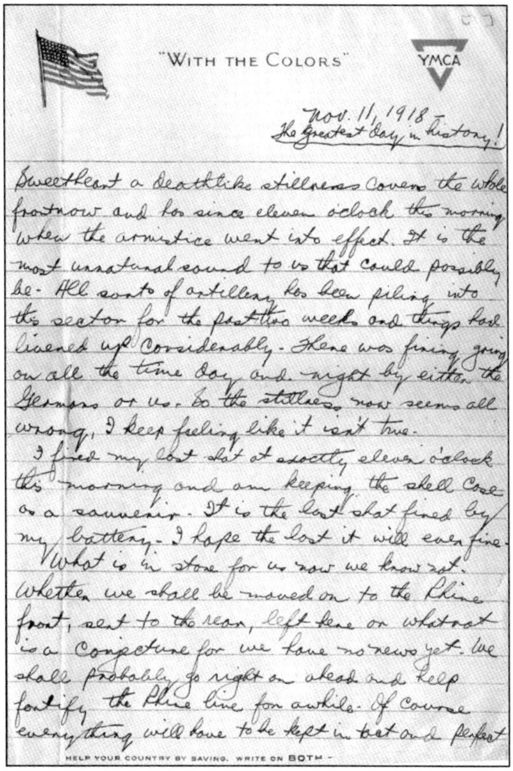

"WITH THE COLORS" YMCA

Nov. 11, 1918 — The Greatest day in history!

Sweetheart a deathlike stillness covers the whole front now and has since eleven o'clock this morning when the armistice went into effect. It is the most unnatural sound to us that could possibly be. All sorts of artillery has been piling into this sector for the past two weeks and things had livened up considerably. There was firing going on all the time day and night by either the Germans or us. So the stillness now seems all wrong, I keep feeling like it isn't true.

I fired my last shot at exactly eleven o'clock this morning and am keeping the shell case as a souvenir. It is the last shot fired by my battery. I hope the last it will ever fire.

What is in store for us now we know not. Whether we shall be moved on to the Rhine front, sent to the rear, left here or what not is a conjecture for we have no news yet. We shall probably go right on ahead and help fortify the Rhine line for awhile. Of course everything will have to be kept in tact and perfect

HELP YOUR COUNTRY BY SAVING. WRITE ON BOTH —

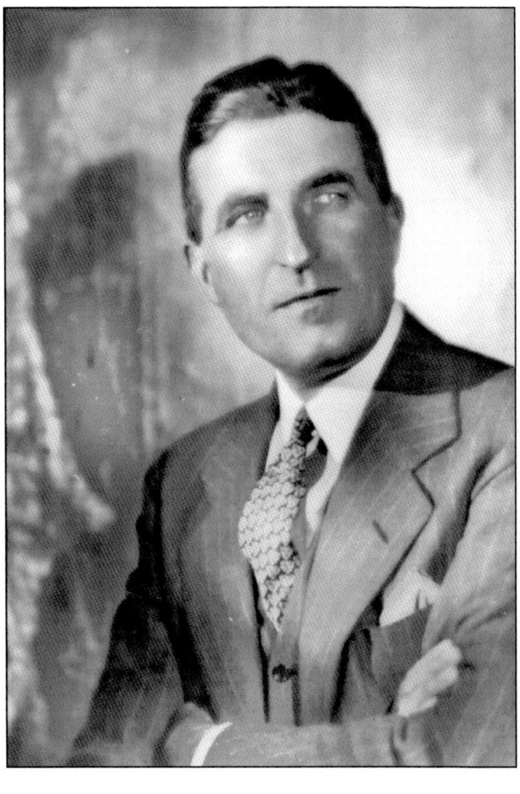

After working for a few years for his brother Alex's Hanes Rubber company, a short-lived tire manufacturer, Robert Hanes rose quickly through the ranks at Wachovia Bank, becoming company president in 1931. He would lead Wachovia Bank for 25 years. He also served two terms in the state legislature, where his good looks and attire earned him the title of "most dapper" legislator. (Courtesy WCCA.)

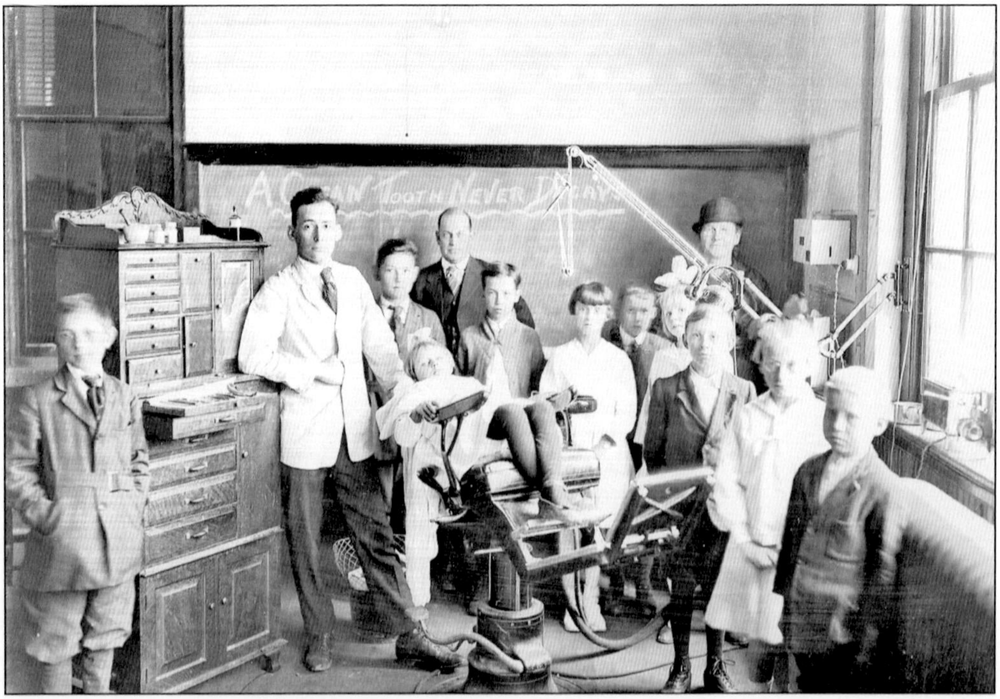

The children's faces seem surprisingly pleasant, given the dental equipment, in this 1919 Winston-Salem school-sponsored dental clinic. "A clean tooth never decays," the blackboard encourages. (Courtesy NCSA.)

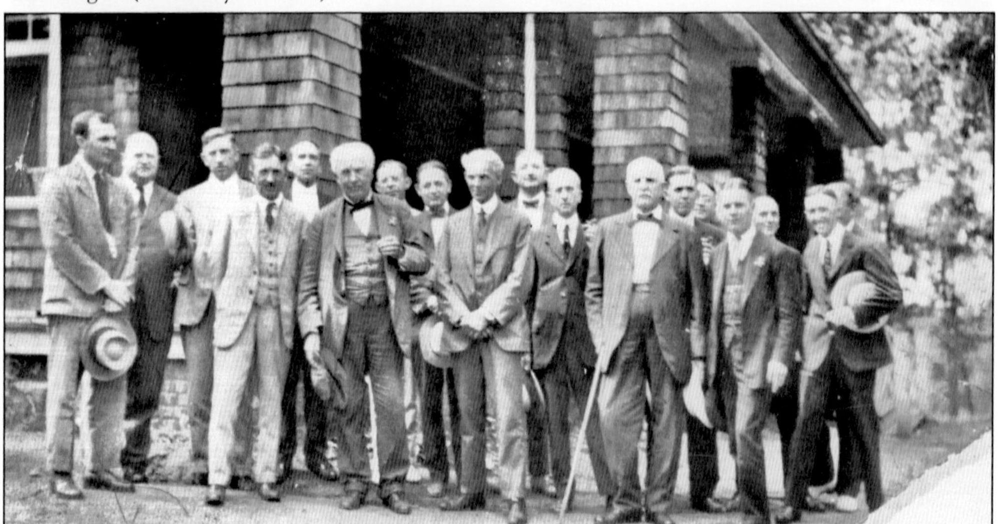

A sugarless but sweet treat happened in 1918 when Thomas Edison and two traveling companions, Henry Ford and Harvey Firestone, were successfully invited to detour into Winston-Salem for a stay. Shown here with many prominent West Enders at Forsyth County Club are, from left to right, James G. Hanes, Henry Dwire, Bunyan Womble, Harvey Firestone Sr., A.H. Eller, Thomas Edison, Frank Dunklee, John Gilmer, Henry Ford, B.F. Huntley, unidentified, Pleasant H. Hanes, Roy Johnson, Powell Gilmer, Harvey Firestone Jr., Will Watkins, Norman Stockton, and unidentified. (Courtesy FCPL.)

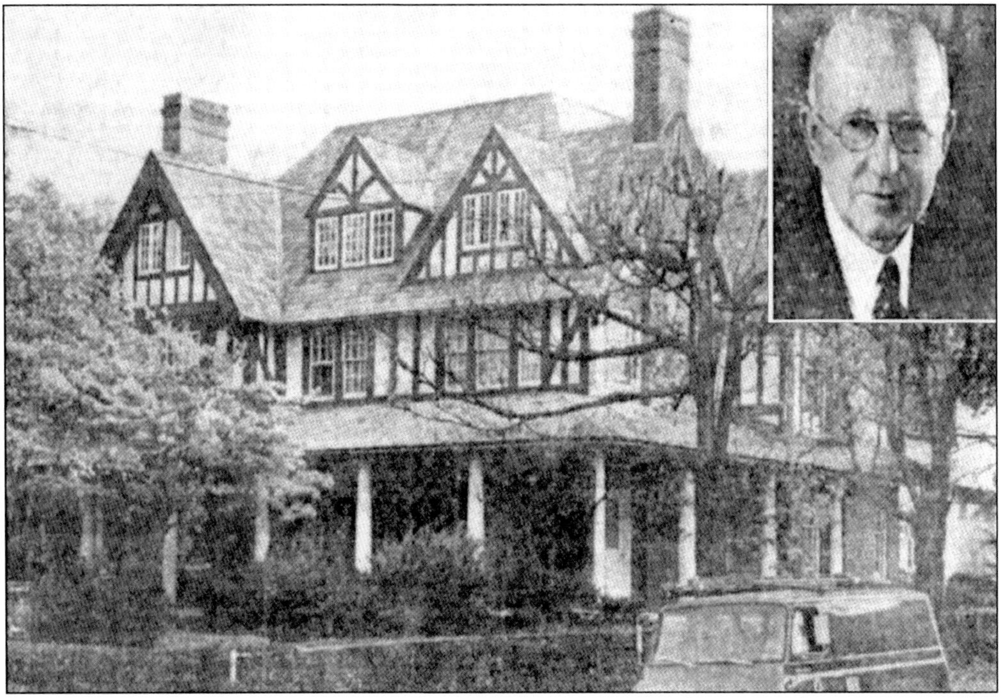

R.E. "Ed" Lasater (inset), a Reynolds family in-law and manager of the Reynolds company's anchor "256" factory downtown, had Reynolda architect Charles Barton Keen design this distinctive home at Fifth and Broad in the mid-1910s. It was, with the neighboring Agnew Bahnson home, the last new residential construction on "Millionaires' Row." (Courtesy FCPL.)

Many of the larger homes built in the 1910s and 1920s were styled "bungalows" for their rambling informality. However, many of the smaller homes in West End are also called by that name in deference to the informality of the Craftsman style, built frequently between the late 1910s and early 1930s. Craftsman homes, as shown here at 1017 West Fifth, often feature low-pitched roofs, angle roof brackets, wide eaves, and wood shingles. (Courtesy the author.)

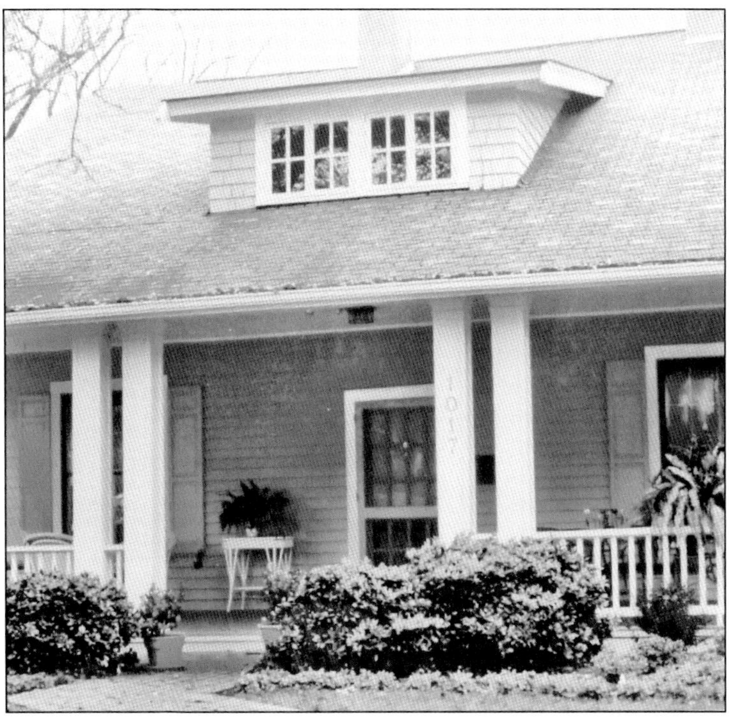

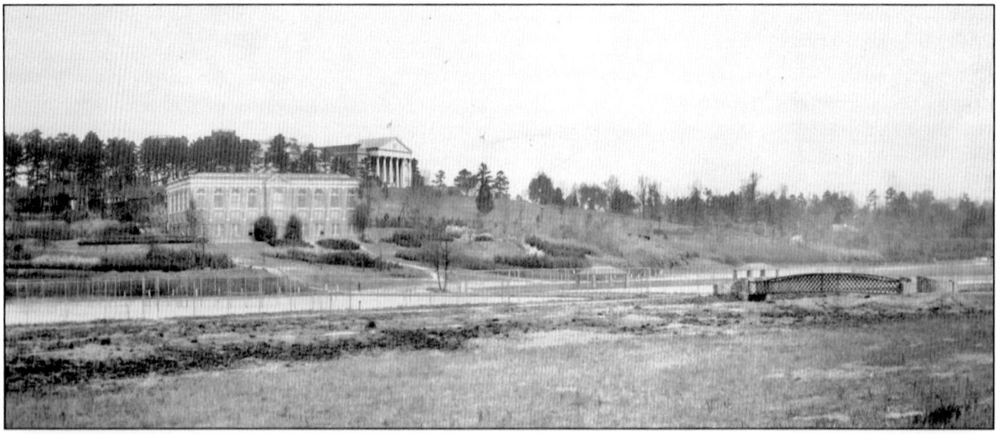

R.J. Reynolds passed away in 1918. Funds from his estate were donated to the city, and P.H. Hanes donated land for the creation of Reynolds High School and Hanes Park. The park is shown here in front in the valley at the western base of West End ridge. The image looks northwest, and the high school can be seen on Silver Hill, so named for its grove of silver maples. (Courtesy FCPL.)

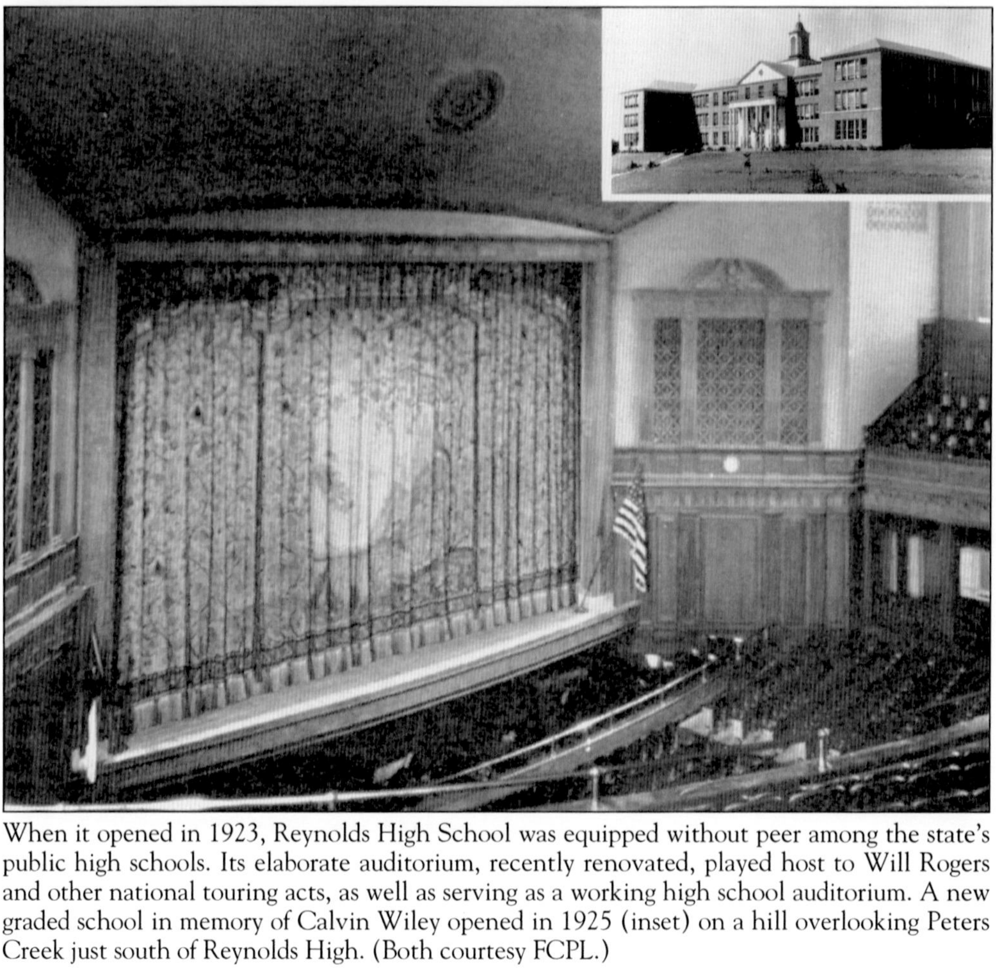

When it opened in 1923, Reynolds High School was equipped without peer among the state's public high schools. Its elaborate auditorium, recently renovated, played host to Will Rogers and other national touring acts, as well as serving as a working high school auditorium. A new graded school in memory of Calvin Wiley opened in 1925 (inset) on a hill overlooking Peters Creek just south of Reynolds High. (Both courtesy FCPL.)

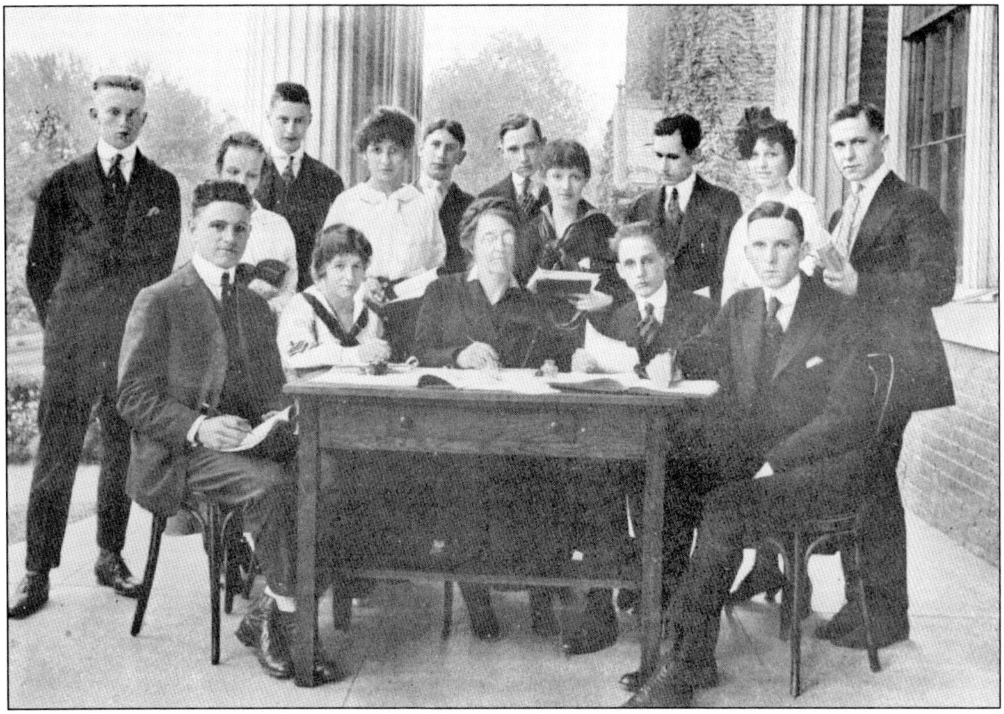

Miss Mary Wiley, daughter of Calvin Wiley and lifelong resident at the family home on Spruce Street, was a teacher at Reynolds and is shown here heading the yearbook staff. Wiley began her teaching career at West End Graded School, then moved with the system to Cherry Street's Winston High School, and then to Reynolds. (Courtesy FCPL.)

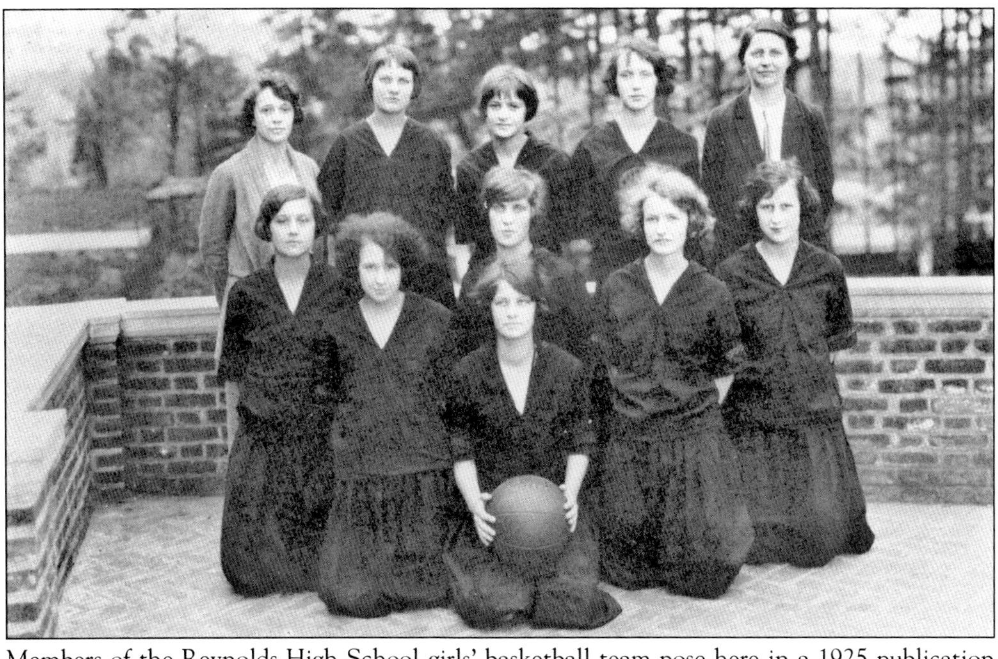

Members of the Reynolds High School girls' basketball team pose here in a 1925 publication advertising the offerings of the new school for prospective students. (Courtesy FCPL.)

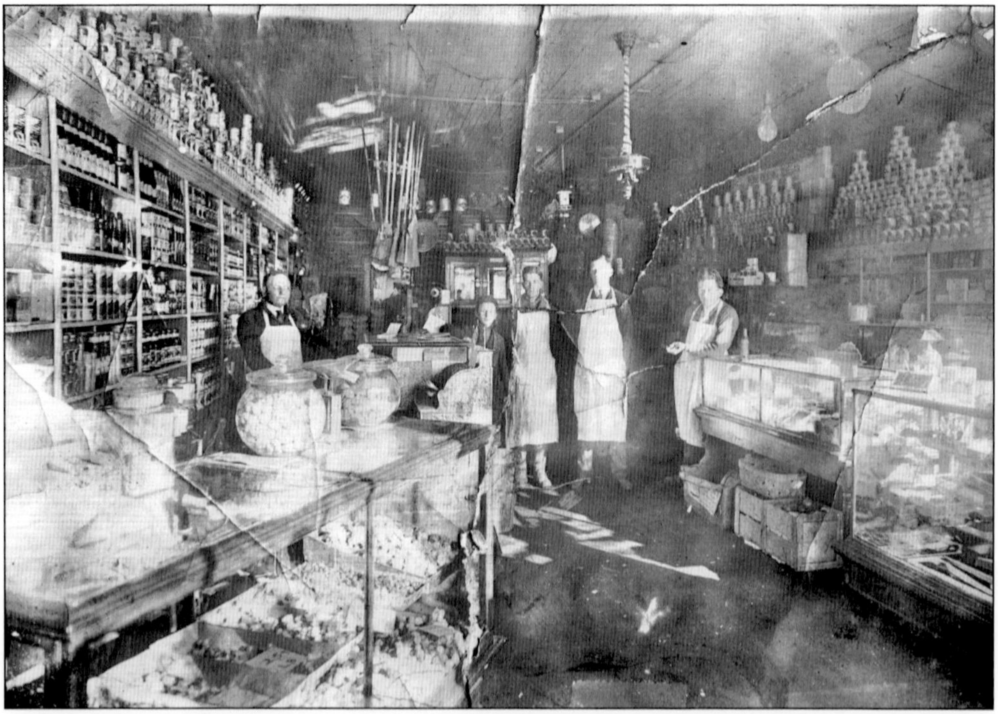

Arthur Kirby opened this store across from the intersection of Summit Street and West End Boulevard in 1923 at what is now 461 West End Boulevard. Business was so brisk that he opened another store next door at 457 West End Boulevard, the interior of which is pictured in the panorama below. Kirby's grocery truck made deliveries throughout the West End. (Both courtesy Alan Southard.)

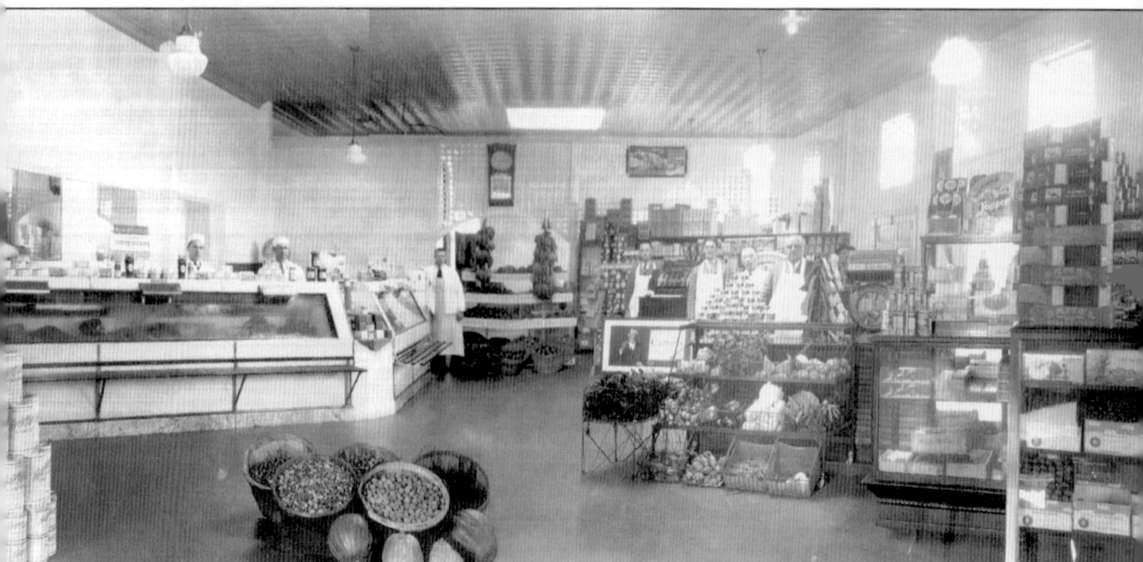

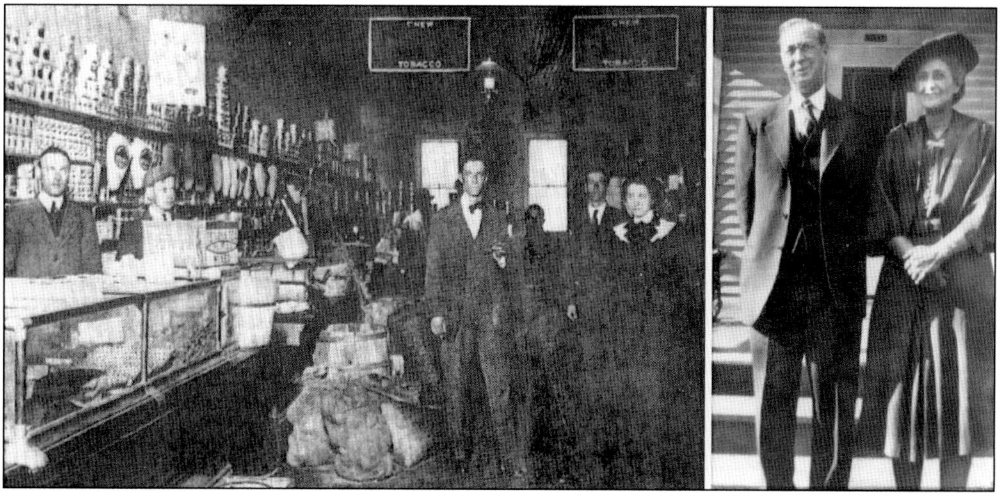

James G. Messick—shown at right with his wife, Sarah, at their home at 1117 West Fourth in the early 1940s—operated this grocery on Trade Street before starting J.G. Messick & Sons Wholesale Groceries. His sons would later open one of Winston-Salem's first modern supermarkets, Food Fair, on Main Street in 1947. (Courtesy Aaron and Brent Messick.)

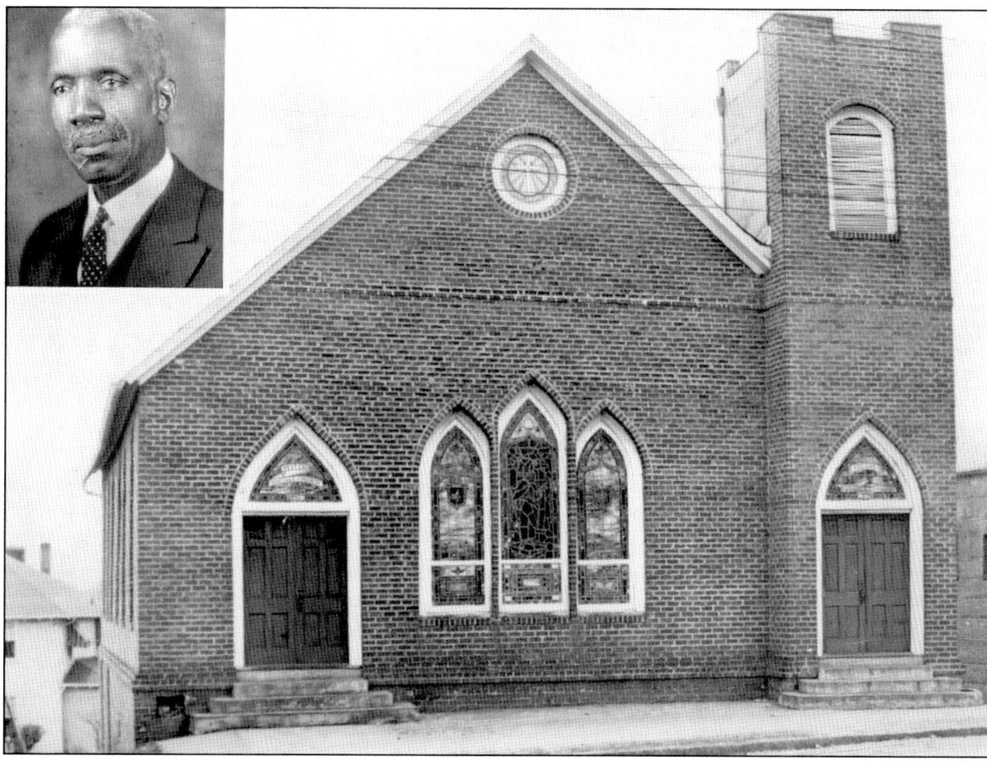

As a deacon, Rev. J. Pinkney Joyce (inset) helped organize West End Baptist Church in 1895 and watched as the congregation moved from small house meetings to this home on Burke Street in the early 1900s. The congregation merged in 1965 with First Institutional Baptist to form United Metropolitan Missionary Baptist Church, one of the last large African-American congregations in downtown. (Courtesy First Waughtown Baptist Church and United Metropolitan Missionary Baptist Church.)

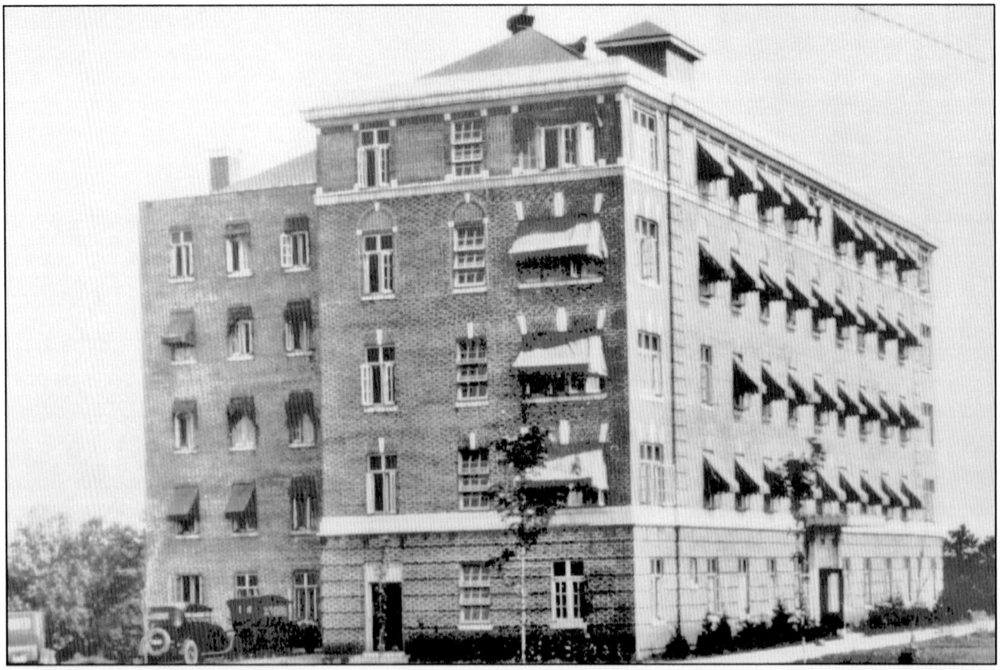

P. Huber Hanes and other local leaders were influential in getting the North Carolina Baptists, who were meeting in Winston-Salem in 1921, to announce sponsorship of a new state hospital in the city that year. Pictured here around 1930 is Baptist Hospital on Hawthorne Hill, just southwest of West End across Peters Creek. (Courtesy Dorothy Carpenter Medical Archives, Wake Forest School of Medicine.)

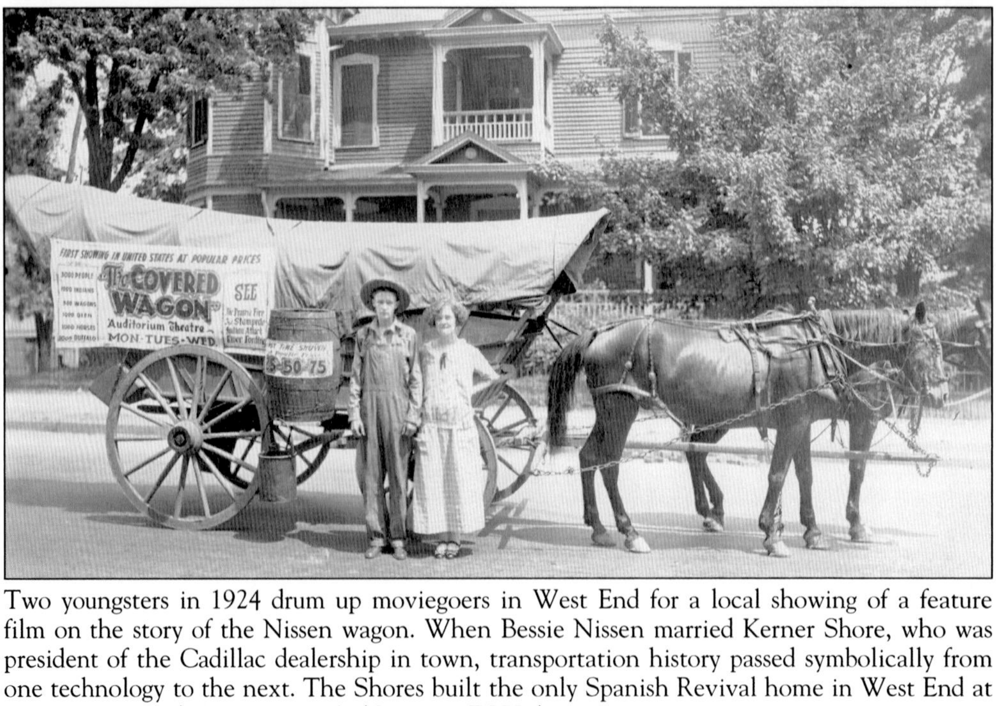

Two youngsters in 1924 drum up moviegoers in West End for a local showing of a feature film on the story of the Nissen wagon. When Bessie Nissen married Kerner Shore, who was president of the Cadillac dealership in town, transportation history passed symbolically from one technology to the next. The Shores built the only Spanish Revival home in West End at 1281 West Fourth Street in 1923. (Courtesy FCPL.)

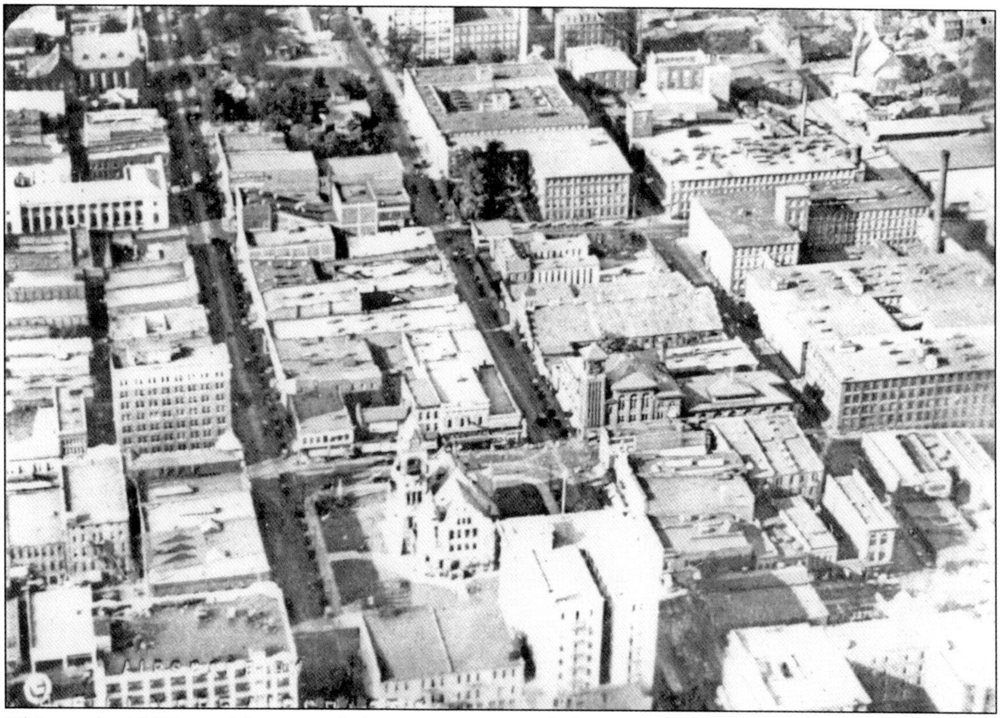

This early 1920s aerial view of the center part of the city depicts in the lower center the Romanesque courthouse that was replaced in 1926 and, to its upper right, the 1895 city hall, site of the R.J. Reynolds headquarters skyscraper, which opened in 1929. The density of tobacco warehouses, manufacturers, shops, and offices in the central business district is impressive. (Courtesy WHS/OS.)

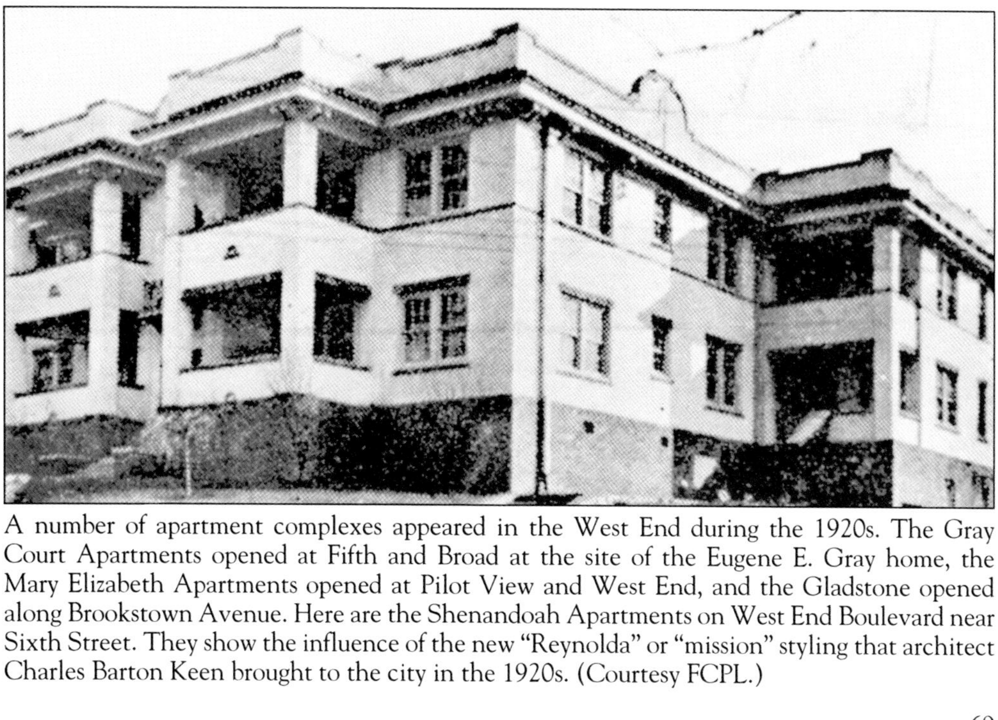

A number of apartment complexes appeared in the West End during the 1920s. The Gray Court Apartments opened at Fifth and Broad at the site of the Eugene E. Gray home, the Mary Elizabeth Apartments opened at Pilot View and West End, and the Gladstone opened along Brookstown Avenue. Here are the Shenandoah Apartments on West End Boulevard near Sixth Street. They show the influence of the new "Reynolda" or "mission" styling that architect Charles Barton Keen brought to the city in the 1920s. (Courtesy FCPL.)

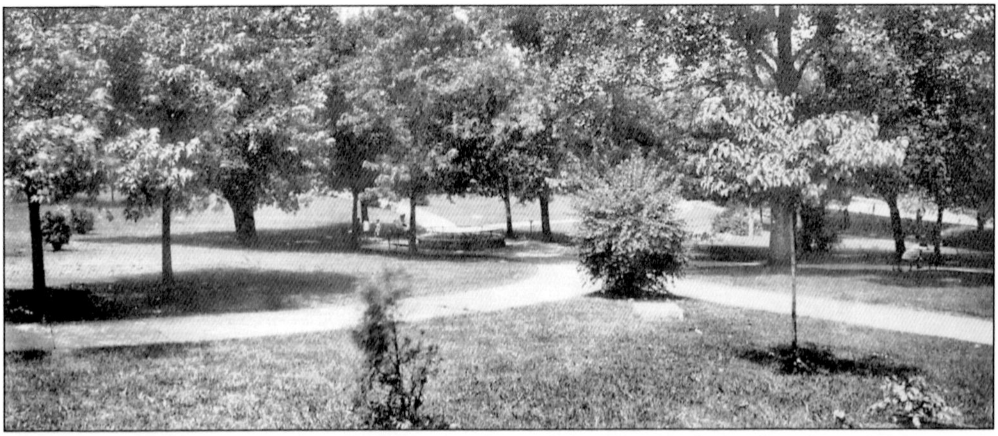

Grace Court, named for Grace Whitaker, daughter of the West End Hotel and Land Company's president, was donated to the city in 1905. In its early years, as one neighbor said, it was "not much more than a cow pasture." Here in 1924 from *Art Work of Piedmont Section of North Carolina*, the park featured a cast-iron fountain and paved sidewalks popular with neighborhood children for skating and go-carts. The iron fountain was removed for scrap during World War II but was replaced by a brick fountain until the 1970s. (Courtesy FCPL.)

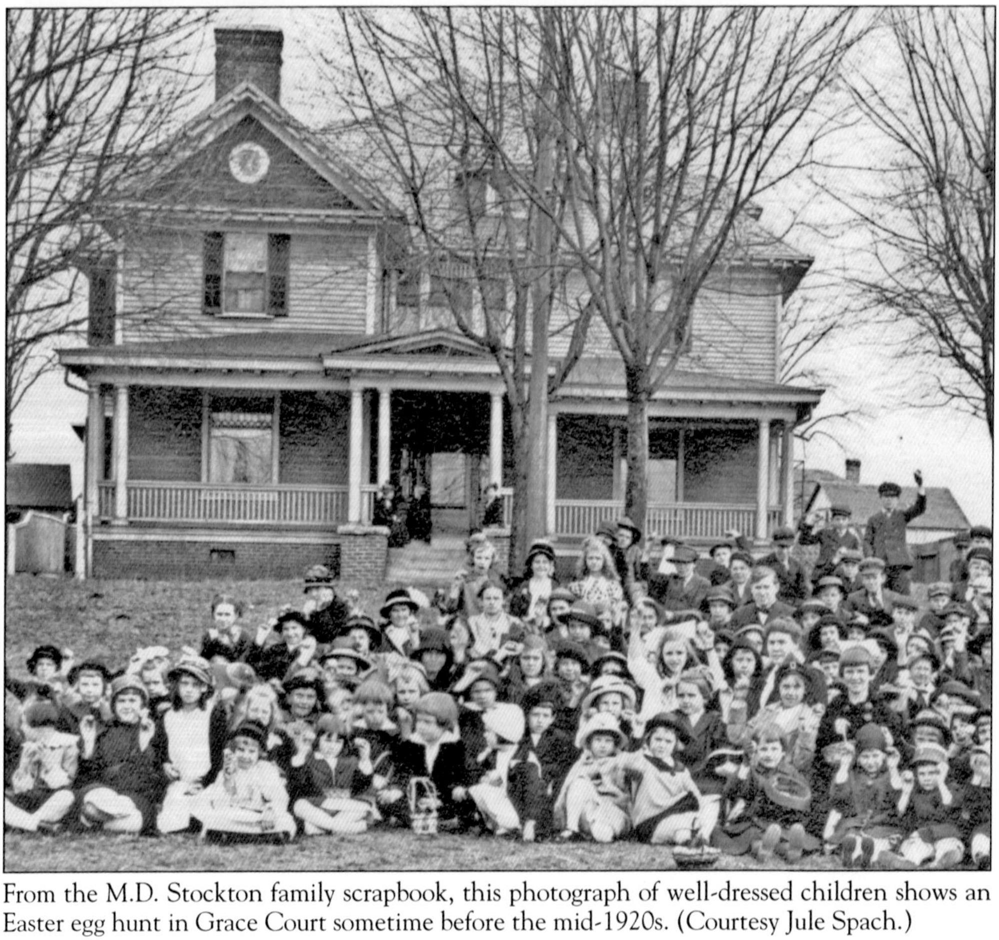

From the M.D. Stockton family scrapbook, this photograph of well-dressed children shows an Easter egg hunt in Grace Court sometime before the mid-1920s. (Courtesy Jule Spach.)

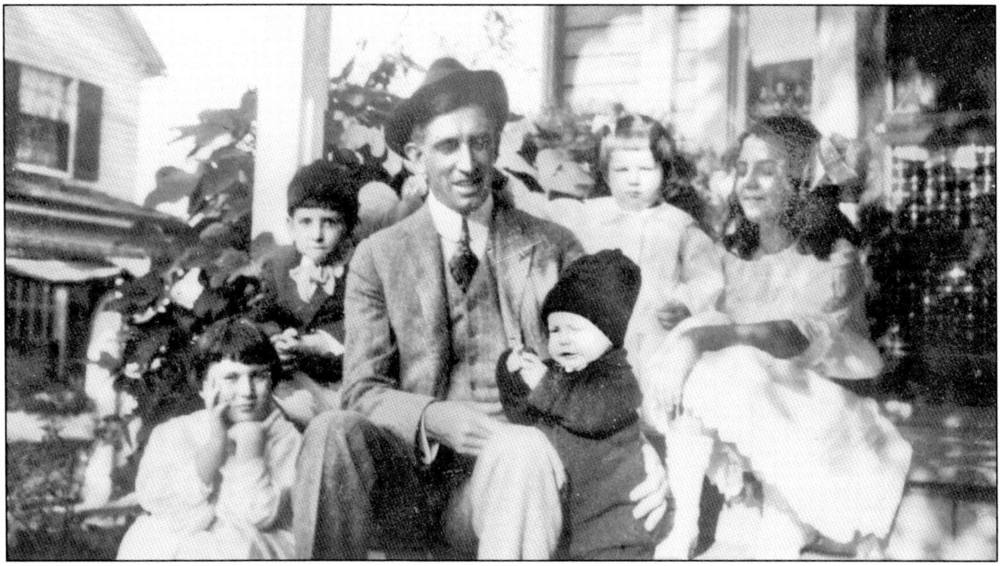

In 1914, attorney B.S. Womble married and moved to 607 Summit Street, near his senior partner, Col. Clement Manly. Above, Womble sits with his children on their front porch in 1923. He told the family of an early West End experience: a simple drive with Huber Hanes and their dates in about 1910, during which they went out from Cherry Street to the end of the pavement at Summit, on to Lovers' Lane (now Stratford Road), and back in on Shallowford Road. What would be no more than a 15-minute drive today was then—with dates, uneven roads, and a flat tire—an all-afternoon adventure. Womble Carlyle Sandridge and Rice PLLC is now one of the state's largest law firms. (Courtesy Bill Womble.)

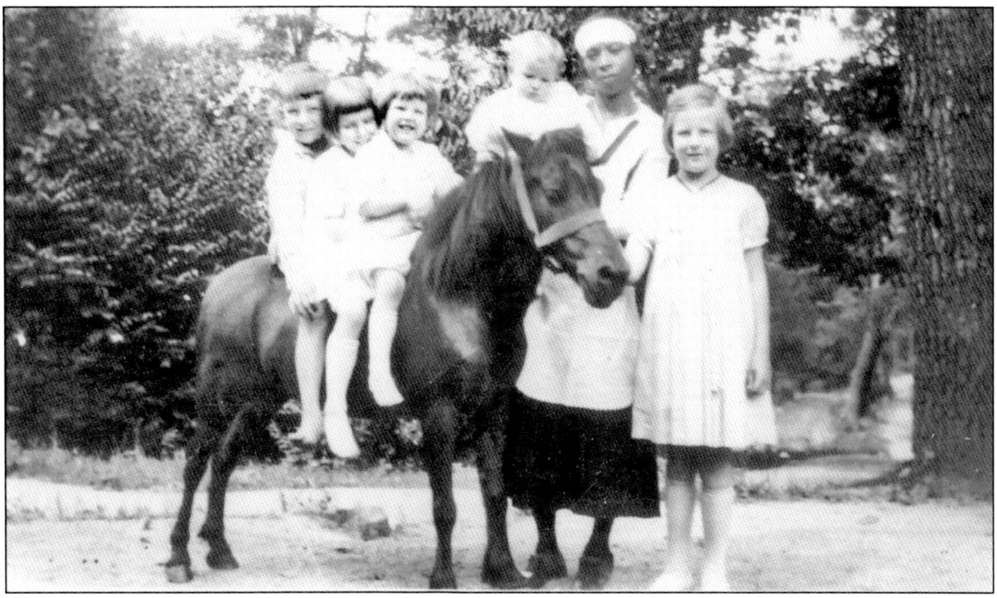

The Womble children—Bill, Olivia, Edith, Calder, and Lila—are pictured here with their nurse and Bill's pony, Gentry. Addie Siewers, their nurse, lived on Liberia Street in Happy Hill near Salem. Other domestic help for West Enders lived in houses in "Brown's Run" along 5 1/2 Street (now Pilot View) and along "Dog Trot" or Burk(e) Street. In 1927, the Womble family moved to a new home at 200 Stratford Road. (Courtesy Bill Womble.)

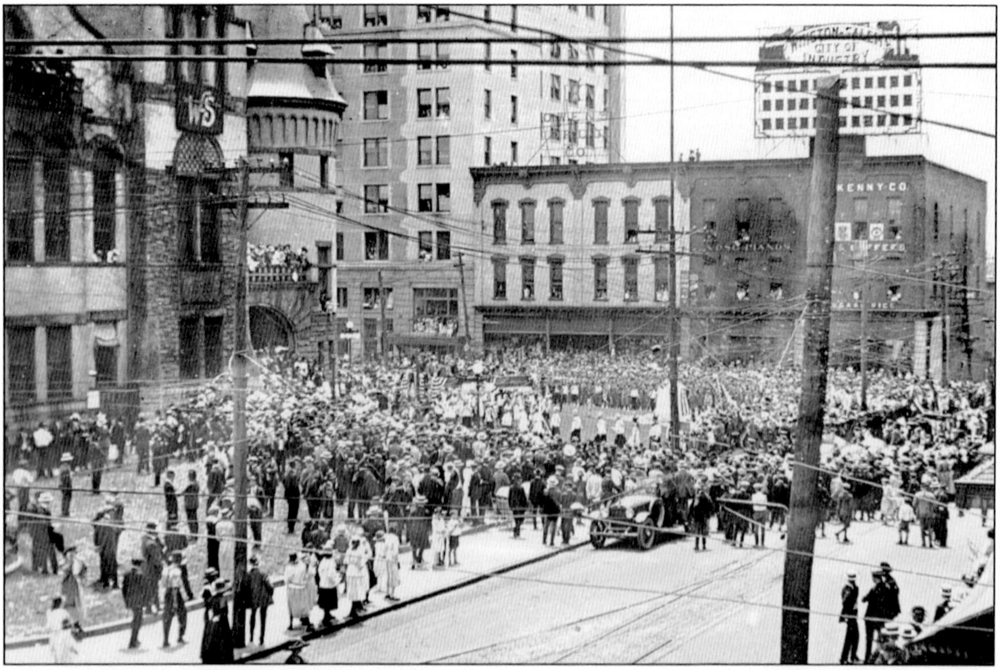

Crowds gather in the Courthouse Square under the sign announcing Winston-Salem as the "City of Industry." By 1924, the city led the nation in production of cigarettes and underwear and was a leader in woolen goods production as well. Over 200 miles inland, it was still the nation's seventh largest "port of entry" for imports and exports. Of the leaders of the chamber of commerce (formerly board of trade) shown below, over half lived in the West End. (Courtesy WHS/OS and FCPL.)

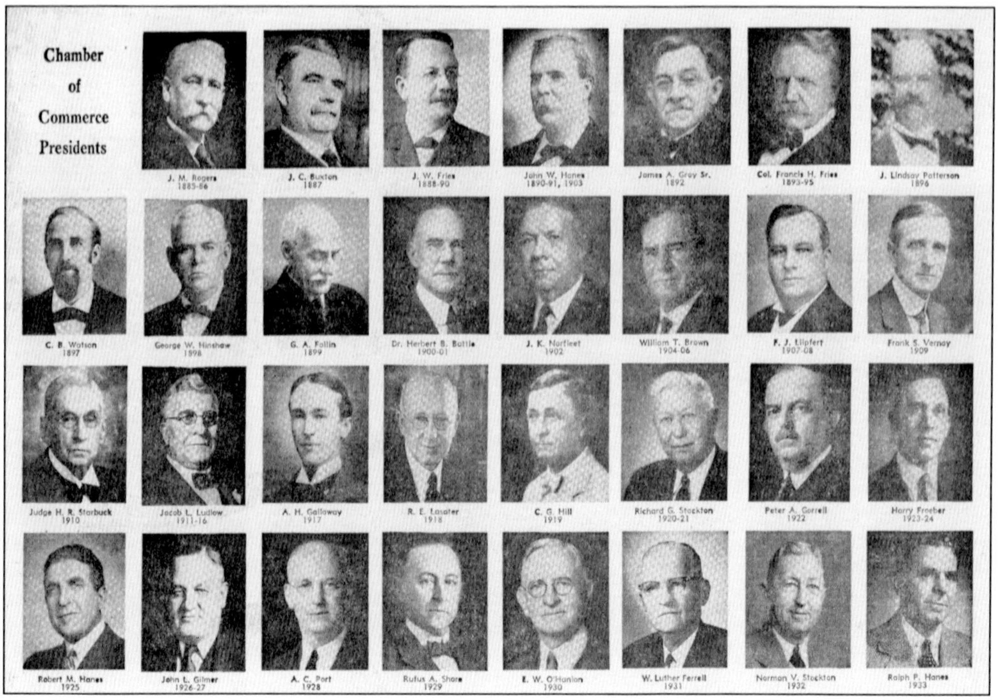

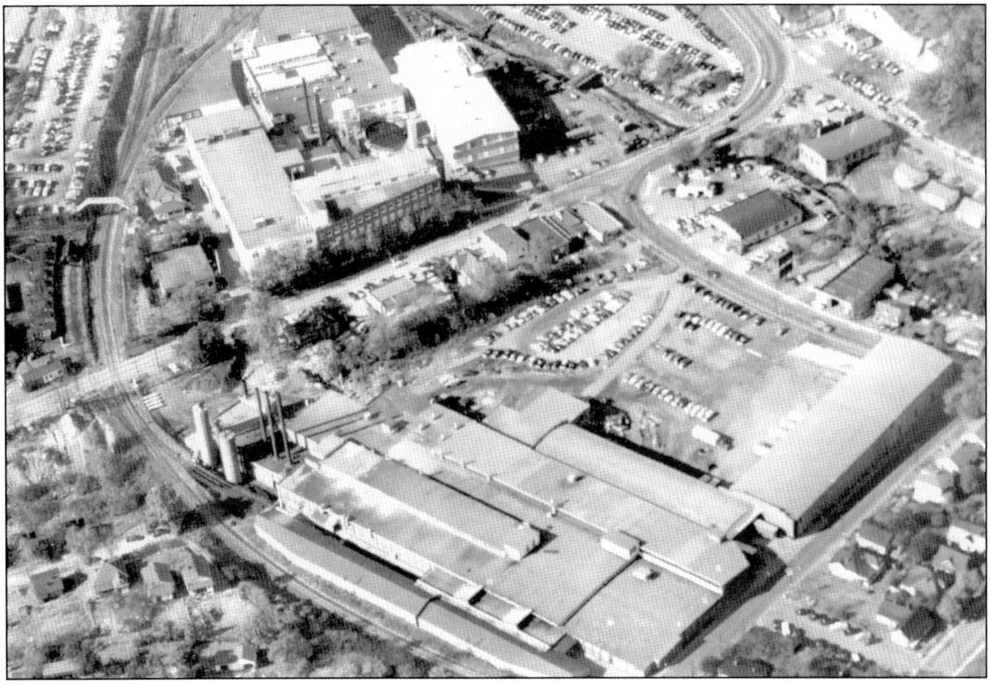

This aerial view shows the northern edge of the West End at left, with the plant of Chatham Manufacturing (top center), a blanket manufacturer from Elkin, North Carolina, built in 1915, and the Hanes Dye and Finishing factory (bottom right), begun by Anna Hodgin Hanes's son Ralph in 1925. (Courtesy FCPL.)

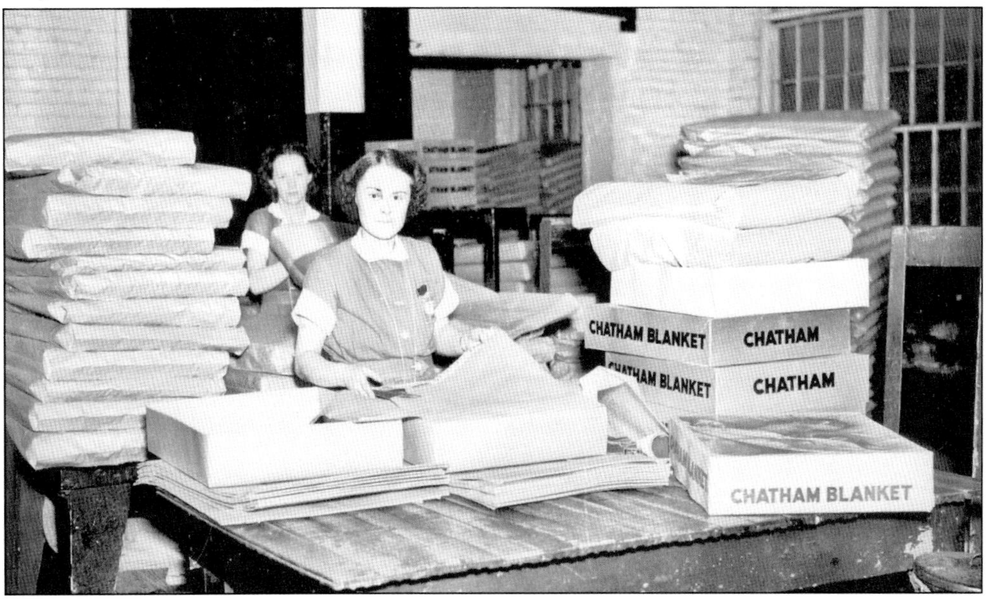

Caroline Singletary recalls as a neighborhood kid on her way home from Wiley School in the 1920s racing with her friends to Peters Creek "to see what color blankets Chatham was making that day." The water-soluble color effluent from the plant was discharged in the creek. Here, a factory worker packages Chatham blankets in the Winston plant in the 1930s. (Courtesy FCPL.)

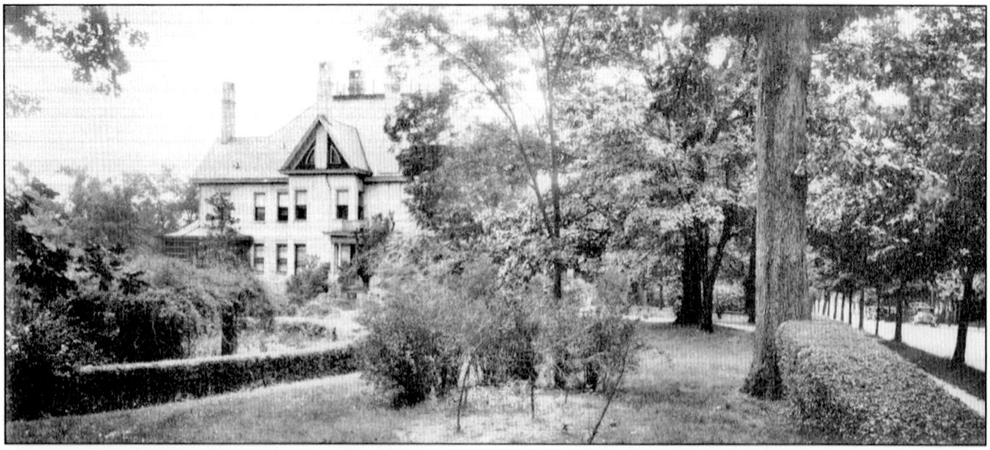

Here in two previously under-labeled photos from the 1924 book *Art Work of Piedmont Section of North Carolina* is the Fifth Street streetscape at the heart of West End's Millionaires' Row: above, the R.J. Reynolds house, and below, the view from half a block long east of the Bowman Gray bungalow (left foreground) with the porch of the Will Reynolds home peeking through next door at the center. (Both courtesy FCPL.)

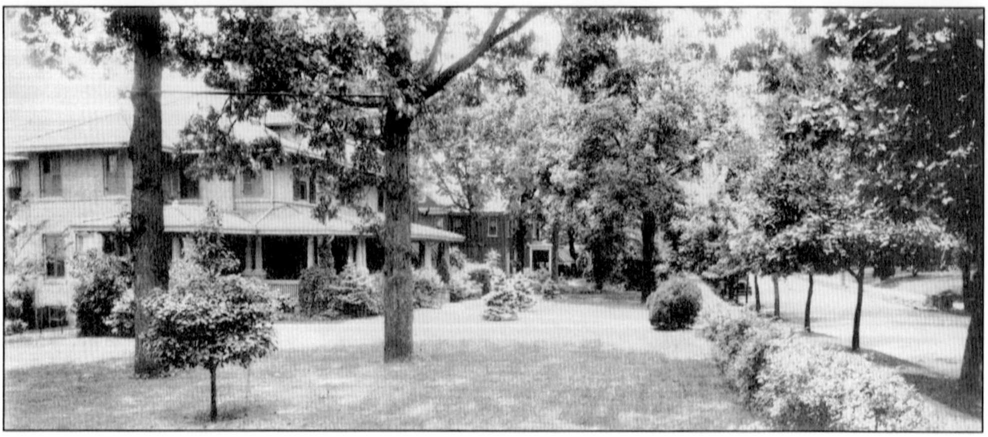

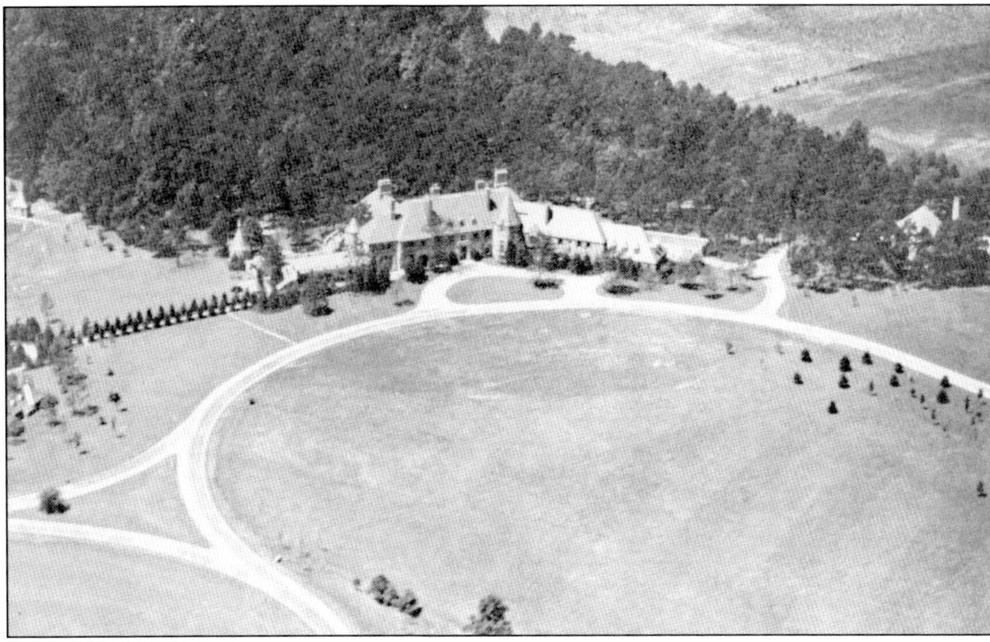

As the Reynolds skyscraper took over the downtown skyline, the West End streetscape began a dramatic change. In 1928, Bowman Gray bought neighbor Will Reynolds's home for $1,000 and then gave the property and that of his own home to Centenary Methodist for a new sanctuary site. Gray opened his country estate, Graylyn (top), in 1932 on acreage acquired from Reynolda. In the early 1920s, Will Reynolds purchased a manor home by the Yadkin River (below) with 1,000 acres of farm to form Tanglewood. (Courtesy Wake Forest University Special Collections, Z. Smith Reynolds Library; and Tanglewood Park/Forsyth County Parks and Recreation.)

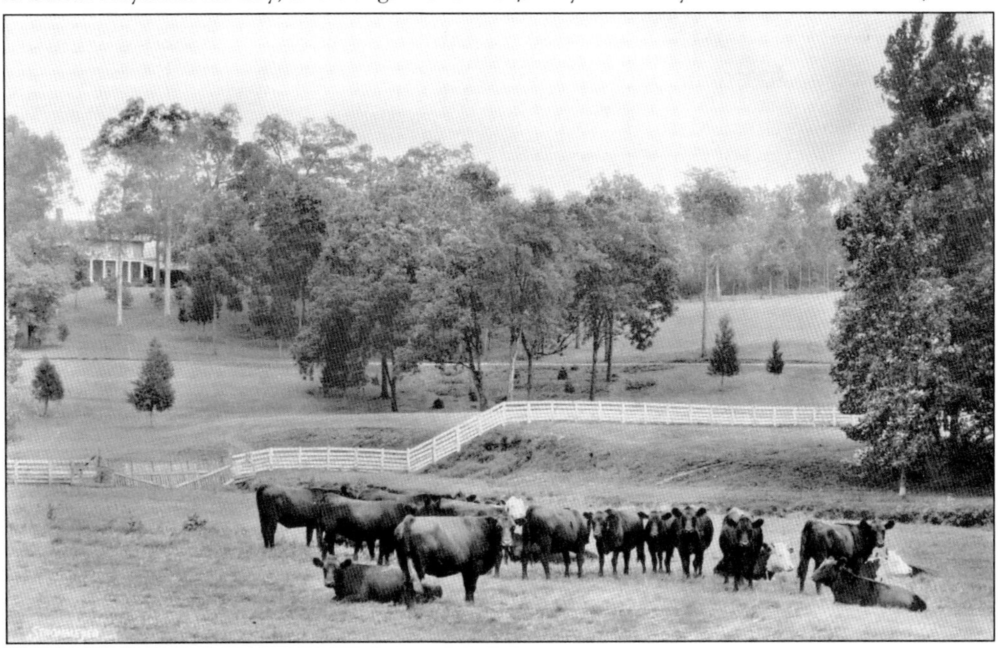

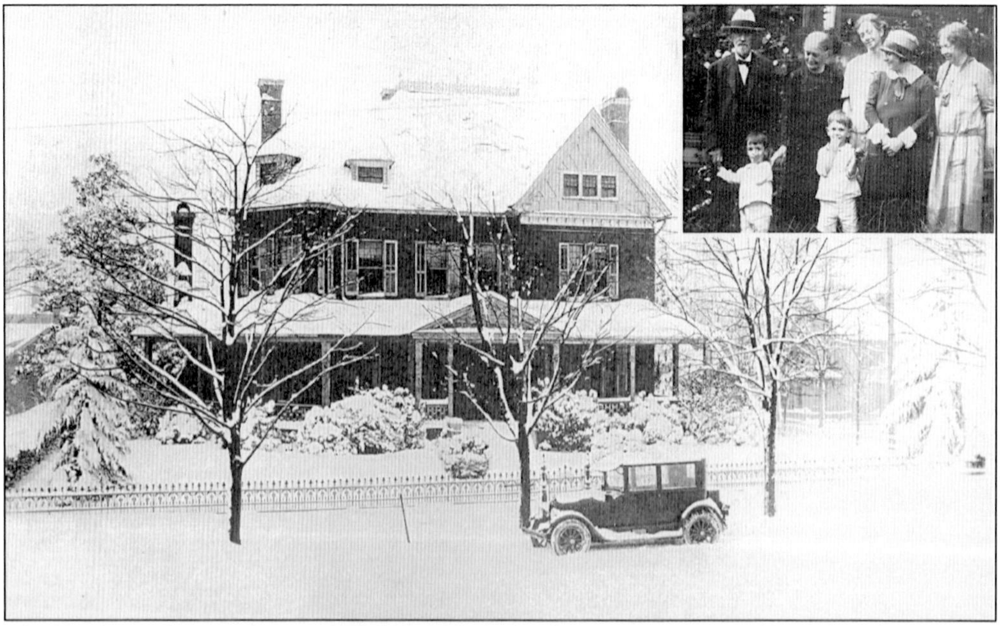

The Frank Liipfert House is captured in a Currier and Ives moment at Fifth and Poplar in 1927. By the late 1920s, it was difficult to build afresh in West End; empty lots were scarce, and new wealth in the 1920s brought the desire for new lands to develop. The first generation of West Enders, like Andrew Mickle (inset, shown in 1927), began either passing on properties to their children or moving westward to new developments. (Courtesy Old Salem, Inc. and Donna and Andrew Mickle.)

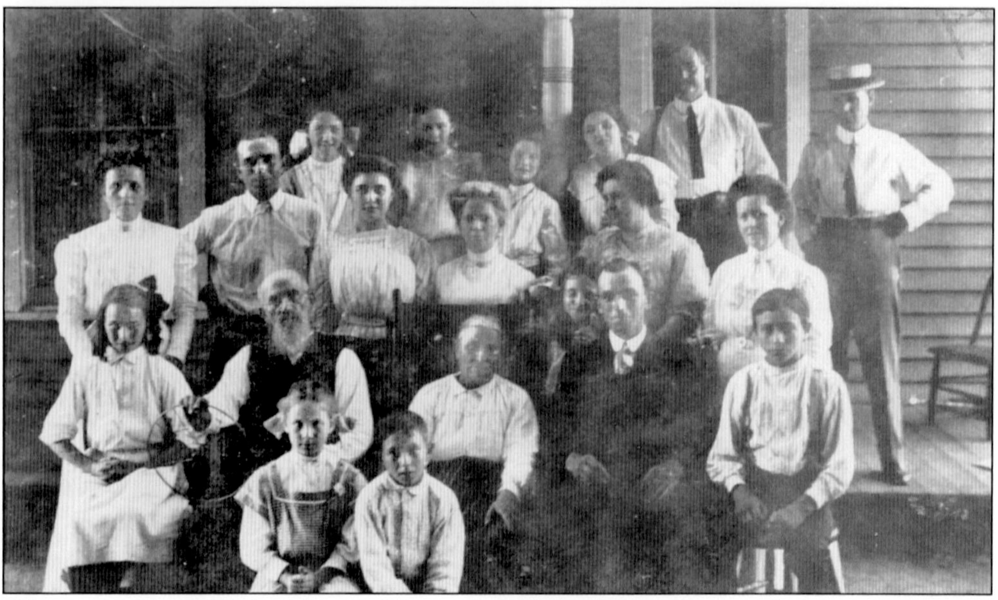

Others moved in to make West End home. Angelo Zaffaroni was an Italian stonecutter who worked on the farm of a North Carolina governor before coming to Winston in the 1880s. Finding no one could pronounce his last name, he became Zaffaroni Angelo. Here, he is pictured with his family around 1910 on the porch at his home near today's Angelo Street. (Courtesy of Tom Angelo.)

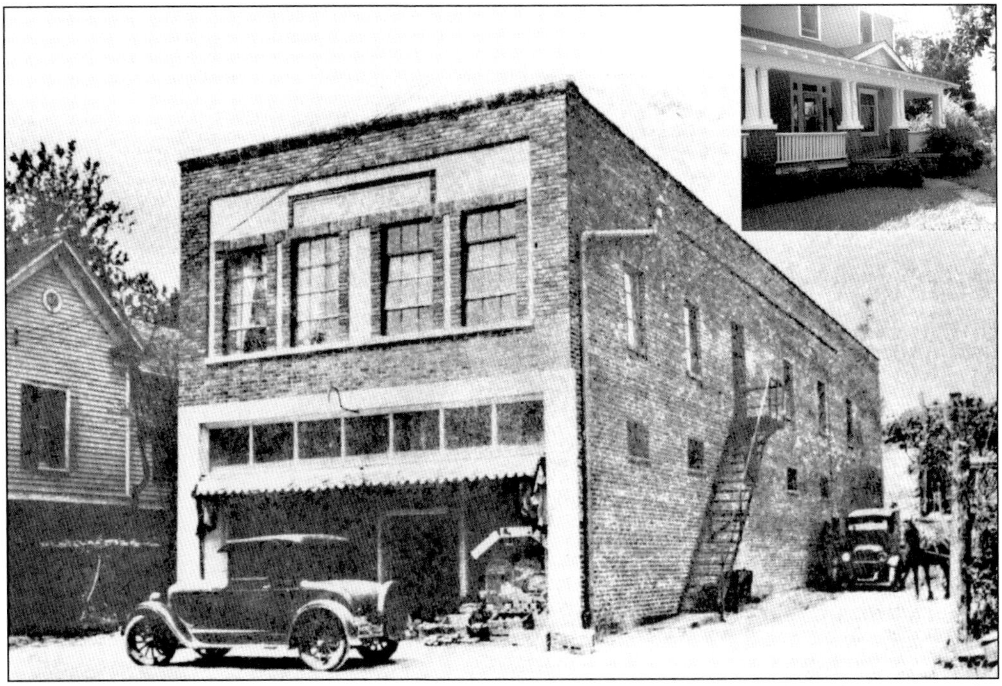

Angelo's son Michael built this house (inset) on the corner of Broad and Sixth in 1916. The family was in the grocery business before concentrating on wholesaling tobacco and candy products for other stores. The family business location on Burke Street, shown here about 1930 with the name of Michael's brother E.J. Angelo over the door, was later expanded with wings on either side and apartments above. It is still a major part of the entrepreneurial district along Burke Street today. (Courtesy Tom Angelo.)

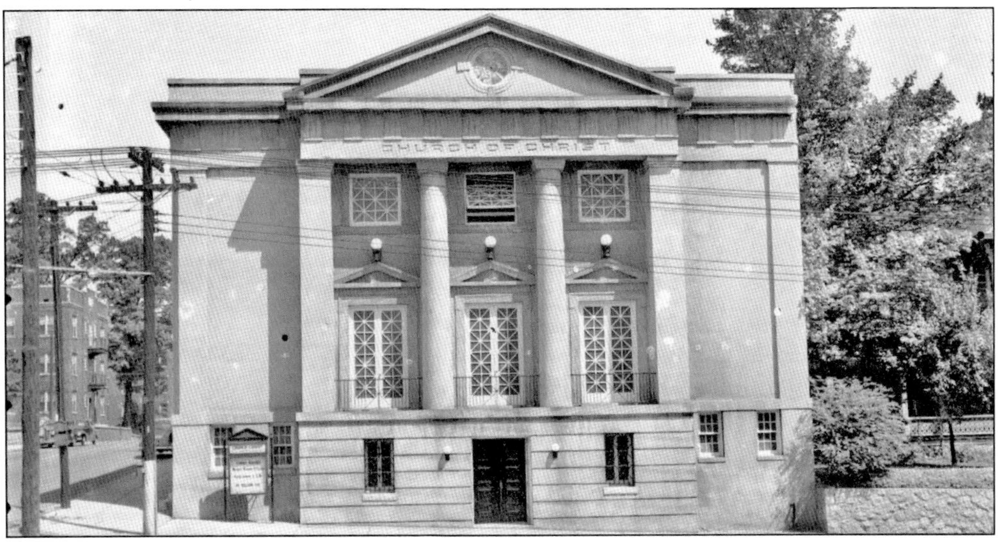

The 1920s witnessed a wave of church construction in and near the West End. First Christian Church (shown here) opened on the northeast corner of Fourth and Broad in 1922, while the First Church of Christ, Scientist, built at Brookstown and Fifth in 1924. The Society of Friends began a meetinghouse at Sixth and Broad in 1926. Augsburg Lutheran opened in 1927 on Fifth Street properties acquired from St. Leo's Catholic Church. (Courtesy FCPL.)

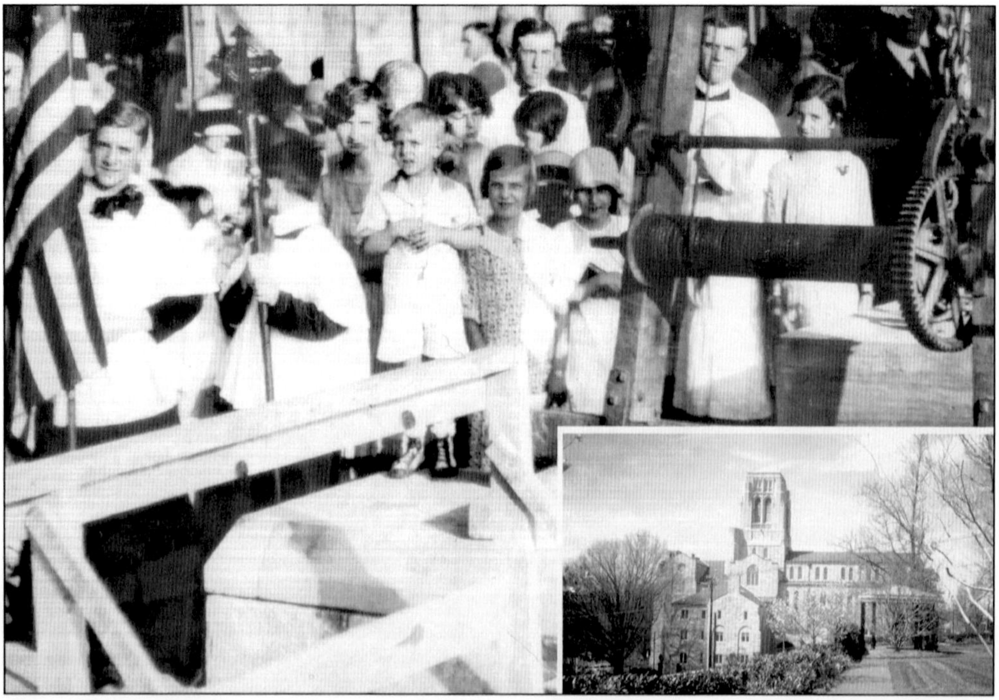

When an offer was made on church property at Fourth and Cherry, St. Paul's Episcopal moved from downtown to the site of the J.C. Buxton house on Summit Street. Located on the most dramatic vista in West End, St. Paul's dominates the view of West End ridge even today (inset). R.E. Lasater helped secure the property in 1927, and the cornerstone was laid in 1928. The church opened on October 6, 1929. (Courtesy StP.)

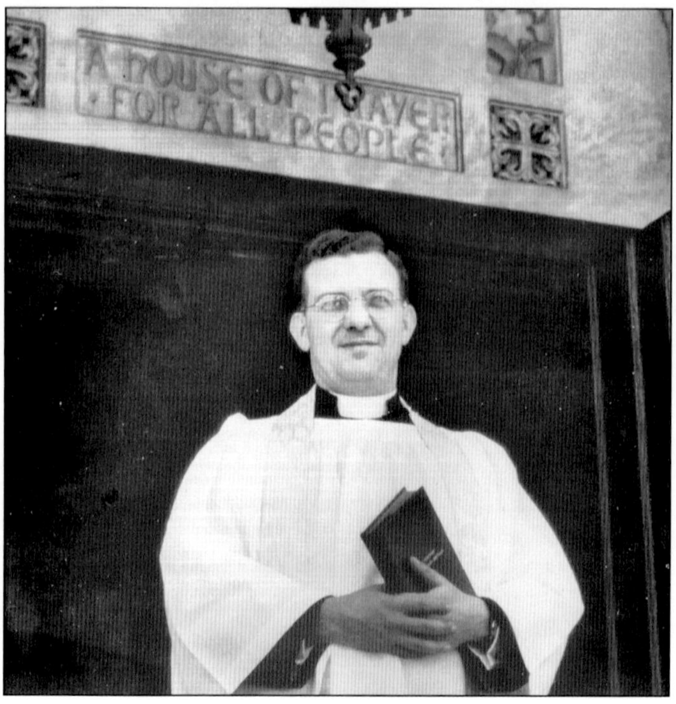

Saint Paul's Church was the first in town to be designed by a nationally known architect. Dr. Ralph Adams Cram signed each of his churches with the same prominently displayed signature phrase. Here in the 1950s, Rector Thomas Fraser stands under "A House of Prayer for All People" at the eastern entrance to the church. (Courtesy StP.)

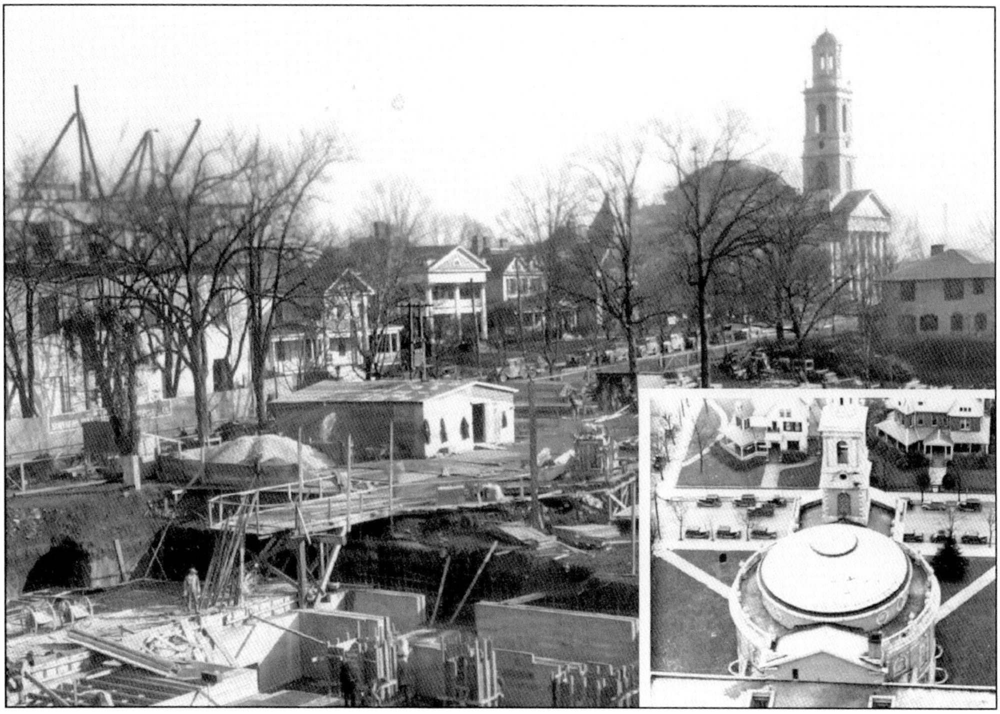

With the help of Reynolds executive D. Rich, First Baptist also relocated, completing their distinctive circular sanctuary (inset) in 1925 at the site of the Dr. Robah Gray home on the northwest corner of Spruce and Fifth. The larger view shows Fifth Street next to First Baptist in 1930, with construction at left on the first commercial intrusion on Fifth, the Bell Telephone building, and in front at the site of the new Centenary Methodist. (Courtesy CUMC and FCPL.)

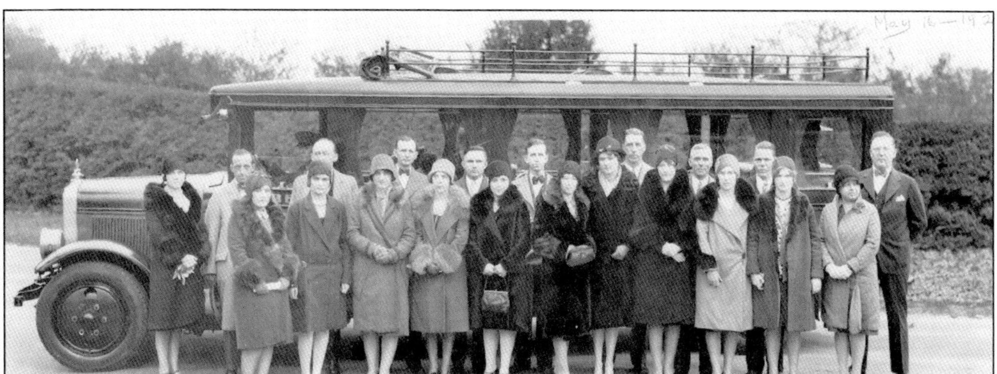

Centenary and West End Methodists joined congregations in 1927, occasionally meeting together in West End School again as the new church was being planned. Here, joint choir director E.R. Clapp (right) leads his musicians on a trip in 1928. (Courtesy CUMC.)

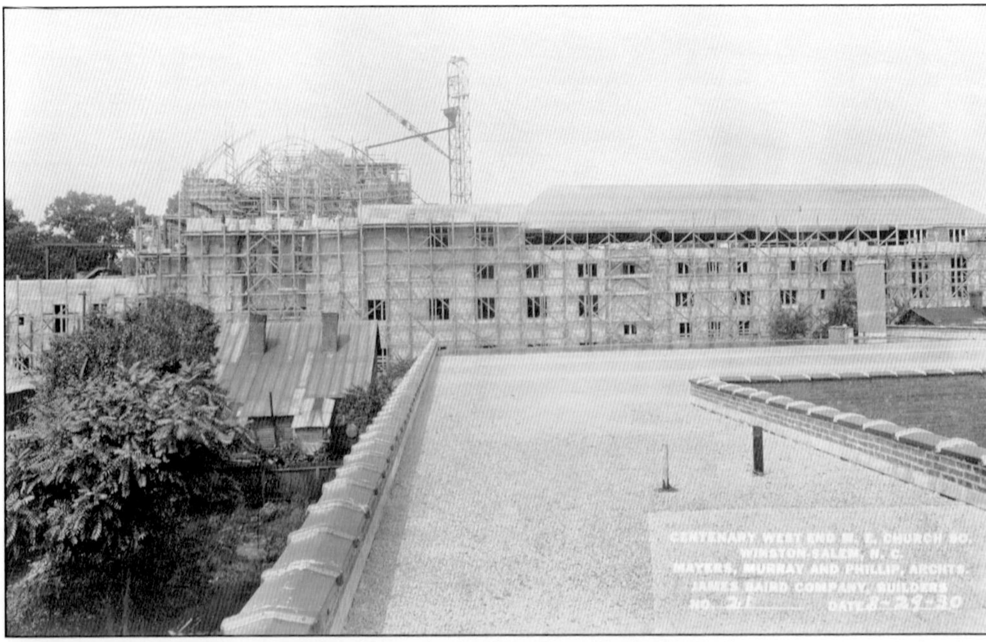

Centenary was the last of the churches to be built in West End. Soon after construction contracts were set in 1929, the stock market crash crippled the prospects of the congregation completing the church. Ten families stepped forward to secure the note guaranteeing the project. The church opened in 1931, and the note was finally retired in 1941. Economic downturn brought change to the way Winston-Salem and the country did business. In 1930, Charlotte overtook Winston-Salem as the state's largest city. (Both courtesy CUMC.)

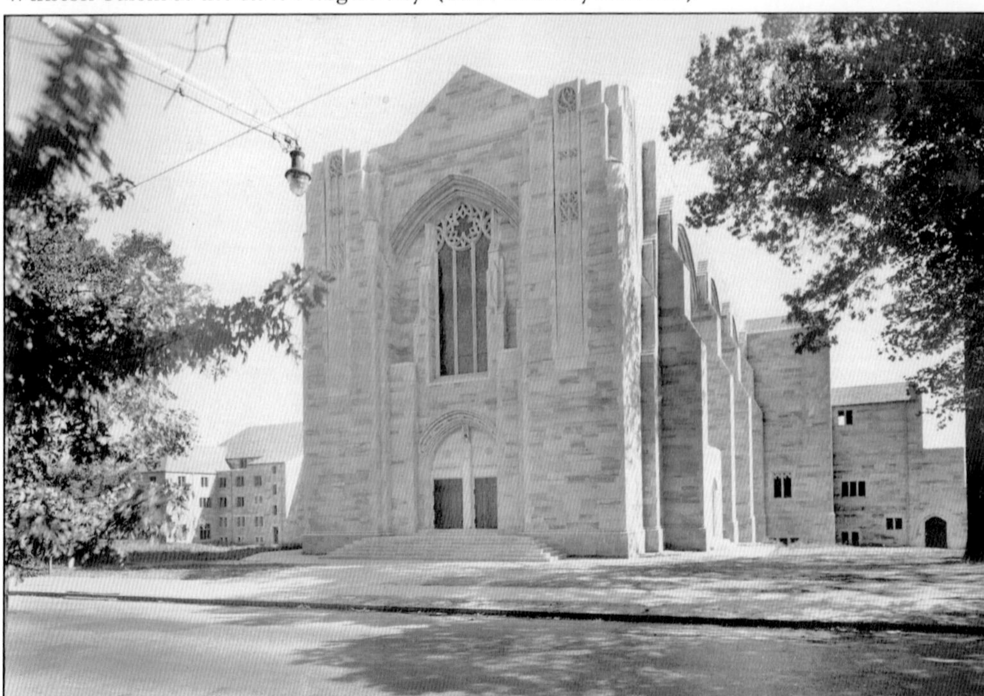

Three

A Neighborhood Matures *1930–1967*

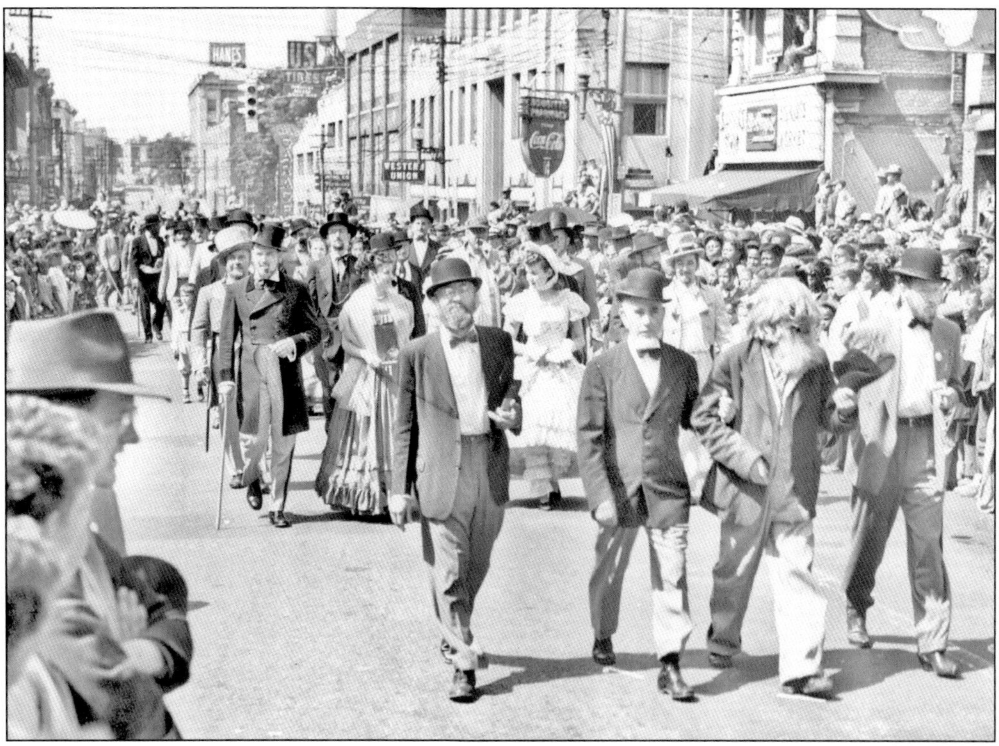

In 1949, Winston-Salem celebrated the 100th anniversary of Forsyth County with a beard-growing contest, costumed re-creations of the antebellum South, and a massive parade with 100,000 people lining the streets. However, as the middle years of the last century came and went in Winston's West End, the parade of success that had seemed so glorious in the years before the Depression was beginning to pass the neighborhood by. (Courtesy FCPL.)

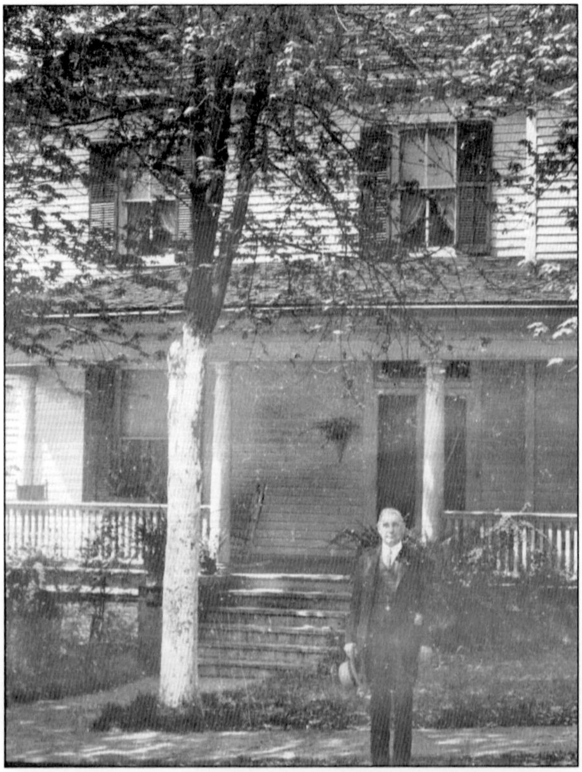

Many fondly remember the days of West End during the Depression—a tight-knit community where people did things to help each other out. Few had cars, enjoyments were simpler, and difficulties made pleasures sweeter. Here, John Still stands in front of the family home where he and his descendants spent 70 years. (Courtesy John Still.)

As West End's wealthier families moved west to Stratford Road, Buena Vista, and elsewhere, larger, older homes found new owners and new uses. The Woman's Club of Winston-Salem moved into the Tise home in 1929 as a bequest of the family. For over 70 years, Tise House was the center for the social and civic programs of this network of the town's leading ladies. Below is a program of the Thursday Morning Music Club at the Tise House in 1951. (Courtesy FCPL.)

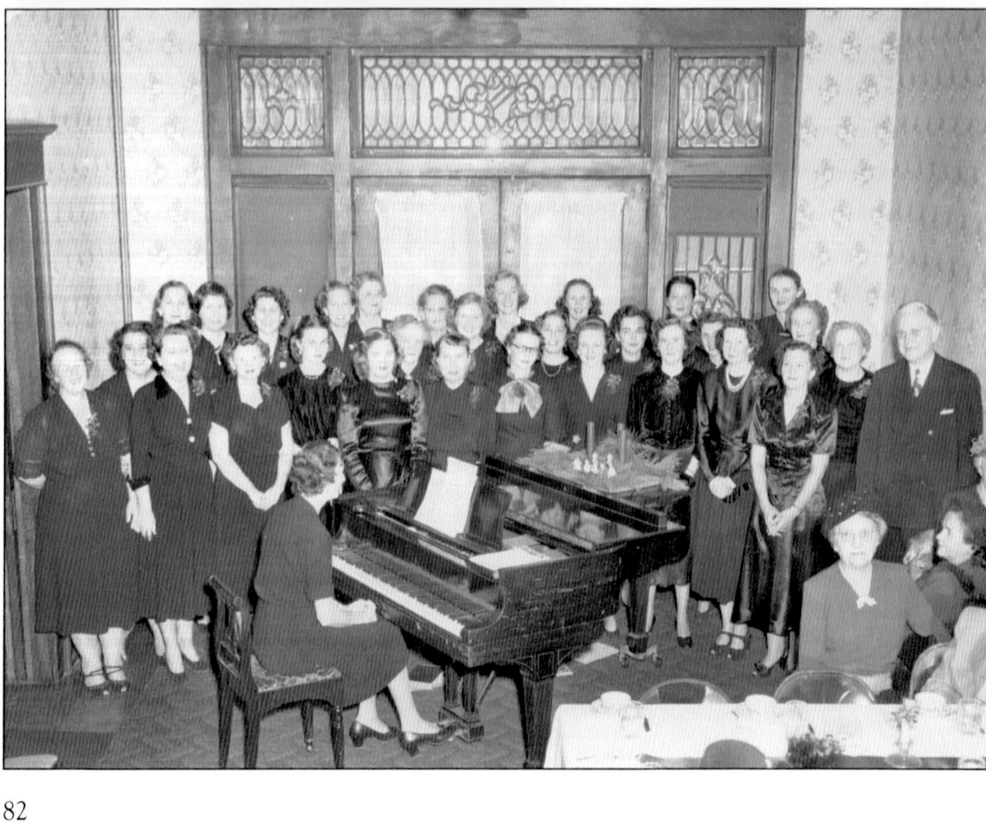

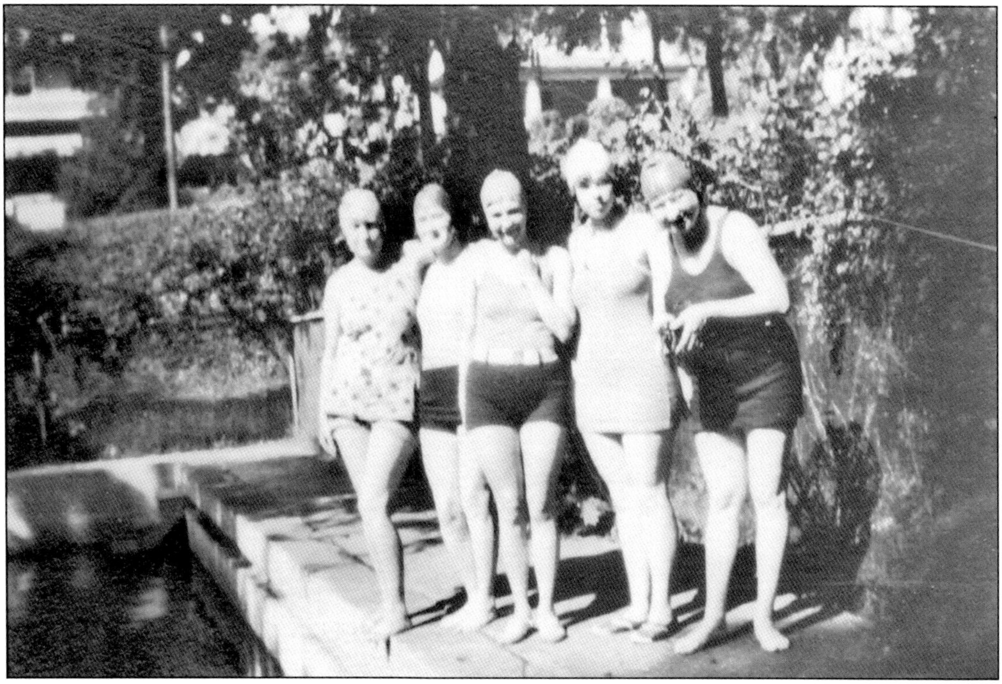

Lucile Perry McCall (left) is pictured with family and friends in the late 1920s at the swimming pool of C.M. Thomas's home at what is now 1300 Brookstown Avenue. Lucile's mom married the widowed Mr. Thomas, owner of a number of construction and supply companies, only after the last of her own daughters was married. (Courtesy Betty McCall Beeson.)

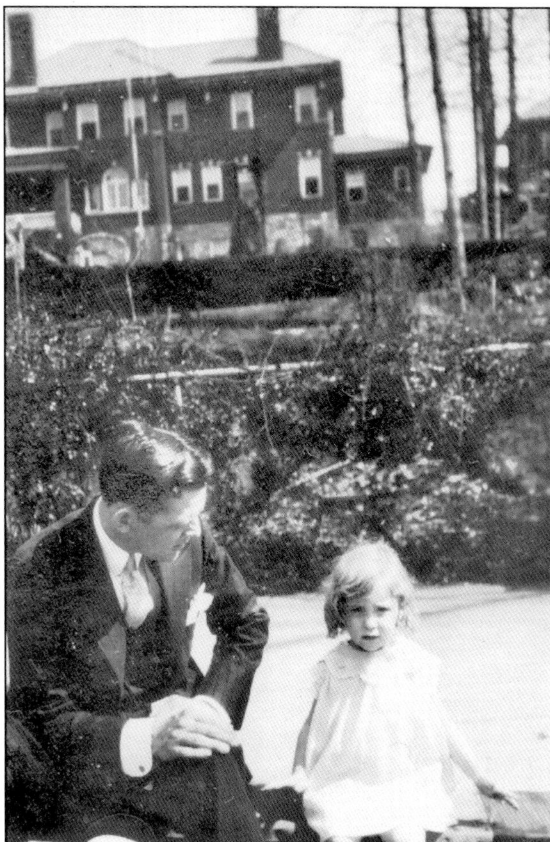

Lucile McCall's daughter, Betty, sits here coyly next to a family friend behind the Thomas home. Mr. Thomas's family income was dependent on folks paying for the products he sold them. With the Depression, fewer were able to pay, and Thomas was forced to leave this mansion in 1930 and downsize to a smaller home. (Courtesy Betty McCall Beeson.)

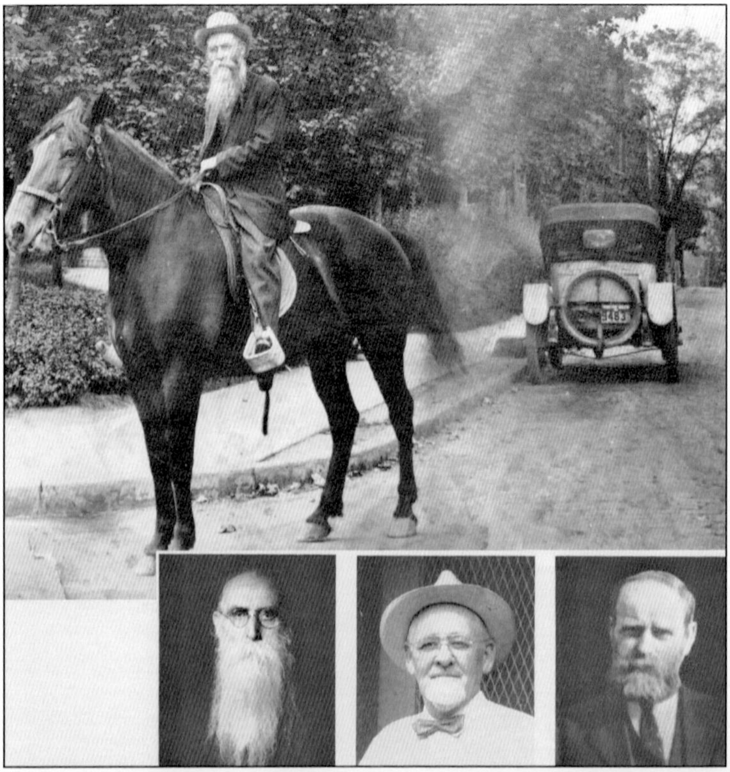

Taylor Brothers was the last family tobacco manufacturer to remain an independent. Bill Taylor, shown here on horseback near his home at Fourth and Brookstown (and inset at left), never bought a car and never wanted one. His brother, Jack, (inset at right) was equally independent politically, being one of the town's few public socialists. Bill's son, Arch (inset center), took over the business at his father's death in 1933. (Courtesy FCPL, and Greg Sawyers/Taylor Brothers Tobacco.)

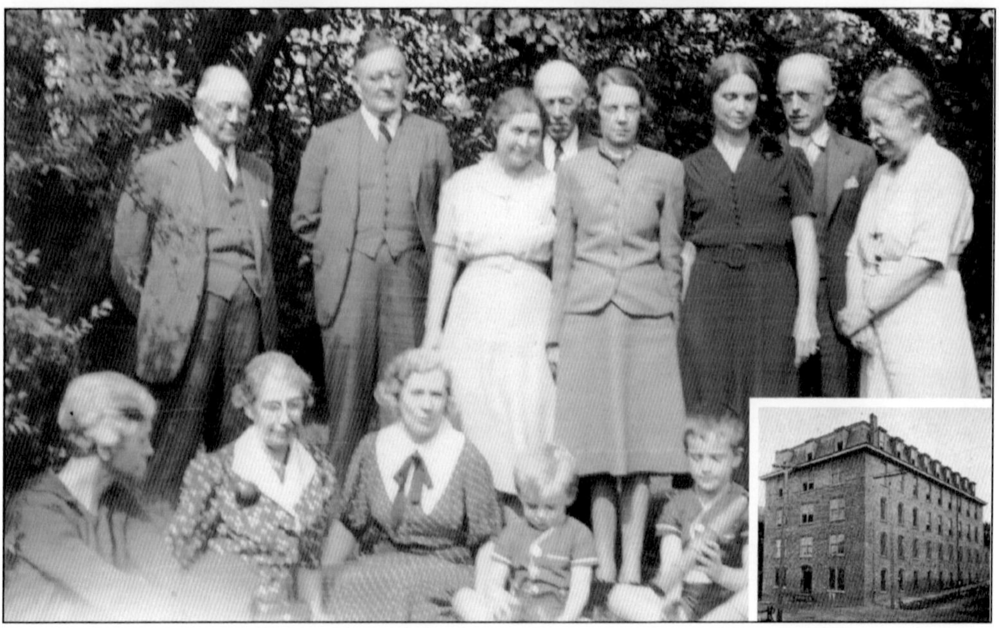

In 1951, when Arch Taylor finally sold the family factory at First and Patterson (inset), a spirit and an era in West End and Winston symbolically ended. However, the Taylors still kept West End ties even after Arch left the neighborhood: he married one of Andrew Mickle's daughters from around the corner on Fifth Street. Arch Taylor is standing second from left in this Mickle reunion photo. (Courtesy RH/MAA and Donna and Andrew Mickle.)

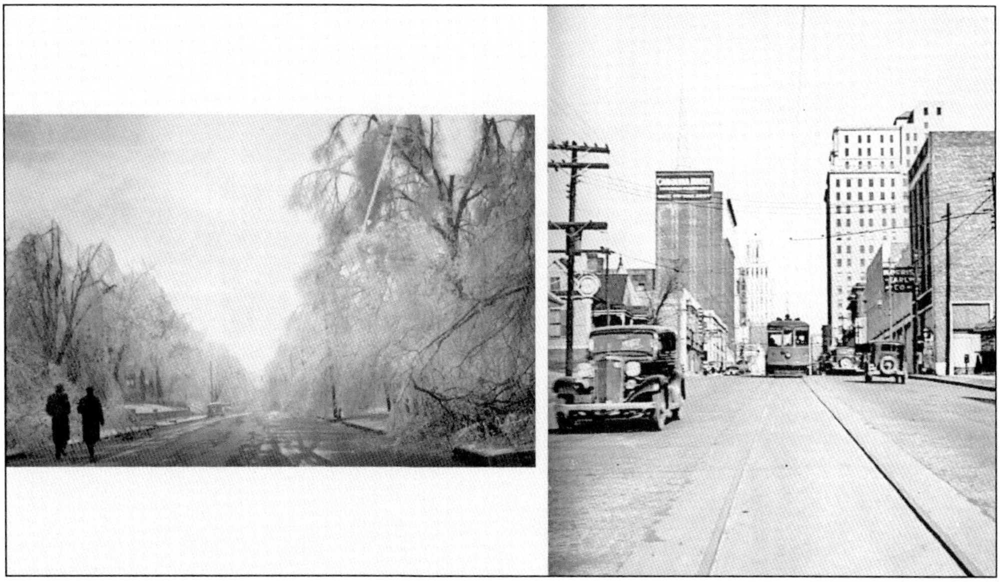

The terrible ice storm of February 1934 was a symbolic freeze for the town in the 1930s; it was a struggle to maintain the fruits of the prosperity of the 1910s and 1920s. In 1936, the last of the city's beloved trolleys made its final run. Here, the trolley passes by two shopping traditions for West Enders on the southside of Fourth Street, Morris Early and Sosnik's. (Courtesy Tom Angelo and NCSA.)

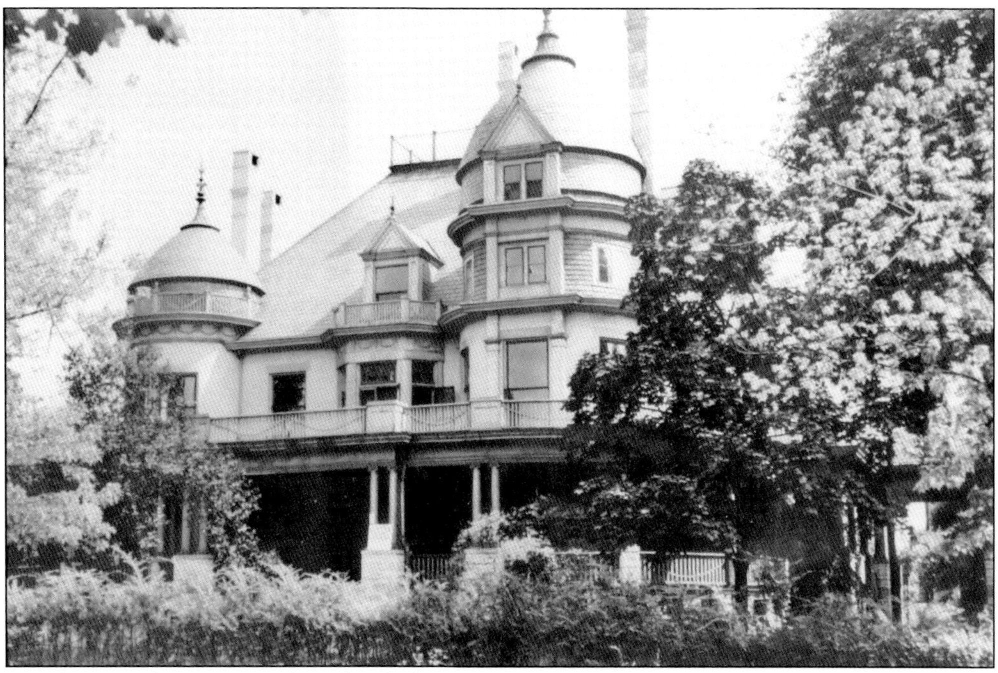

Caroline Singletary remembers fondly how children from families with great wealth lived and played with average folks in the West End of the 1920s. She used to skate with Smith Reynolds on the townhouse porch. After his New Year's Day marriage in 1933, R.J.'s son Dick Jr. even opened the closed townhouse for one big party that included the neighbors. By 1936, the townhouse was overgrown, and its celebrations were few. (Courtesy KBRT.)

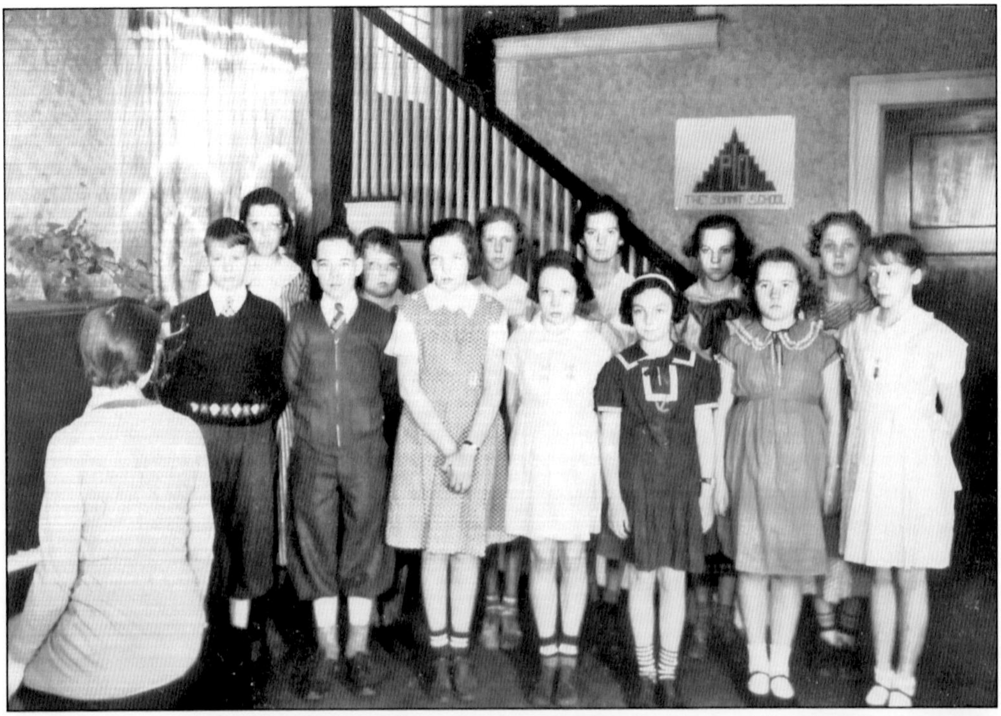

A group of parents concerned about the tight economy's impact on public education started a school in West End at 405 Summit Street in 1933, hiring Miss Louise Futrell to organize and administer the program. Summit School, named for its aspirations rather than the location of its building, had both the distinctively stair-step logo, representing the climb to the top in educational success, and motto, "PIO—Personality, Individuality, and Originality," as seen in the rear of this picture. (Courtesy Summit School.)

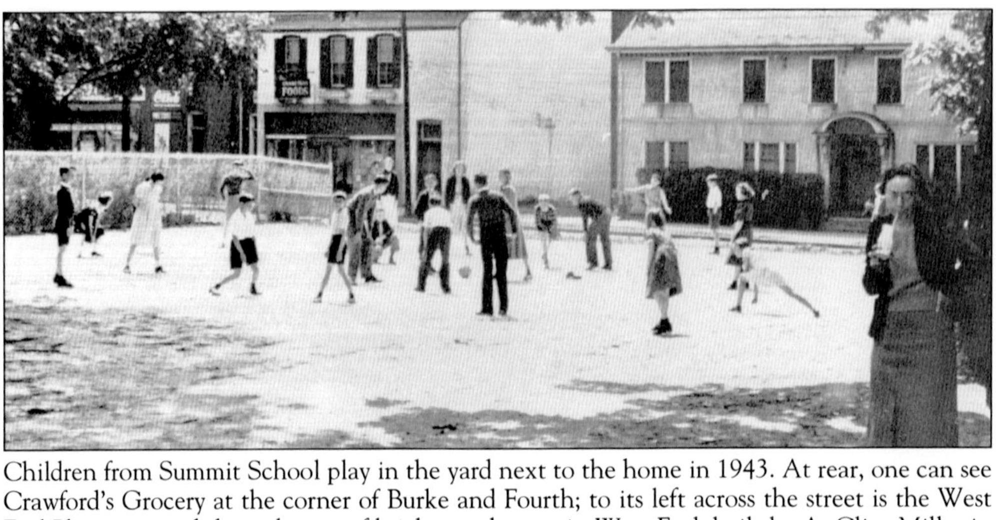

Children from Summit School play in the yard next to the home in 1943. At rear, one can see Crawford's Grocery at the corner of Burke and Fourth; to its left across the street is the West End Pharmacy and the only row of brick townhouses in West End, built by A. Clint Miller in the 1920s. (Courtesy of Summit School.)

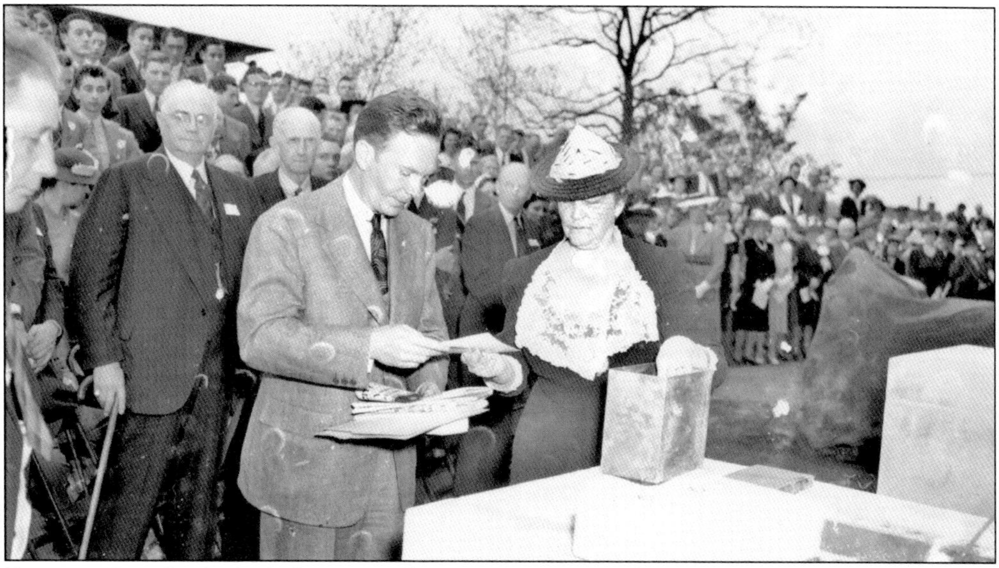

Bowman Gray Sr. died of a heart attack in 1935. Four years later, his family gave monies in his memory to start a medical school in Winston-Salem affiliated with Baptist Hospital. Pictured at the cornerstone laying ceremony are Bowman Gray Jr. and his aunt, Bess Gray Plumly, who lived at the northwest corner of Forsyth Street and West End Boulevard. "Aunt Bess" was a friend to many of the neighborhood children. (Courtesy FCPL.)

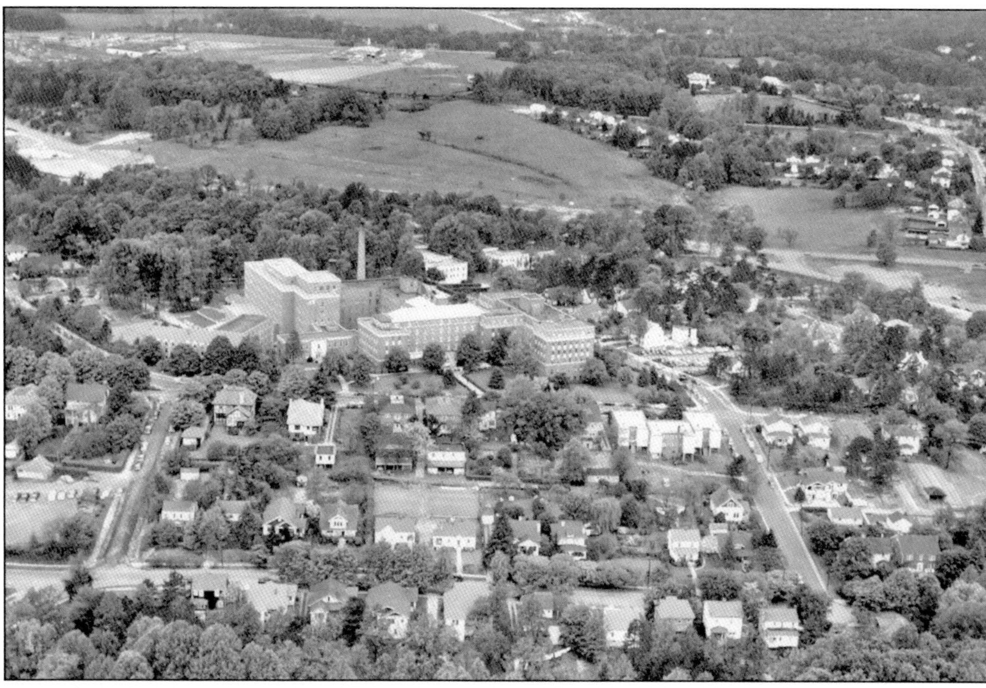

By mid-century, Baptist Hospital and Bowman Gray School of Medicine took up a substantial portion of Hawthorne Hill. Still, the Hanes farm and adjacent Lasater farm left a sizeable amount of open space just to the west of West End. The intersection of Cloverdale and First marks the edge of the farm land, just to the upper right of the hospital complex in this picture from 1950. (Courtesy Dorothy Carpenter Medical Archives, Wake Forest School of Medicine.)

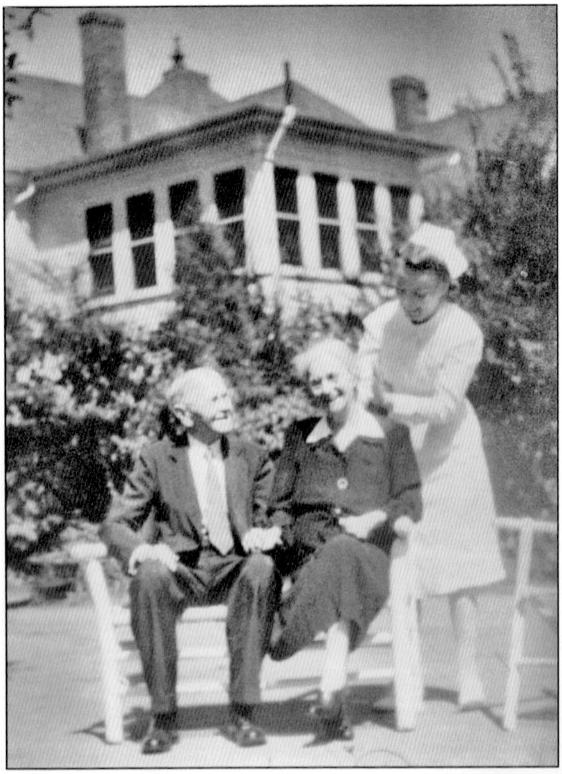

Madison D. Stockton's family grew up with Winston-Salem. An anchor in the West End community, he is shown here with his wife, Martha Vaughn, in the back yard of their home at 936 West Fourth Street. Huntley, Hill and Stockton sold furniture and coffins at the turn of the century. B.F. Huntley lived just east of Stockton on Fourth Street for many years. (Courtesy Jule Spach.)

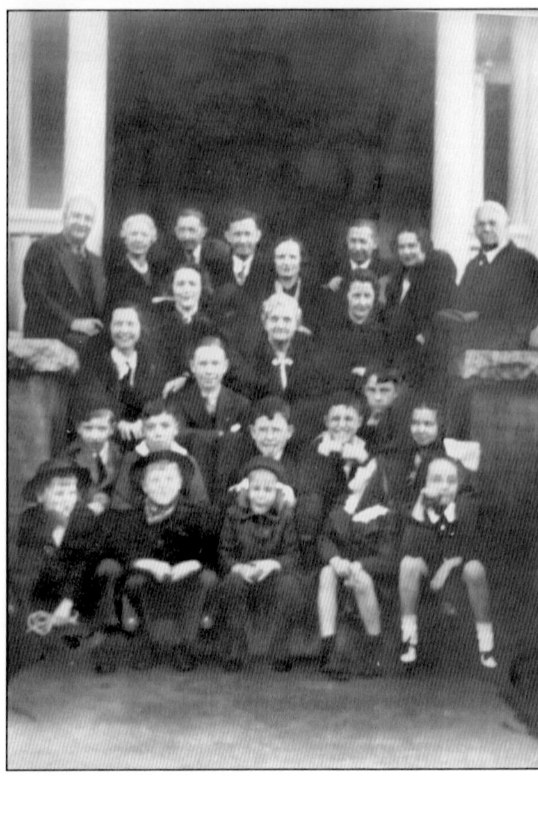

Here is a Stockton family portrait from 1936. Although M.D. Stockton had purchased homes for his children in the West End near the intersection of Fourth and First, several Stocktons moved to new developments along Arbor and Stratford Roads. The 1930s bring back memories to family members of football games between the West End Stocktons and the Stratford Road Stocktons, as well as the occasional mischief that came from greasing the trolley tracks along steep Glade Street. (Courtesy Jule Spach.)

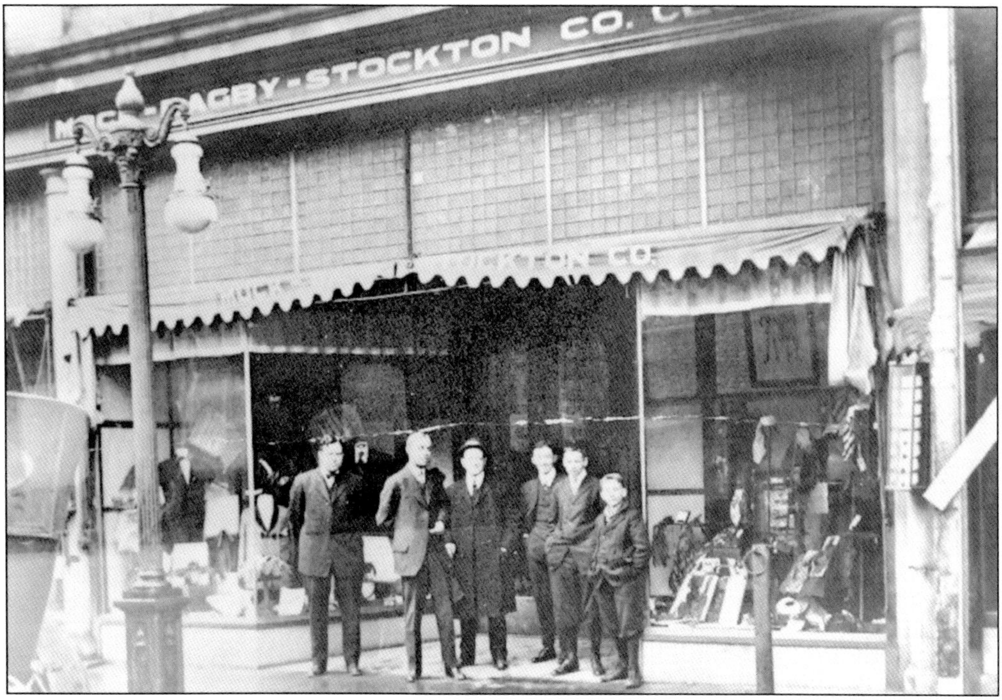

M.D.'s children were accomplished in their own right. Son Norman is shown third from the right in front of Mock-Bagby-Stockton store in 1915. Norman's son Dick and grandson Hill continue Norman Stockton Clothiers in town today. Norman's son Tom was elected a bishop in the Methodist Church. M.D.'s daughter Nancy (Mrs. Linville K. "Hap" Martin) became president of the National Junior League in 1943. (Courtesy Dick Stockton.)

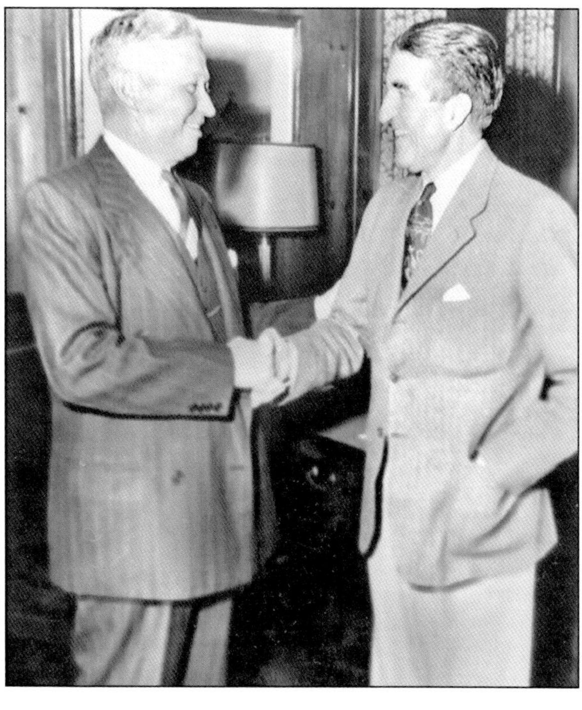

M.D.'s son Richard Stockton (left) served as acting president of Wachovia Bank from 1949 to 1950, when Robert M. Hanes (right) was asked to help implement the Marshall Plan in Europe. M.D.'s attorney grandson Ralph became a partner in Kilpatrick Stockton LLP, one of the state's largest law firms, now located in the West End across Grace Court from his grandfather's former home. (Courtesy WCCA.)

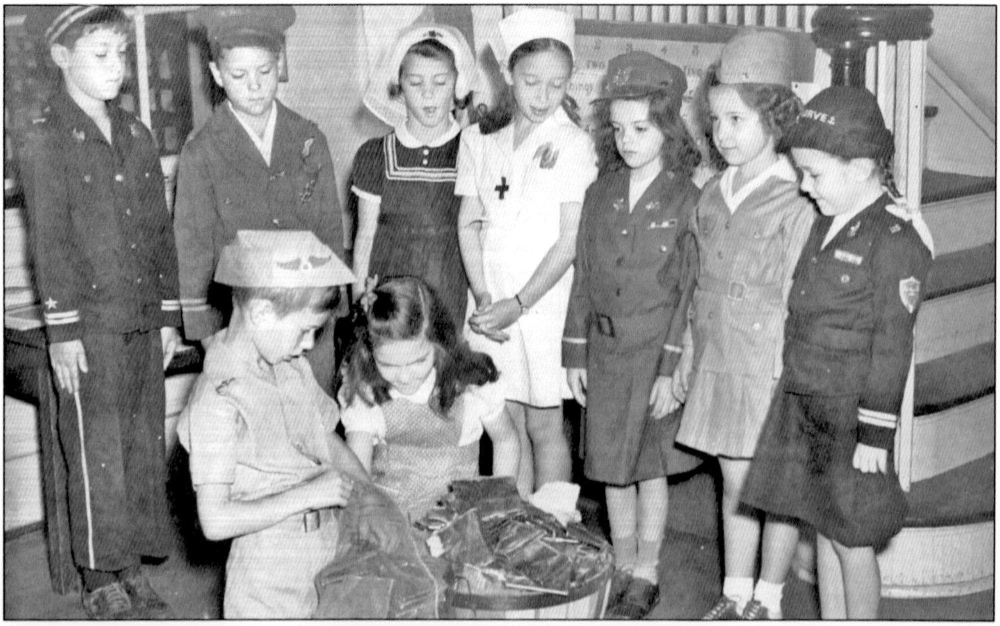

World War II arrived suddenly in West End as in the rest of the nation, but the neighborhood's cohesiveness helped band together both men and women in the war effort and on the home front. In 1944, children at Summit School collect material for a scrap metal drive, each dressed in a uniform from a different branch of the service, WAVES, WACs, and Red Cross included. (Courtesy of Summit School.)

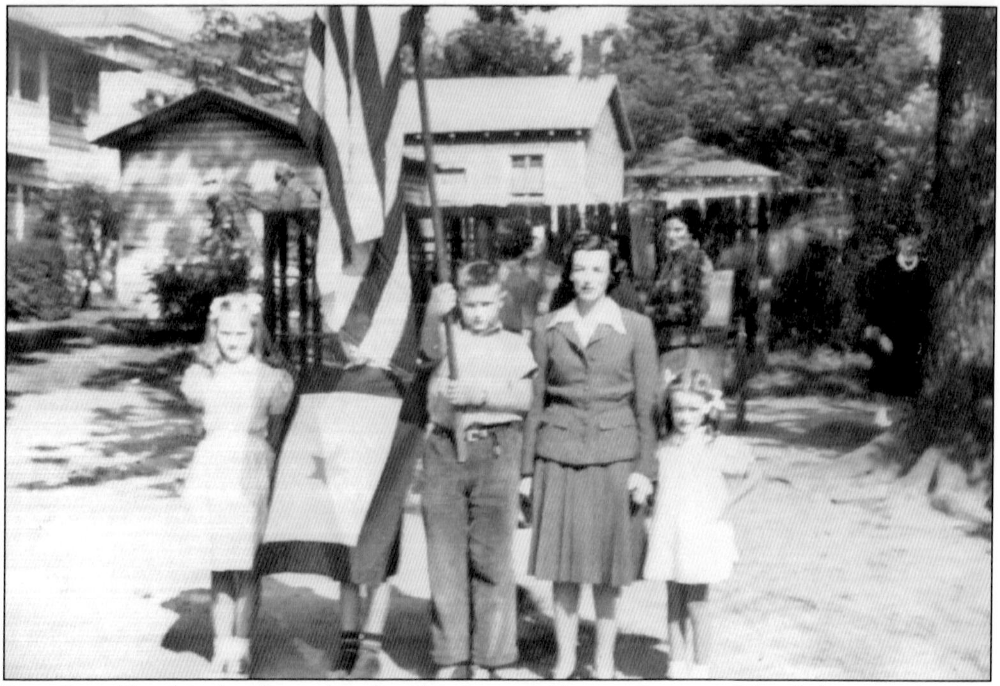

Bess Gray Plumly's daughter, Aurelia Plumly, a teacher at Summit School, became the first WAVE from Winston-Salem in 1943. Schoolchildren parade with her Blue Star flag of service at a ceremony at the Summit Street campus. (Courtesy of Summit School.)

M.D. Stockton's grandson, Jule Spach, who grew up in his grandparents' home with his mother and brother after his father died, was a cadet at Virginia Military Institute in 1943 when nearly the entire class was called to active duty. Spach trained as a pilot and once flew his aircraft low over Hanes Park, buzzing his friends and neighbors in West End. During World War II, his plane was shot down in Italy, and he became a German POW. After a happy return home, he spent many years in mission to Brazil. Spach was elected moderator of the General Assembly of the Presbyterian Church, U.S. in 1976. (Courtesy Jule Spach.)

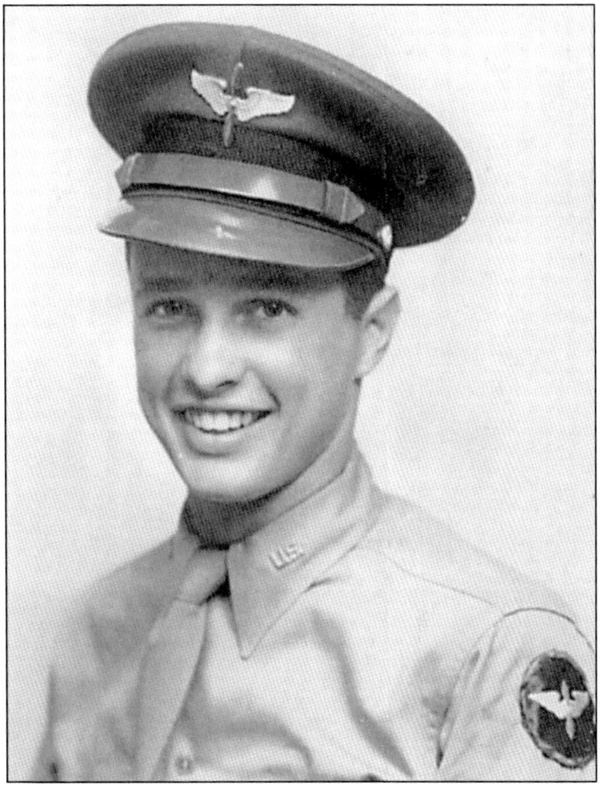

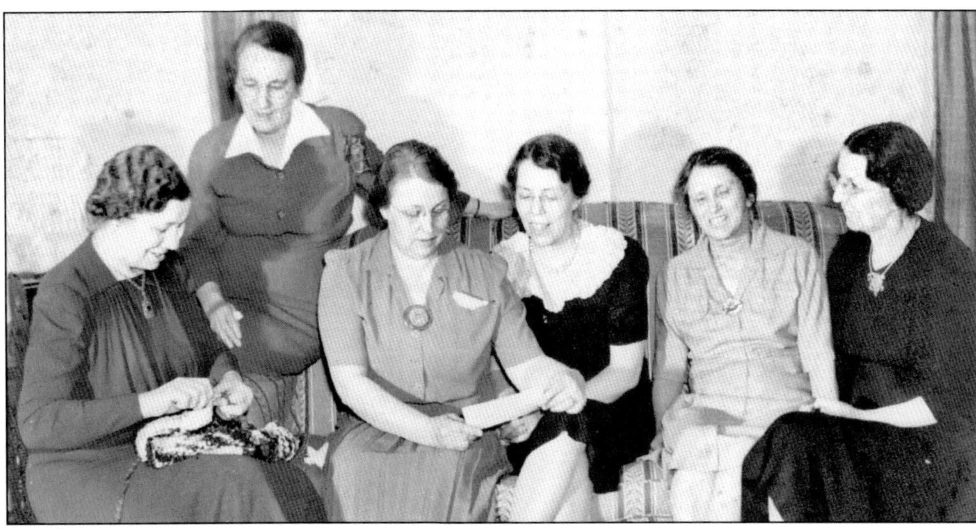

Here are women of First Baptist Church meeting to help organize the Fifth War Bond Drive in June 1944. Ninety percent of the population of Winston-Salem was native to North Carolina in those days. Only at war's end, with the move of Western Electric to the old Chatham plant in West End in 1946, did a substantial influx of out-of-state investment and people to the area occur. (Courtesy First Baptist Church.)

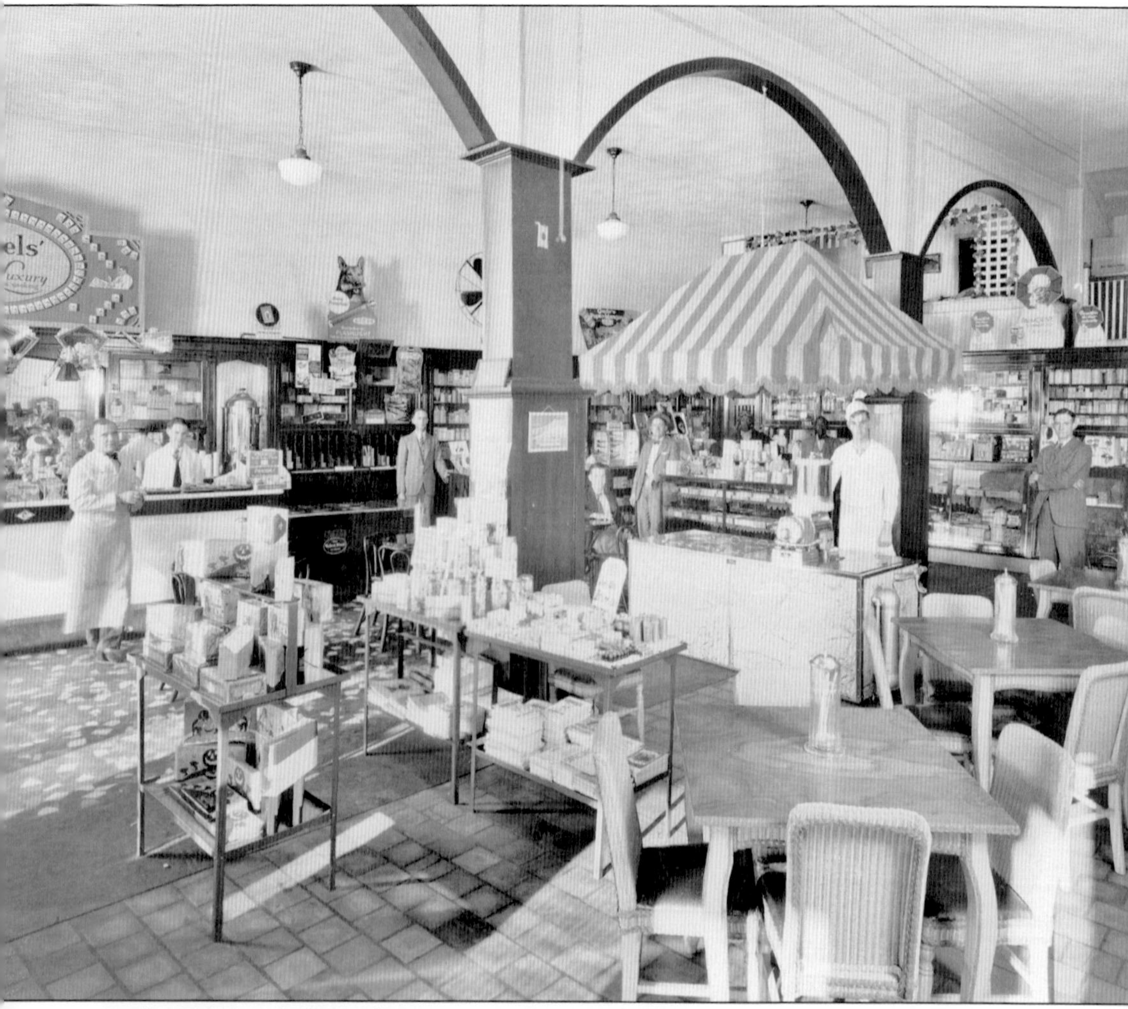

In the 1930s and 1940s, there was no more popular hangout for kids than the Summit Street Pharmacy at the corner of Summit and West End Boulevard. Convenient to neighborhood schools and local residences, the pharmacy featured carhops to bring its soda shop patrons curbside service. (Courtesy FCPL.)

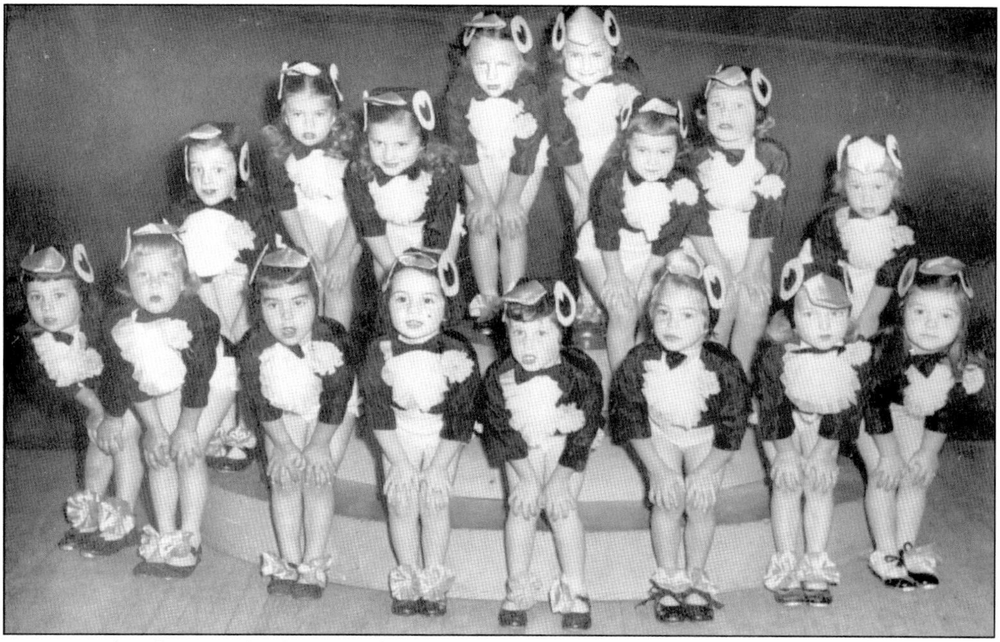

Vinni Frederick opened a dance studio for young talents in 1947 at the southeast corner of First and Hawthorne. Hers is one of the longest continually operating businesses in the West End and a source of happy memories for many locals. Wanda Plemmons succeeded Miss Frederick and expanded the studio in recent years. (Courtesy Academy of Dance Arts.)

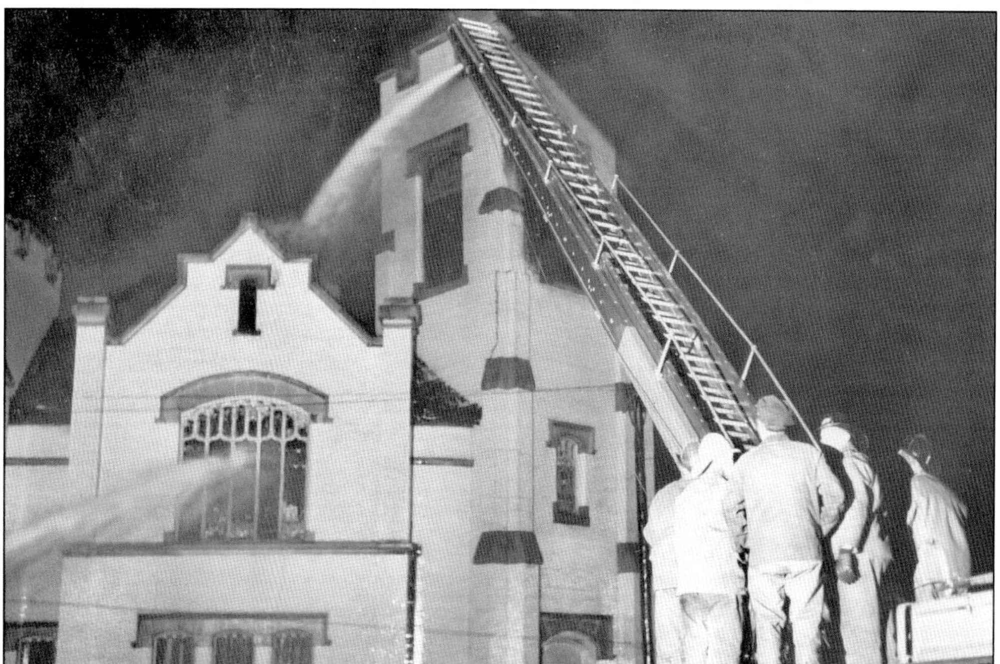

The building that once housed West End Methodist and later served as a short-term home to other groups burned in March 1947, causing the loss of one of the neighborhood's most distinctive landmarks. (Courtesy FCPL.)

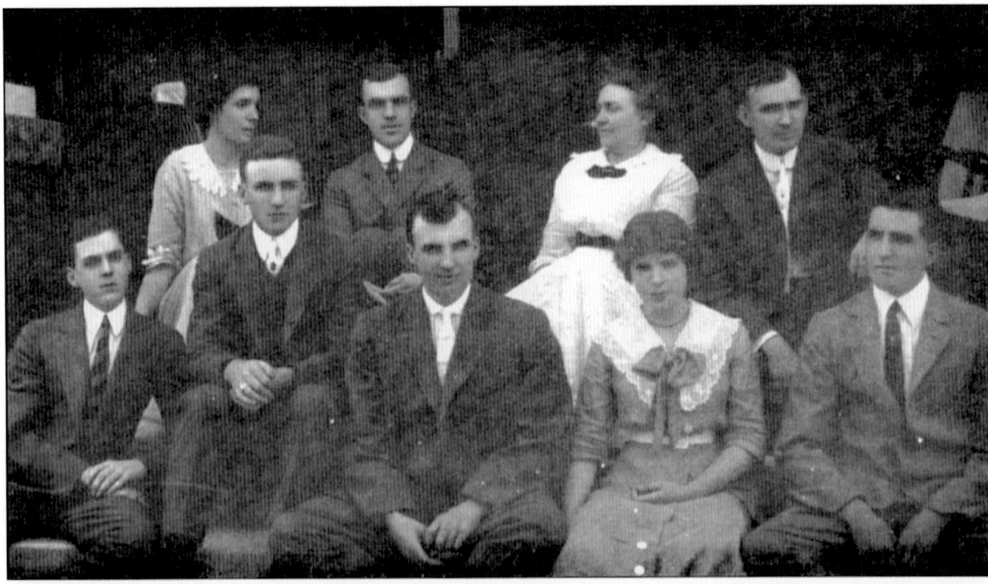

Anna Hodgin Hanes died in 1947 and her proud children later established a fund in their parents' memory for the betterment of the county and state. Here, she sits on the Fourth Street front porch with her young family, with a few family accomplishments not yet noted. From left to right are (front row) Ralph, John (undersecretary of the treasury under Roosevelt), Jim, Lucy, and Robert; (back row) Daisy, Fred (chair of Duke Medical School,) Mother Hanes, and Alex. (Courtesy Borden Hanes and Jo White Linn's Hanes family history.)

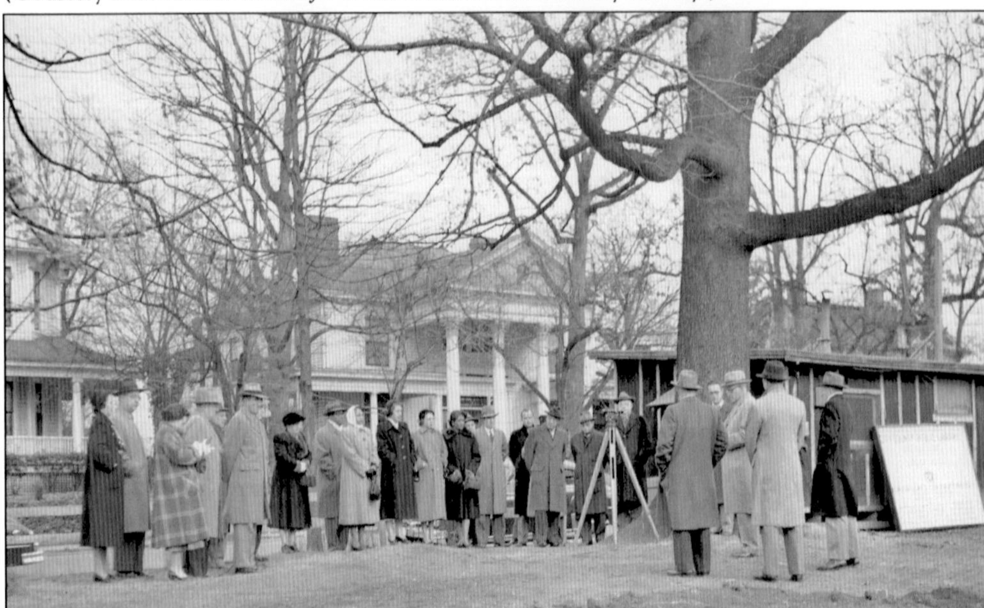

R.J. Reynolds Jr., briefly mayor of Winston-Salem in the 1940s, donated the family townhouse to the city as a site for a new public library. The groundbreaking ceremony in 1951 shows that a substantial amount of the housing stock across from the heart of old "Millionaires' Row" still existed at the time. The Coan home's distinctive triangular pediment (see page 47) can be seen behind the group of dignitaries at the ceremony. (Courtesy FCPL.)

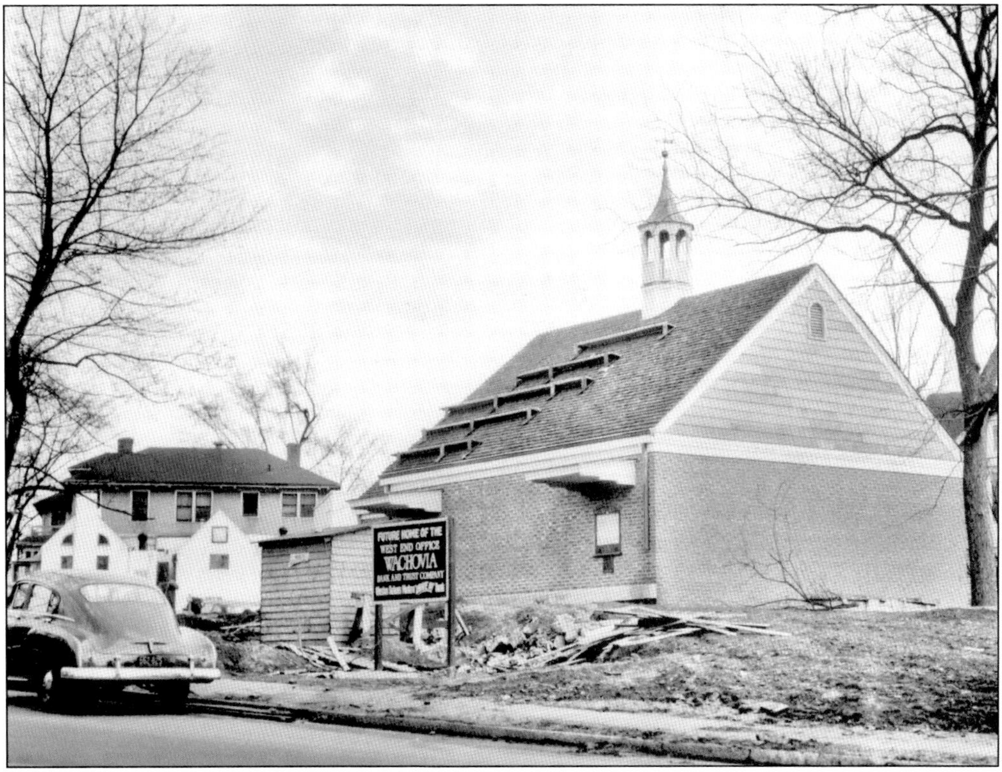

In 1950, at the site of the West End Methodist Church, "modern drive-in banking" was introduced to Winston-Salem at the new West End branch of Wachovia Bank. The pedestrian neighborhood built around the streetcar was now touted as a convenient location for downtown commuters to do their banking on the way to and from work. (Courtesy FCPL.)

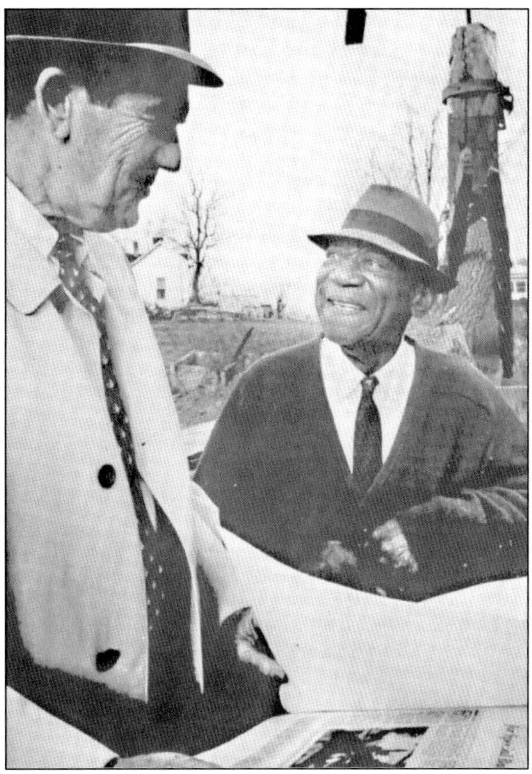

The bank building was constructed with handmade bricks from the kiln of George Black, one of the most successful African-American businessmen in Winston-Salem. Black's bricks formed many of the structures built by Winston-Salem leaders over the years and were used in the reconstruction of the village of Old Salem in the 1950s. Here, Wachovia's Meade Willis Jr., whose family lived on the Boulevard in the 1920s, presents Black in 1970 with a scrapbook of articles saluting his career and work. (Courtesy WCCA.)

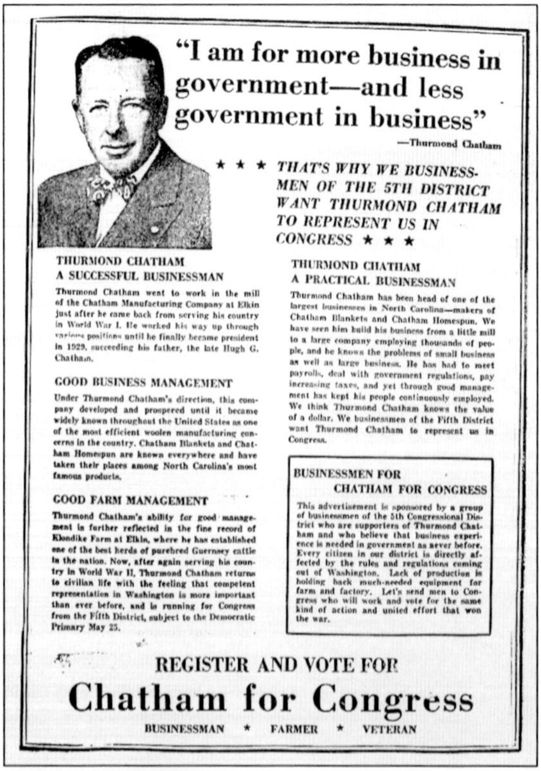

Thurmond Chatham, who lived in a house on West Fourth Street when he married West End's Lucy Hanes, then lived next to Robert Hanes on Stratford Road. Chatham ran for congress in 1948; he won the race and served 10 years in the U.S. House of Representatives. (Courtesy NCSA.)

Pictured at the 1949 Truman inauguration are Mr. and Mrs. Ralph Hanes, Mr. and Mrs. Thurmond Chatham, and Mr. and Mrs. Robert Hanes. Truman appointed Robert Hanes administrator of Marshall Plan funds for Belgium and later tapped Gordon Gray, Bowman's son and the local newspaper publisher, to become secretary of the army. In 1951, Truman came to town to dedicate a new campus for Wake Forest College on part of the Reynolda estate. (Courtesy WCCA.)

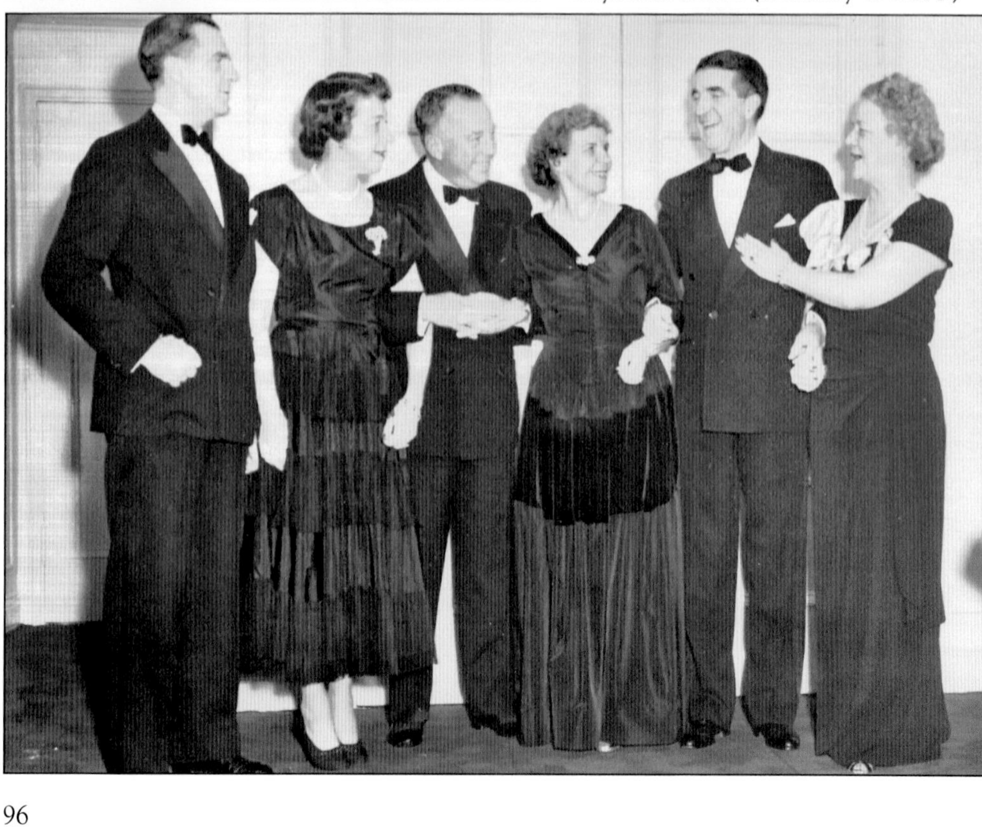

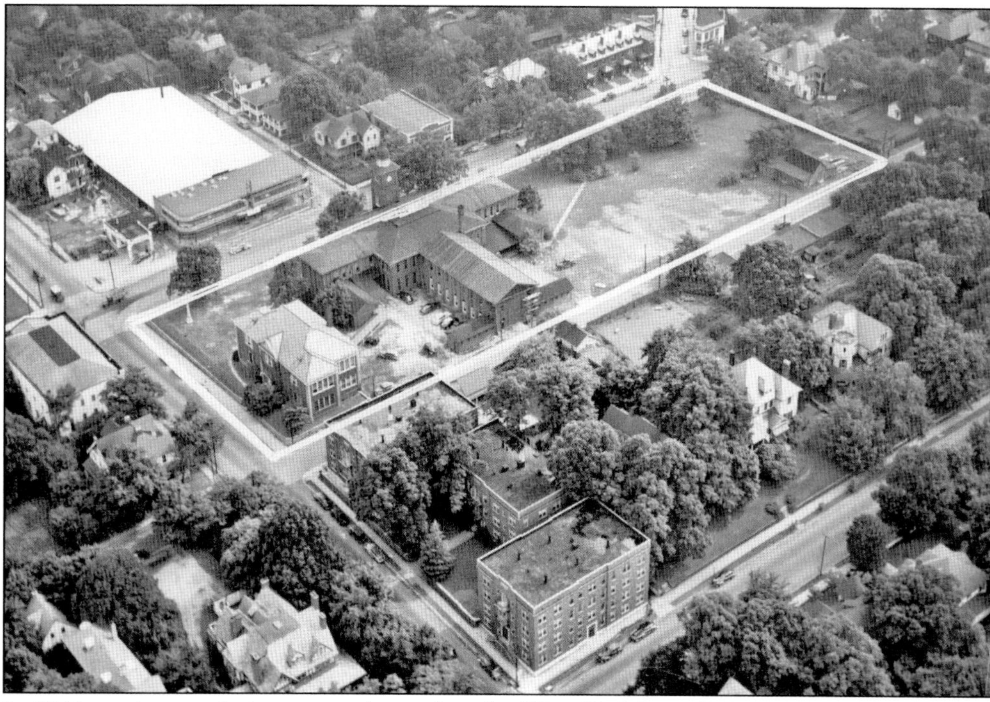

In 1948, zoning regulations were changed in the West End from "RC" to "R-1" to allow more intensive commercial development. The change was not felt overnight, but a slow increase began in the number of commercial buildings infiltrating the West End along Fourth and Fifth Streets. In the picture above, the lot of West End School is marked for demolition for a new department store. A memorial obelisk to Calvin Wiley at the corner of Fourth and Broad is now at Wiley School. Of the half-dozen stately homes along Fifth Street visible at the bottom of the picture, only the Agnew Bahnson home at Spring and Fifth in the lower left is still standing. (Courtesy FCPL.)

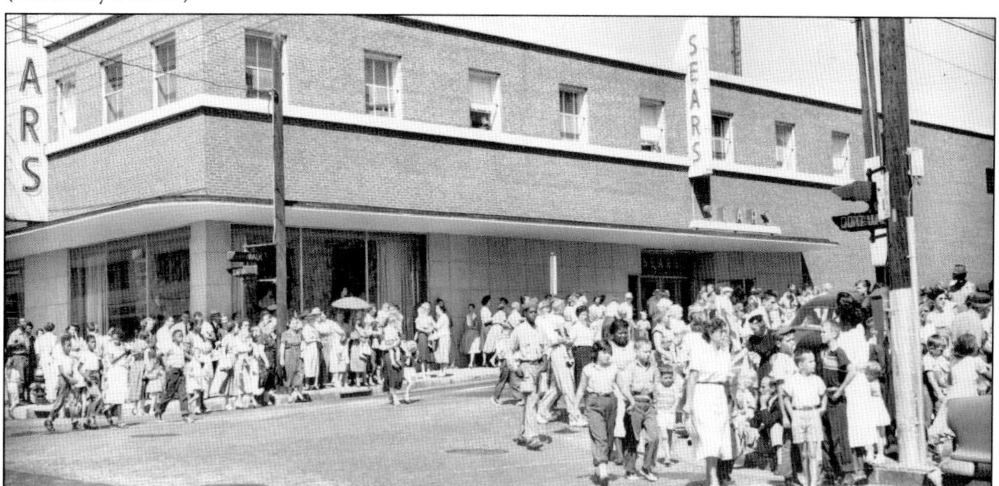

Here, crowds greet the grand opening of the new Sears store at Fourth and Broad in 1949. Sears became the largest store in town and stayed at that location until 1975, when it closed and then reopened as part of the Hanes Mall on Stratford Road west of town. Hanes Mall remains one of the largest shopping developments in the state. (Courtesy FCPL.)

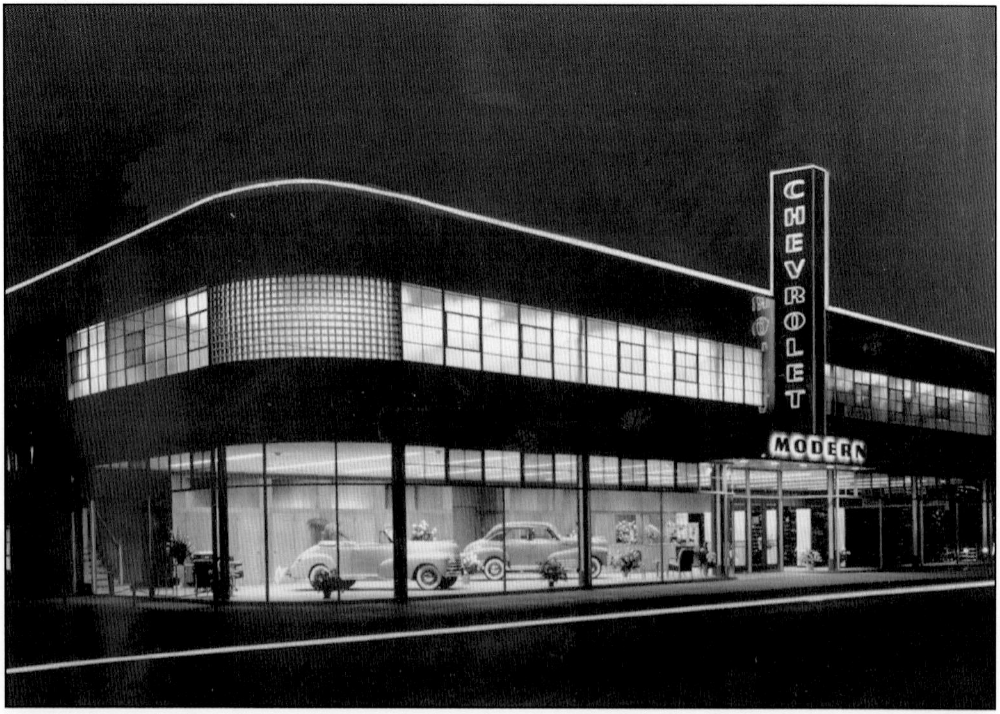

Distinctively built in the International style of architecture, Modern Chevrolet opened at the southwest corner of Broad and Fourth in 1947. When O.F. Fowler moved the family's dealership to the new location from North Main Street, company officials in Detroit complained that he had moved "too far from town." (Courtesy Modern Chevrolet.)

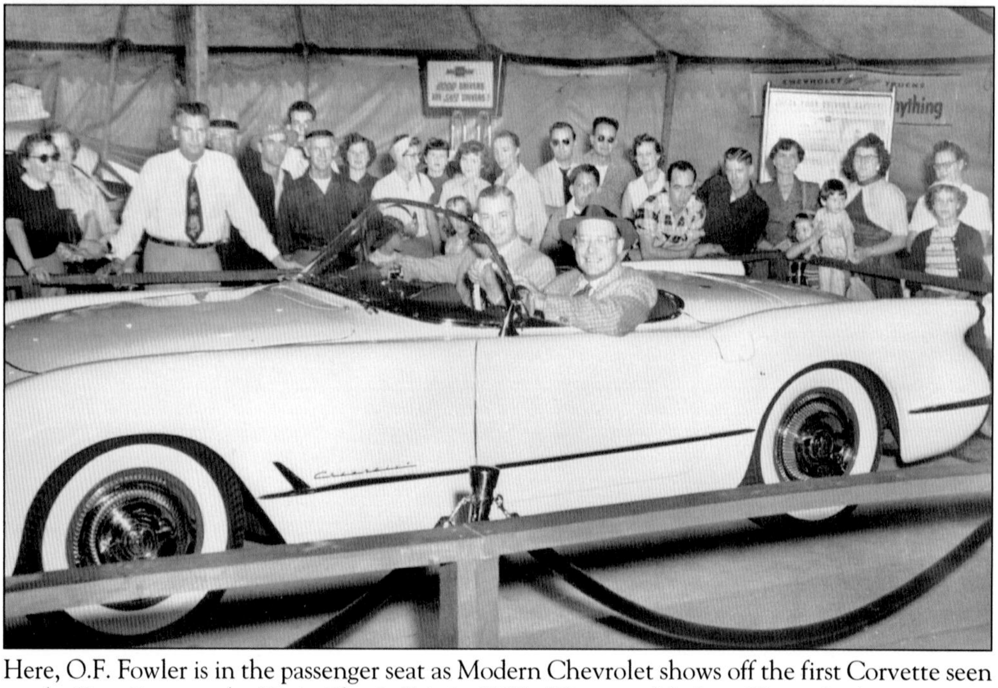

Here, O.F. Fowler is in the passenger seat as Modern Chevrolet shows off the first Corvette seen on the East Coast at the Dixie Classic Fair in 1953. (Courtesy Modern Chevrolet.)

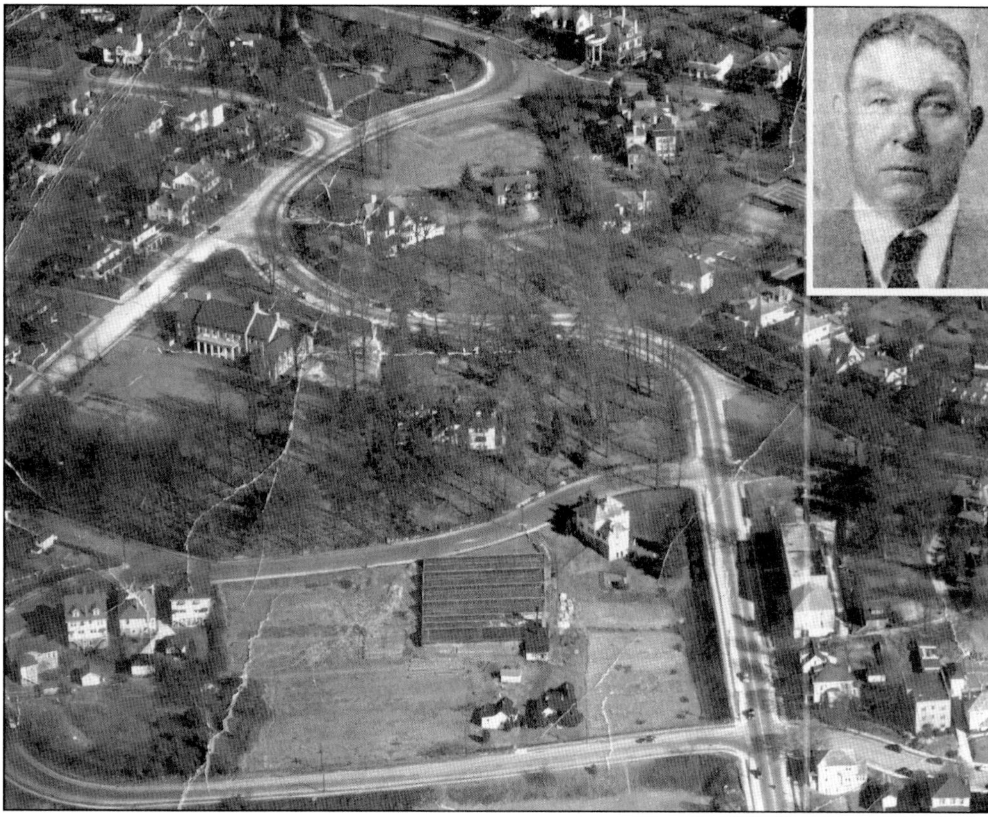

In the lower half of this view of West End Boulevard and Glade Street in the 1940s is the McNulty Greenhouses, a near half-century presence in the West End that was cleared after the late 1950s. Martin McNulty (inset) operated both a local florist in town and this greenhouse complex. The Central Family YMCA relocated to this site in the early 1970s. Above the greenhouses can be see a then-new YWCA next to the wooded property of James G. Hanes. (Courtesy Barbara Martin and Tommy McNulty.)

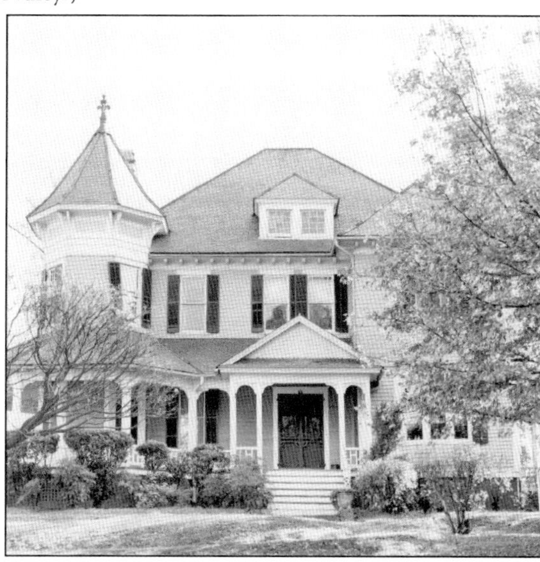

Planning for entertainment for the Forsyth Centennial led to the creation of a permanent Winston-Salem Arts Council in 1949. Their home for several years was the former J.C. Trotman house on West Fifth Street. Other offices opened in West End homes. M.D. Stockton's house became headquarters for the local Red Cross and later the Piedmont Craftsmen artists' guild. (Courtesy FCPL.)

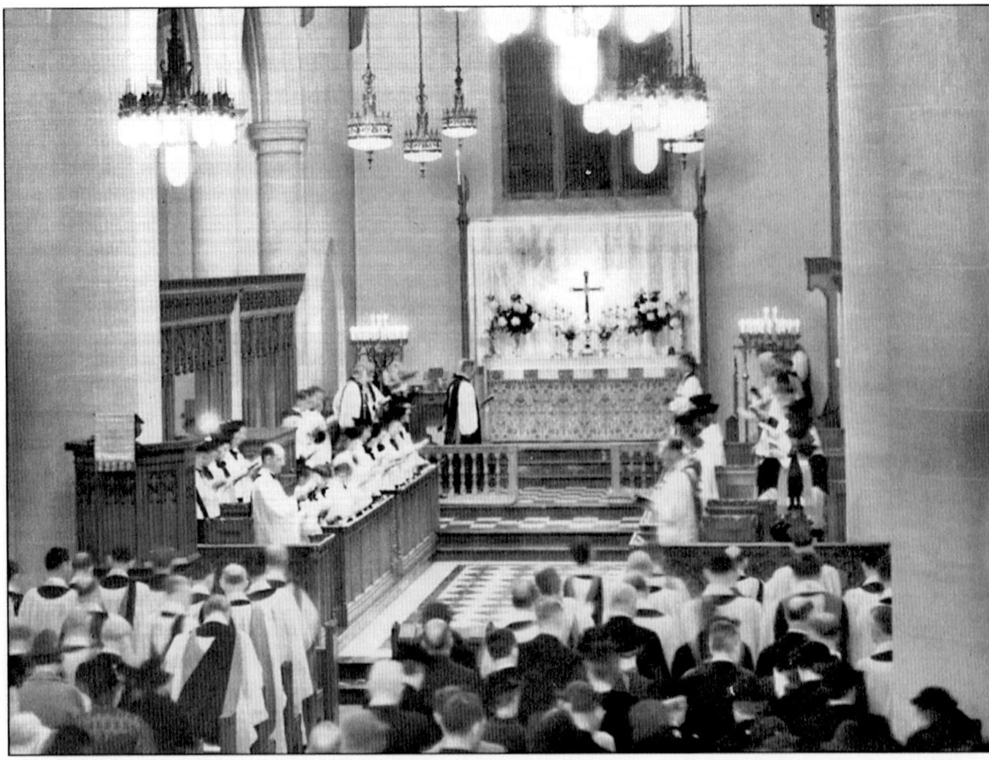

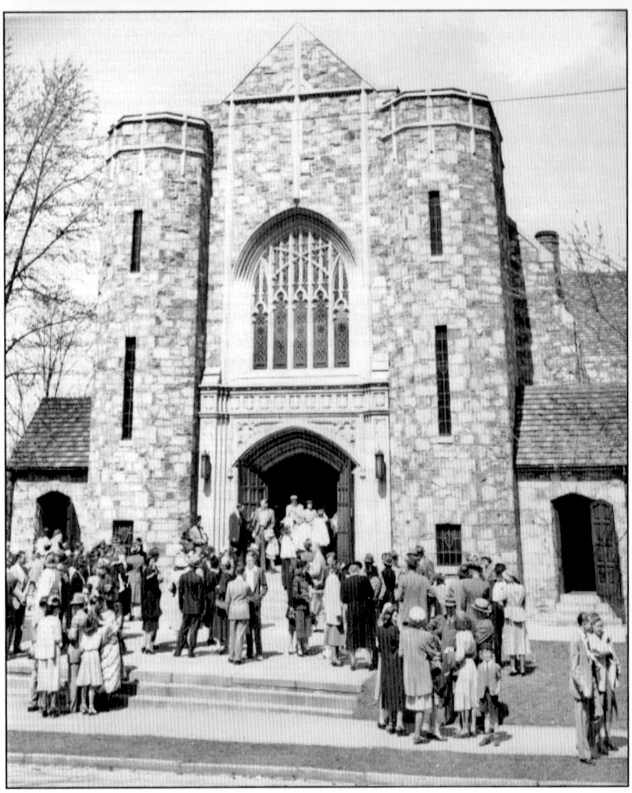

Mid-century was a time of both stability and steady growth for West End's downtown churches. St. Paul's (above), Augsburg (left), Centenary, First Baptist, and the Christian Science congregation each added to their physical presence in the neighborhood with education buildings. For even as the city expanded its boundaries outward, these churches remained anchors for their faith communities and kept their members' interest in the health and livability of the West End area. (Courtesy of StP and FCPL.)

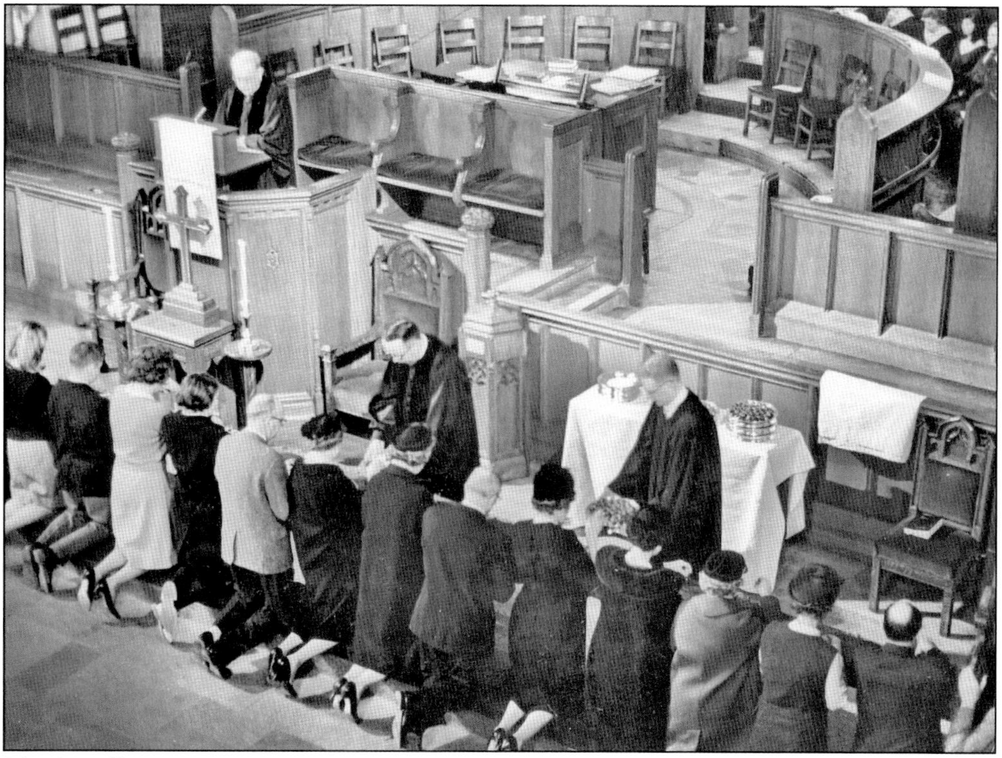

The friendly competition between West End churches wasn't just over the number of worshippers at Centenary Methodist (above) or the new construction at First Baptist (right). At noontime, parishioners scurried for table space at Myrtle Yokely's boardinghouse in the old Frank Liipfert Home on Fifth. Originally an assistant in Mrs. Viola Allen's business on Spruce Street near Fourth, Yokely fed 400 guests every Sunday in addition to boarders. Yokely later moved to a smaller operation in the R.E. Dalton House at 870 West Fifth. It ran through the 1970s and was the last boardinghouse in town. (Courtesy CUMC and First Baptist Church.)

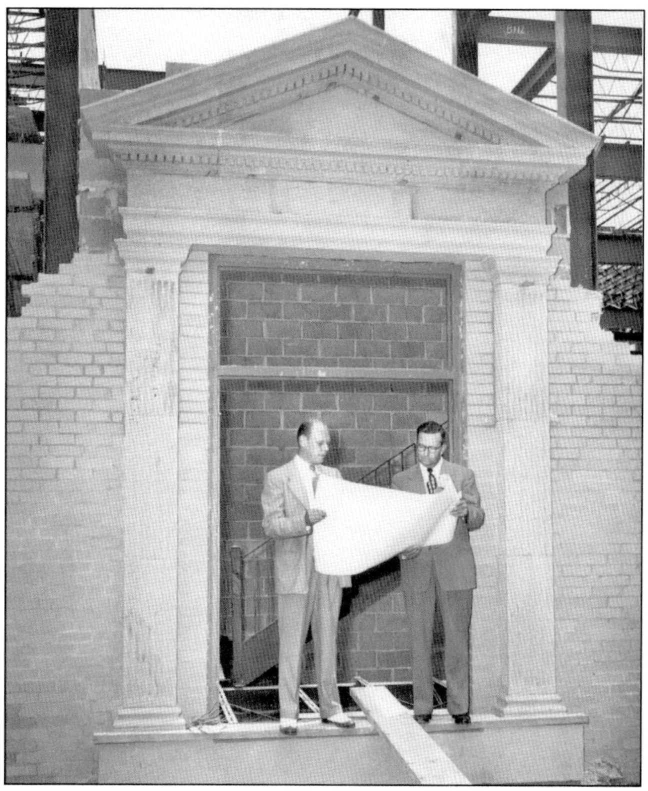

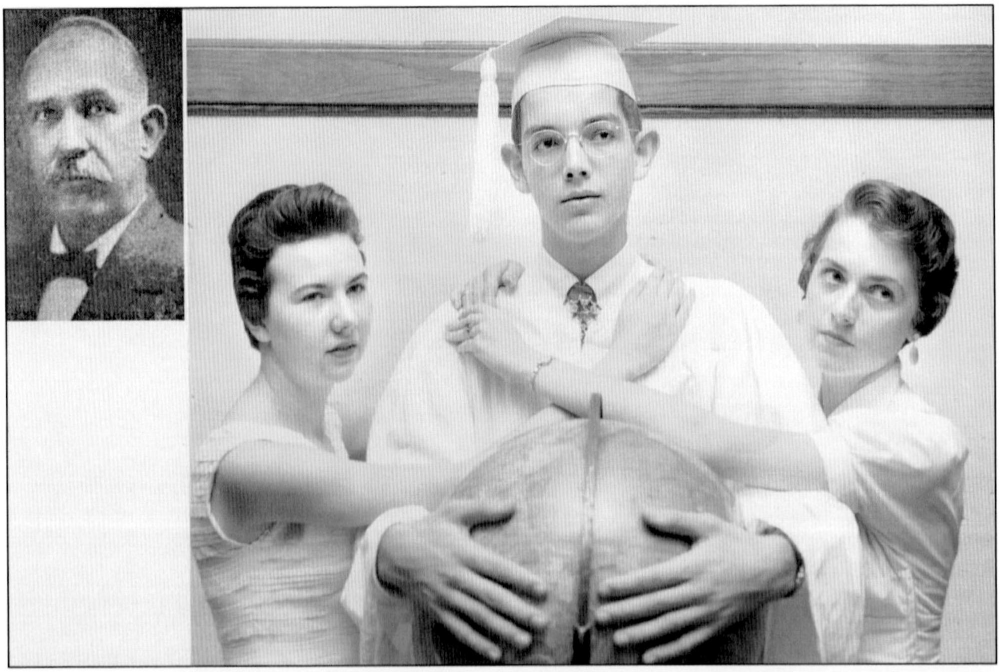

The Montague Medal began as an award in the 1880s to the senior with the highest grade average at the Winston Graded School. Col. H. Montague (inset), a local attorney, endowed the medal competition, which in later years came to be awarded to the senior with the highest average at Reynolds High. Here is the 1955 winner in a pose that had to be the envy of every brainy guy in school. (Both courtesy FCPL.)

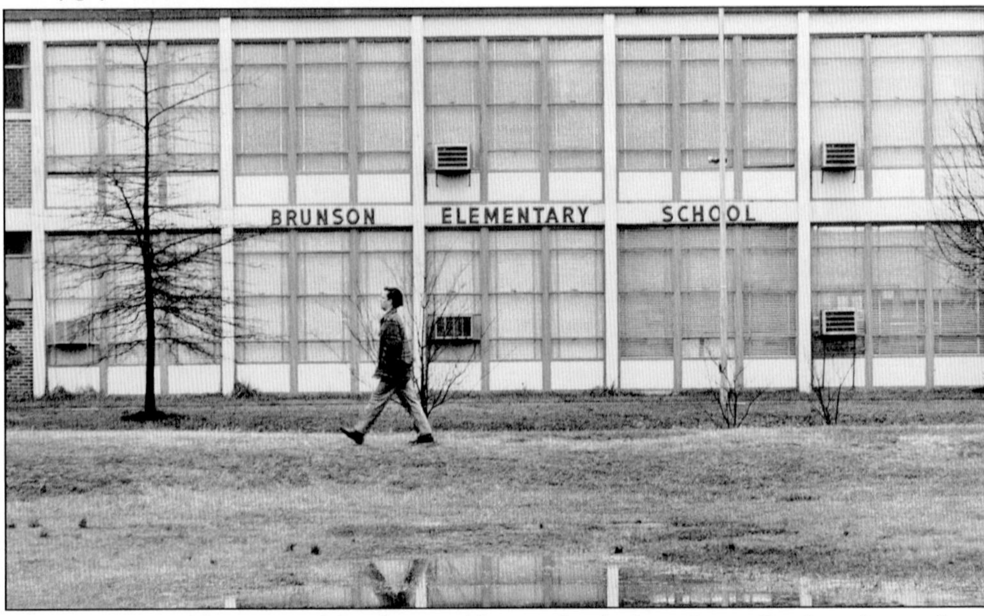

In 1959, Brunson Elementary School opened here in lands along Peters Creek at the northeast corner of Hawthorne and First Streets. Brunson was one of the leaders in school integration, and its highly academically gifted programs coupled with a diverse cultural mix make it one of the county's most well-regarded schools. (Courtesy Winston-Salem/Forsyth County Schools.)

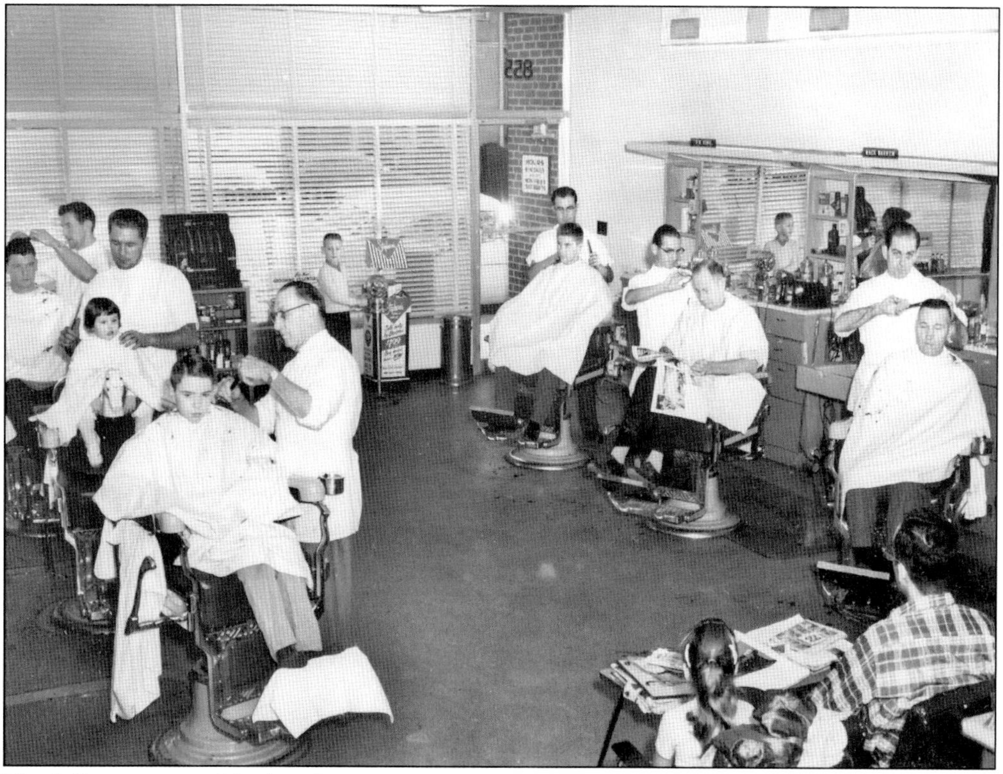

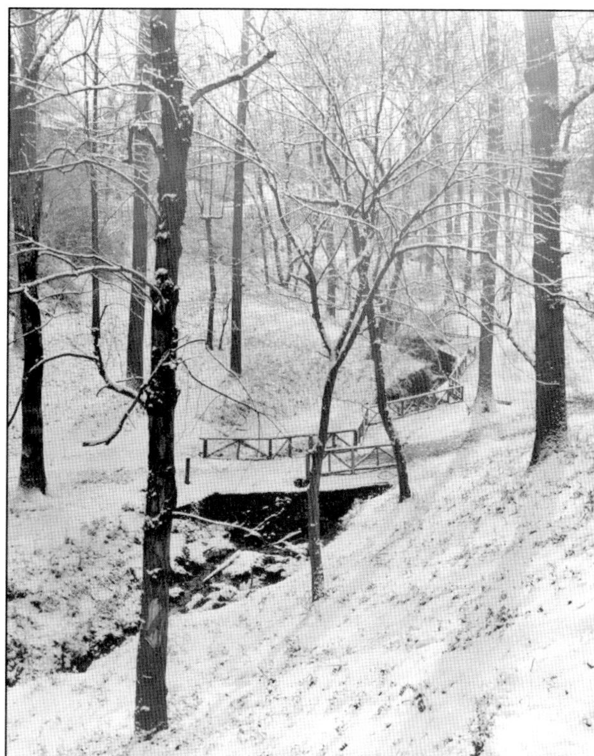

The full service neighborhood barber shop was found not just in Mayberry, but also in West End in 1957 at Fourth Street's Hair Den. So many barbers and hairstylists have had a shop in West End that by the 1970s, the local paper wrote about the "war of the barbers," as too many shops battled over too few parking spaces. Then, as now, the neighborhood barber was a place to relax and share news. (Courtesy Hair Den.)

The West End Hotel and Land Company never fully developed The Springs park. Many simply drive past the wooded notch in the hill as they drive into town up Reynolda Road and then Broad Street, not knowing Spring Park is still there on the right. It has rarely looked more beautiful than on this snowy winter's day in 1959. (Courtesy FCPL.)

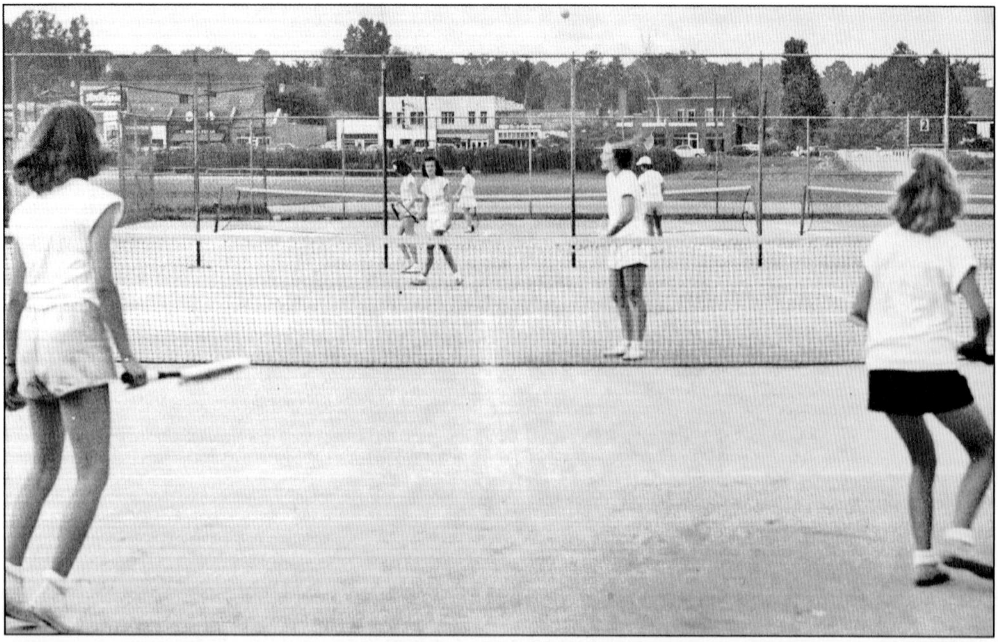

Tennis star Bill Tilden's visit to Hanes Park energized the community and its love for tennis in the 1930s, and tennis courts have long been a part of Hanes Park. The Joe White Tennis Center was built there in the 1970s. Tennis players enjoy a match here around 1960, about the same time Winston-Salem's population crested past 100,000. In 1965, the two Hanes companies from West End merged into one corporation. (Courtesy Recreation and Parks Department, City of Winston-Salem; hereafter listed as RPD.)

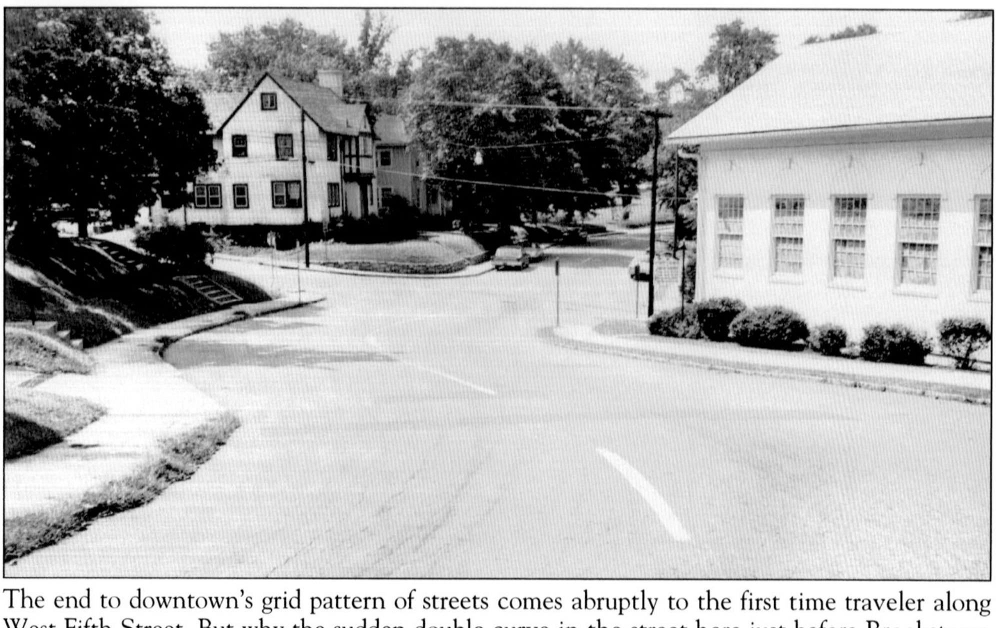

The end to downtown's grid pattern of streets comes abruptly to the first time traveler along West Fifth Street. But why the sudden double curve in the street here just before Brookstown Avenue? The plot map of 1891 on page 26 hints at a spring emerging near the spot, but locals will tell you the road simply follows the path livestock wore into the hill following the easiest way around the ridge. (Courtesy FCPL.)

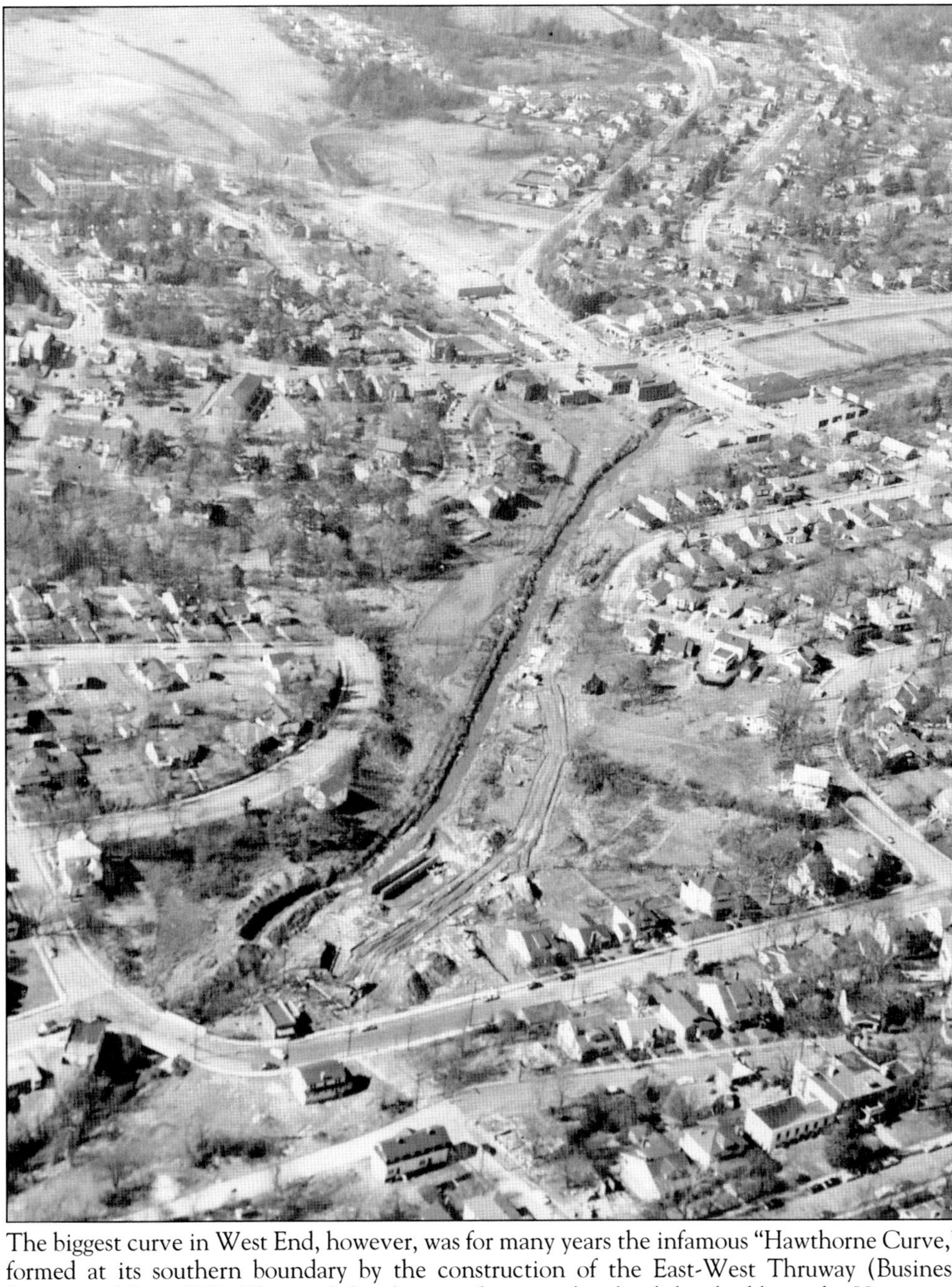

The biggest curve in West End, however, was for many years the infamous "Hawthorne Curve," formed at its southern boundary by the construction of the East-West Thruway (Business Interstate 40) in 1957. The road sliced across the open farmland that had been the Hanes and Lasater farms and rested over Peters Creek along the West End, swerving to avoid a row of politically-connected businesses. West End is on the right in this view, with the bridge over Peters Creek at Crafton Street. West Fourth Street is at the bottom right of the picture. Peters Creek and its floodplain had been a natural boundary for West End before the highway gave it a concrete border. Hawthorne Curve was straightened finally for safety reasons in the 1990s. (Courtesy FCPL.)

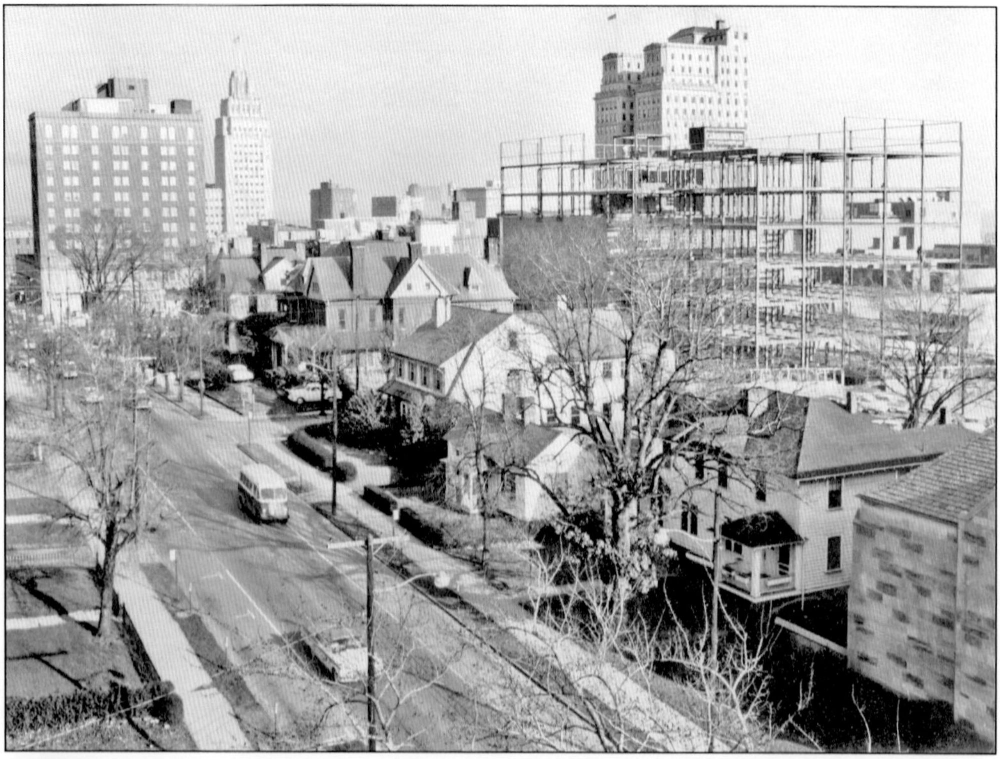

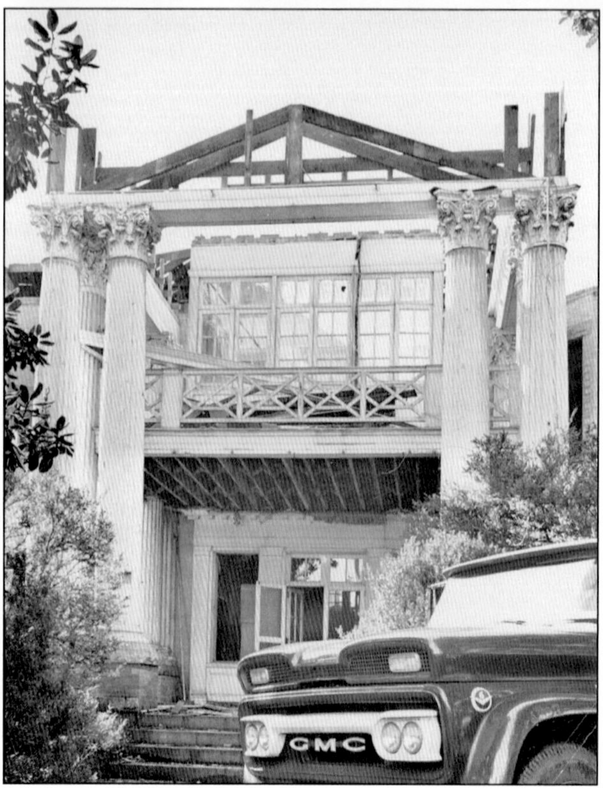

Integon Insurance was Security Life and Trust when it operated out of the former Shore home on West Fourth Street in 1931. In 1962, Integon constructed a headquarters skyscraper downtown on Fifth Street. Commercial development and time were putting a squeeze on West End's old housing stock. The C.G. Hill property, formerly the Hanes family home Westerleigh, came down in 1963. A grand 200-year celebration of the town was held in 1966. The paper's commemorative issue for the event said of West End, "A few of the ornate old homes still stand, housing a die-hard oldtimer, a business or an apartment complex, waiting for the day they, too, will fall to progress." (Both courtesy FCPL.)

Four

Saving Grace, and the Rest of West End *1968–2000*

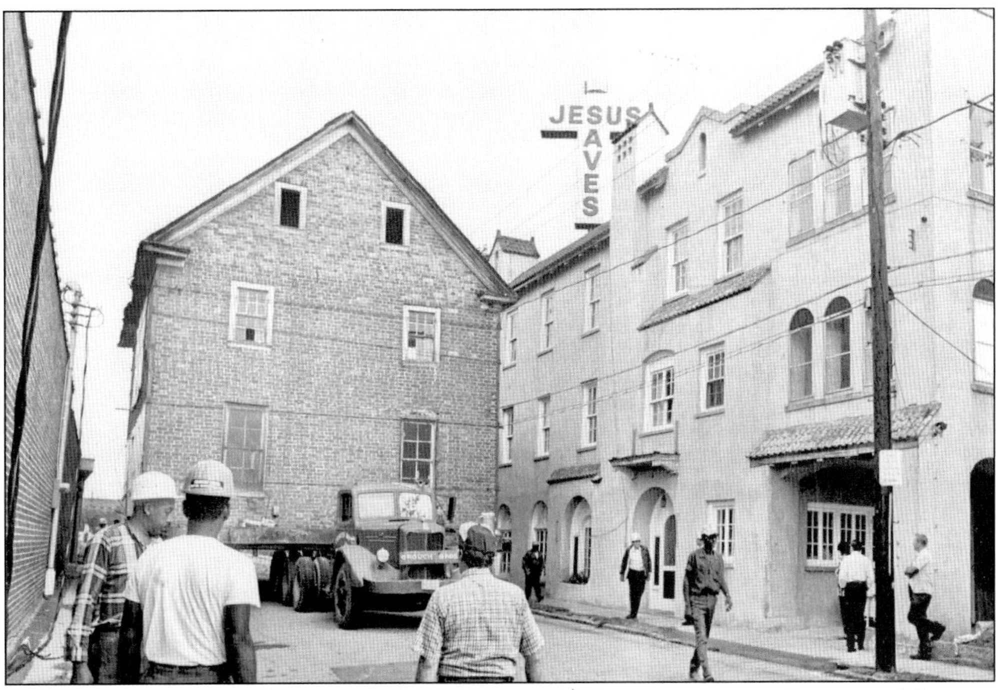

To oppose wholesale urban renewal, plus win partners to an untested vision of historic preservation, seemed a task only for true believers. However, West End today endures and thrives. A symbolic resurrection came in September 1974 when the 1815 Zevely House, the oldest home in Winston, was wrested from its foundations on Oak Street and carted right through town onto a lot at Fourth and Brookstown. (Courtesy FCPL.)

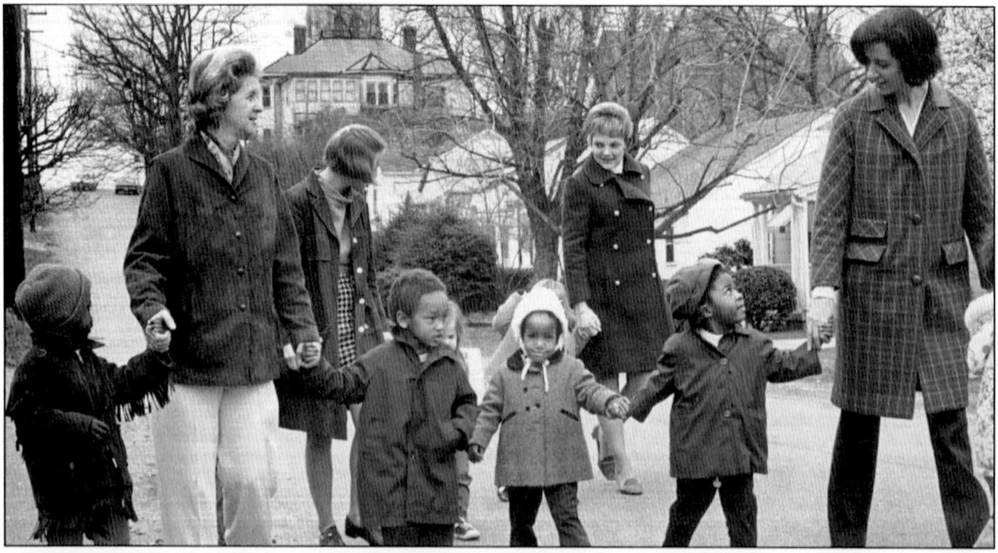

Tensions caused by changing civil rights and a growing climate of civil disobedience were palpable in Winston-Salem's downtown in the 1960s. In 1968, six West End and downtown churches opened the Downtown Church Center in a house at 123 West End Boulevard, later with a "pocket park" for kids across the street. It was an effort to reconnect to the neighborhood and offer child care, social services, ministry, and trust to those living at downtown's periphery. (Courtesy Winston-Salem Churches in Ministry.)

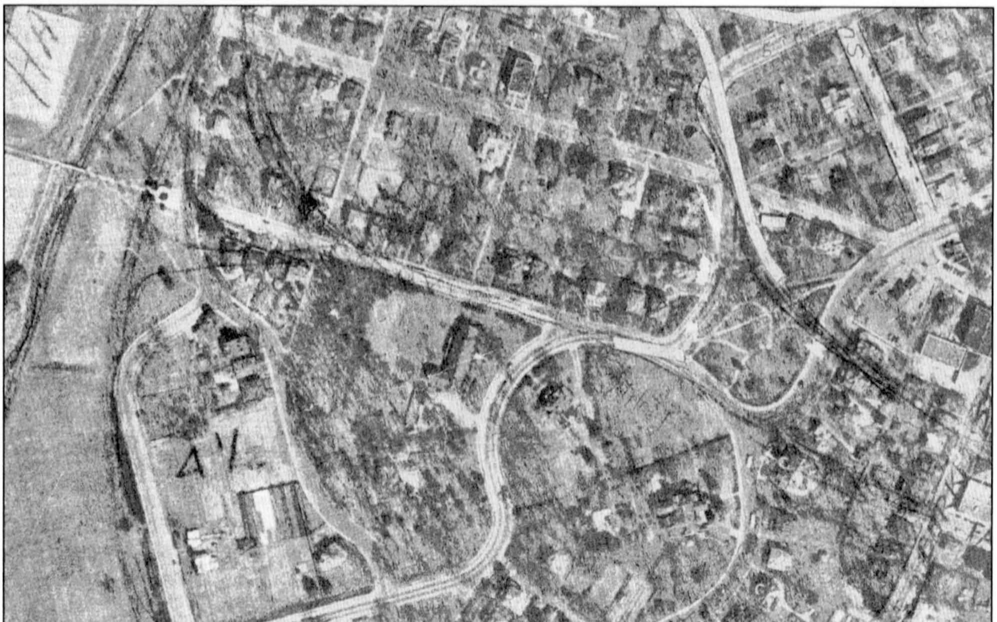

West Enders felt under assault when plans for a Ninth Street Expressway were kindled in 1967. Shown here as a series of tentative marks and tape lines on a 1951 aerial map of West End, the highway would have widened Northwest Boulevard and a Reynolda Road interchange at Hanes Park as it connected to Business I-40, and its on-ramps and exit ramps through downtown would have ridden roughshod over much of West End's western edge. (Courtesy City-County Planning Department, Winston-Salem/Forsyth County; hereafter listed as CCPB.)

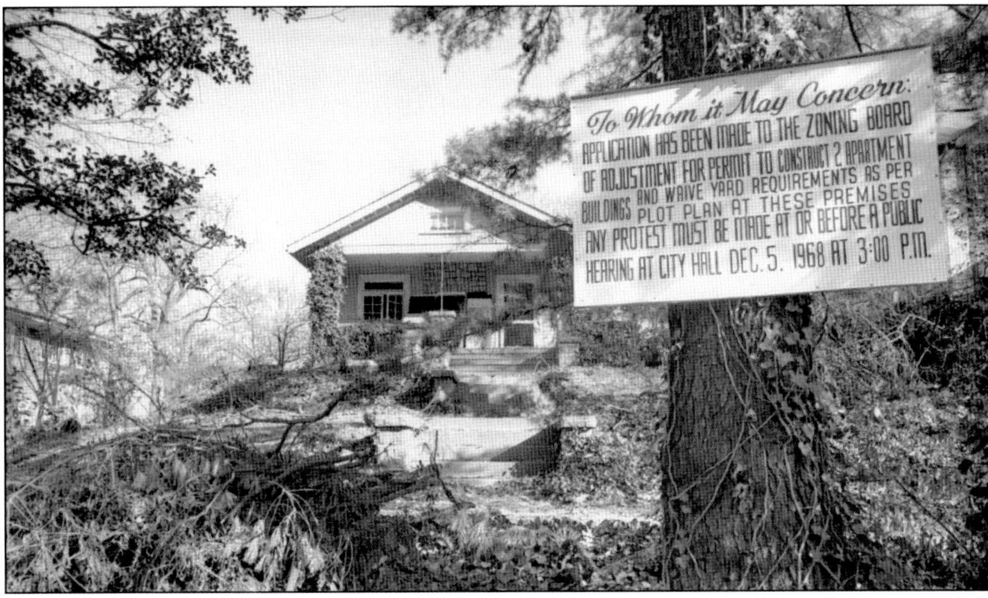

In 1968, the Henry Nading property at 651 Summit Street was demolished and a modern apartment complex was built, one the neighbors derisively called the "Summit Street Motel." It certainly was an aesthetic intrusion onto a street with 50- to 70-year-old homes, but zoning laws at that time had little allowances for aesthetic considerations in the permit process. (Courtesy FCPL.)

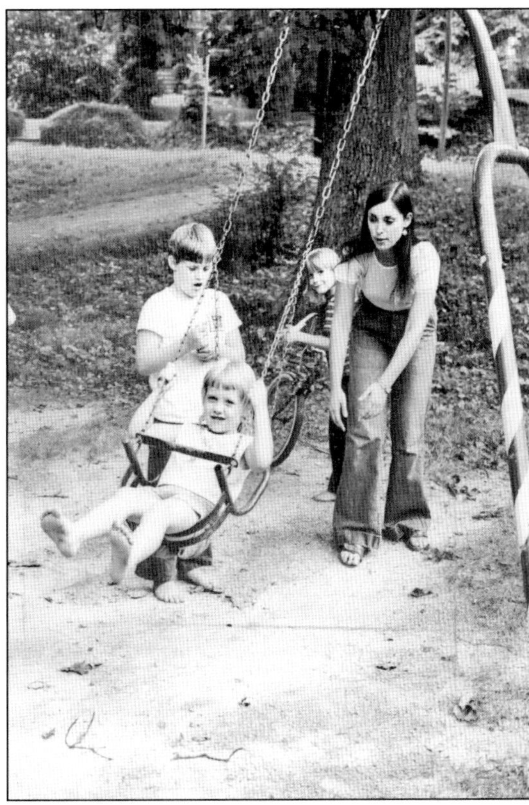

In response, people began to discuss their concerns and organize their objections to plans for their neighborhood at the same place they always met—with their children at the neighborhood parks. In May 1969, Ellen Yarborough and Ellie Clayton distributed a flyer asking folks to come to the first meeting of what would become the West End Association at the Glade Street YWCA. The expressway plans were rebuffed. (Courtesy RPD.)

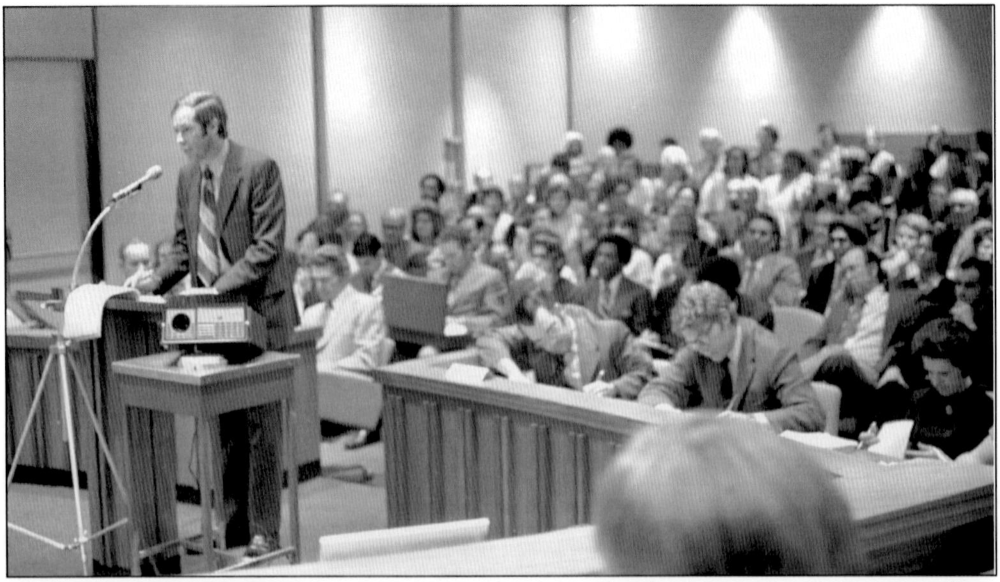

In July 1971, the West End Association re-energized under the leadership of Tom Ross (here at podium), a passionate attorney and neighbor to the unwanted apartments on Summit. West Enders switched tactics from house-to-house battles, seeking to have the entire West End back-zoned to more commercially restricted R-2 zoning. They won a major victory in October 1972 with the reclassifying of a large portion of the West End. In order to get to a vote, the association had to give up rezoning along the central Fourth and Fifth Street corridor from Broad Street to Grace Court. (Courtesy FCPL.)

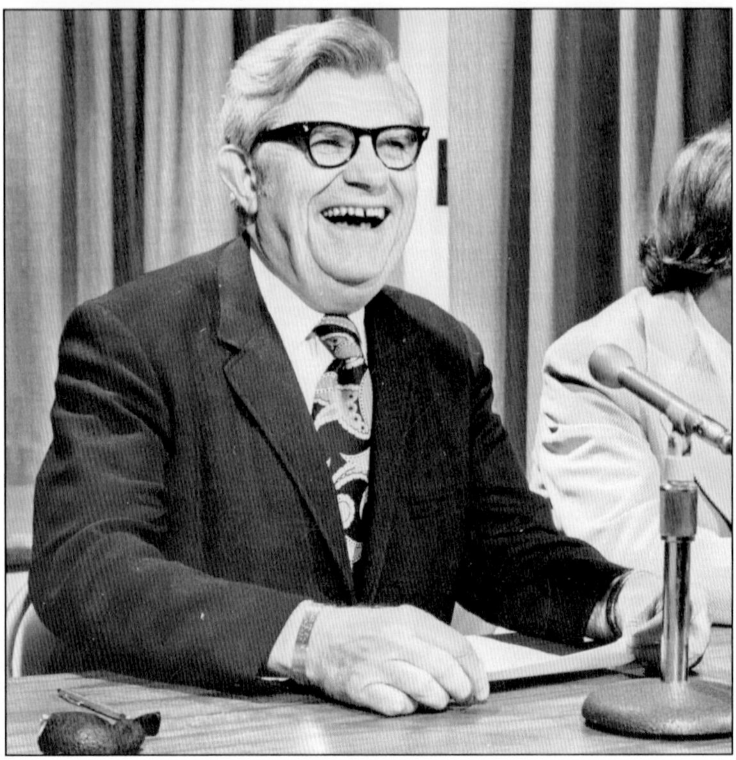

Mayor Franklin Shirley was an early supporter of the West End efforts and helped form Historic Winston to look at property issues in "Old Winston" generally. Despite considerable opposition from the planning board and commercial developers, Mayor Shirley helped keep dialogue between the two groups open. (Courtesy City of Winston-Salem.)

With his wife, Robin, and two other West End couples, Peter and Barbara Smitherman and Ray and Charlotte Troxell, Tom Ross formed Adelaide, "a group with an old-fashioned name to save old-fashioned houses." Here, part of the group celebrates with a toast the successful move of Zevely House (see page 107), which still serves today as a fine dining restaurant. Such West Ender efforts were a significant awakening of neighborhood power in the leadership of the city. (Courtesy FCPL.)

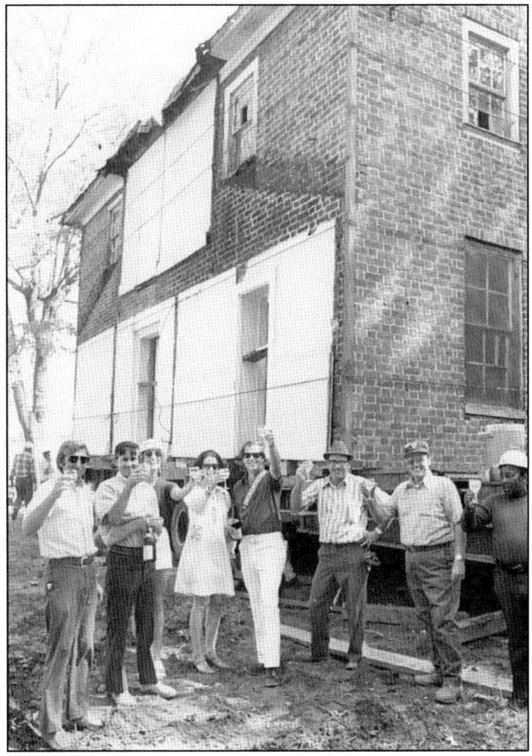

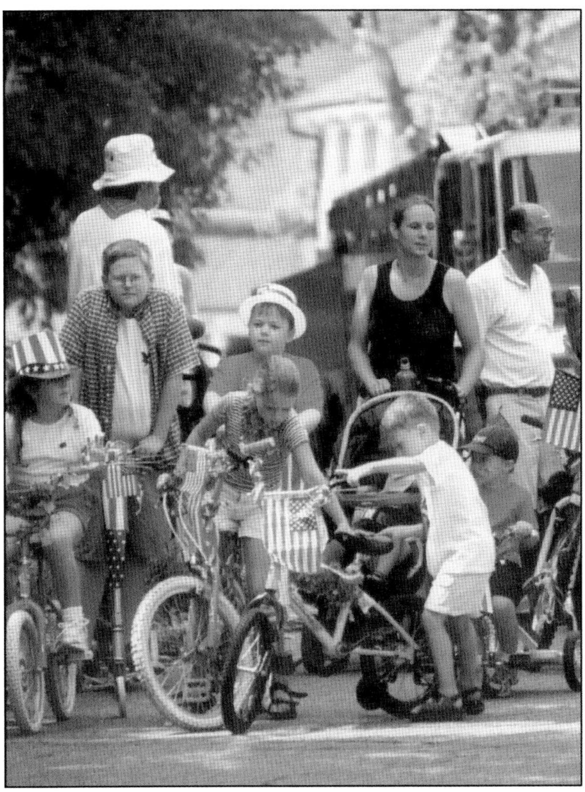

West Enders' response to the zoning change was not just a return to the neighborhood parks to celebrate the lessening pressures on their community but also an invitation to others to come and discover the potential of West End properties as part of a revived downtown. Since the 1970s, neighbors have held parades, organized concerts in Grace Court, and held yard sales and potlucks to build excitement and community spirit. (Courtesy the author.)

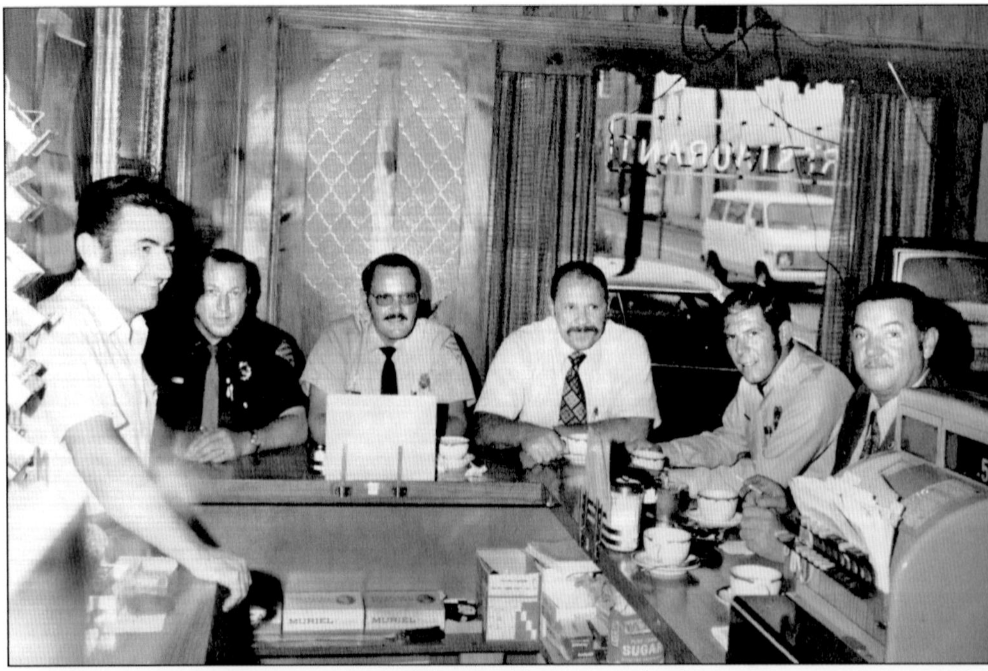

The zoning vote and the enthusiasm of the neighbors started to have a positive invasive effect on the city. Places that people had taken for granted as always having been there were suddenly realized to be vulnerable and highlighted as worth preserving. Neighborhood gathering spots like Nick Doumas's Lighthouse Restaurant, at the corner of Brookstown and Burke, were held up not just for good eats but for the goodwill they brought to the community. (Courtesy Lighthouse Restaurant/Harold Doumas.)

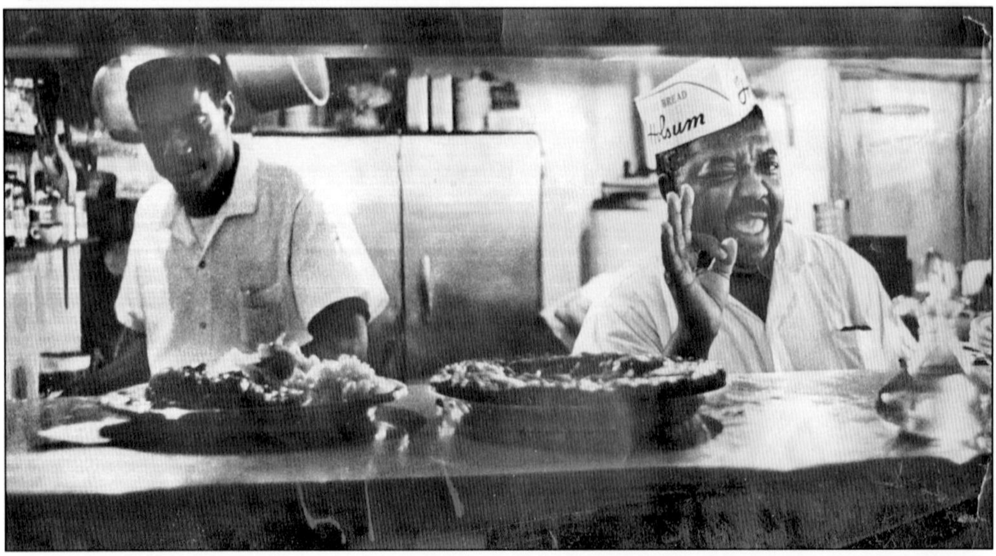

By the mid-1970s, fresh eyes at the newspaper, which had declared West End dying a decade earlier, now called it "a small Georgetown." A photographer for the Wake Forest yearbook took this shot of the cooks at the Lighthouse, one of the favorite hangouts for him and his Wake friends. West Enders were helping the entire community realize the hospitality of their pedestrian-friendly place. (Courtesy Lighthouse Restaurant/Harold Doumas.)

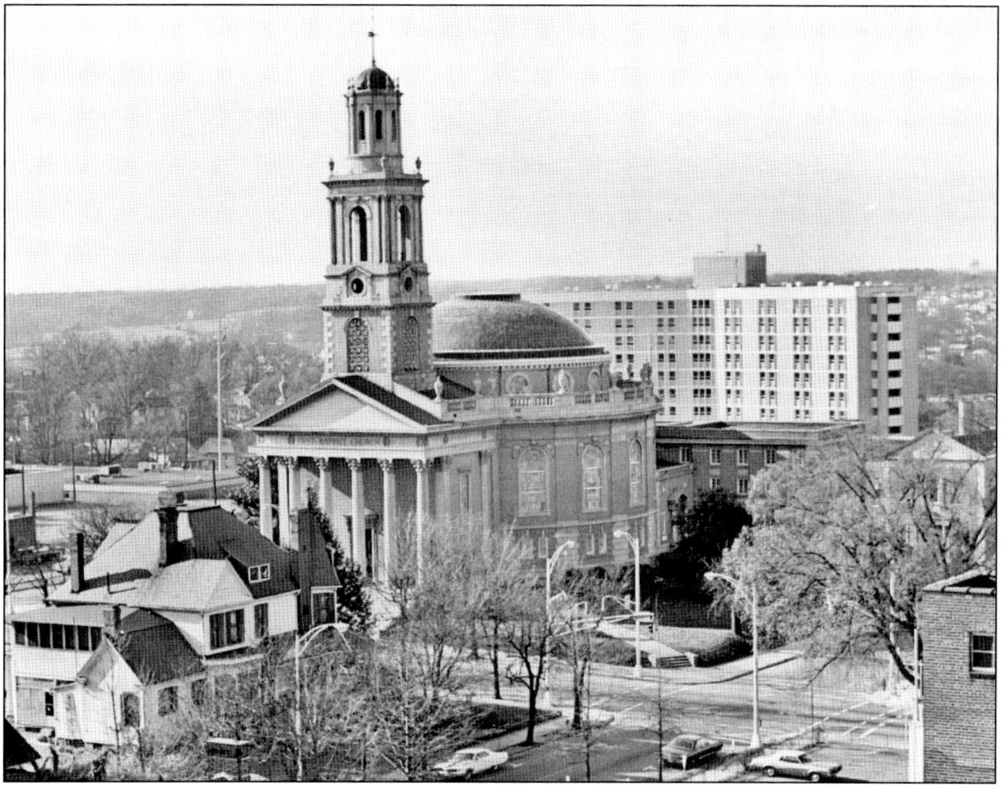

In the early 1970s, Crystal Towers Apartments were built at Sixth and Spruce Streets on lands that would have been a part of the original West End development. This part of West End, north of Sixth between Broad and Spruce, had suffered such a severe economic downturn and loss of housing stock that it became known as the Crystal Towers neighborhood. From left to right are the H.D. Poindexter house on Fifth, First Baptist, and Crystal Towers. (Courtesy FCPL.)

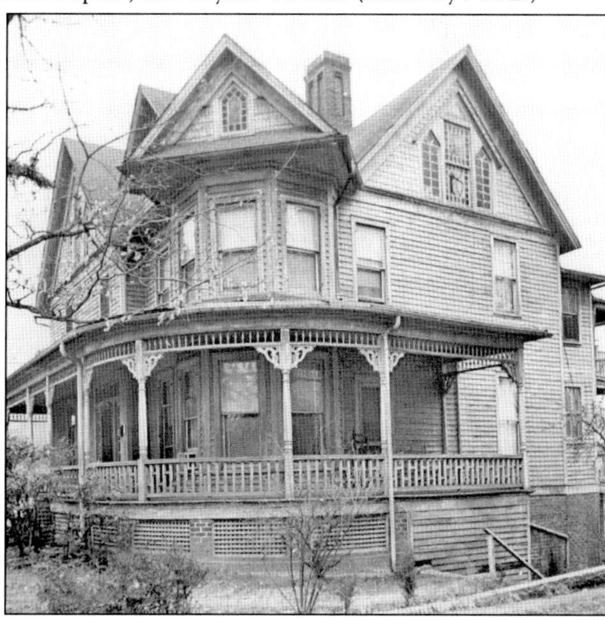

As part of an urban renewal grant, the city secured $1 million to improve the housing and livability of the Crystal Towers neighborhood. Sites were prepared for the removal and relocation of seven historic homes from commercially pressured areas in West End and elsewhere to the area. Here is the Jacquelin P. "Jack" Taylor house near the northeast corner of Fifth and Summit. The house was moved to 236 West End Boulevard to make room for a parking lot. (Courtesy FCPL.)

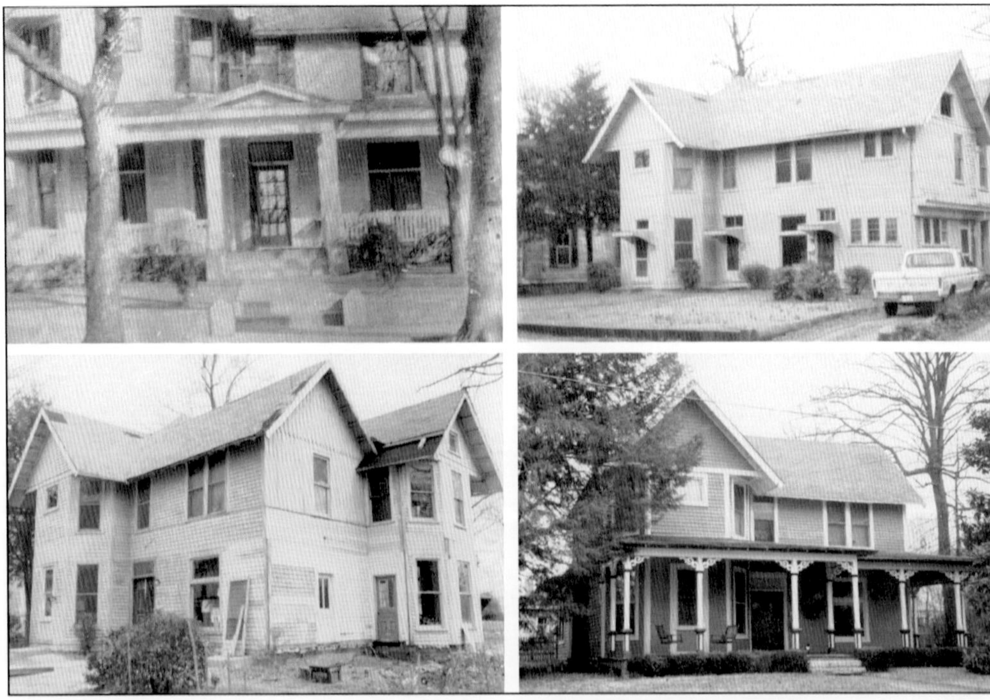

Charles and Laura Phillips bought the Moir-Salmons house at 637 North Spring Street in 1977. By the 1920s (upper left), the 1898 home had already undergone alterations from its original Victorian look. By the time of their purchase (upper right), the home's charms had been stripped into four apartments. Several years worth of work uncovering (lower left) and recreating the house have resulted in a beautiful home (lower right). Such time-consuming yet rewarding renovations are an important part of the West End story. (Courtesy Laura Phillips.)

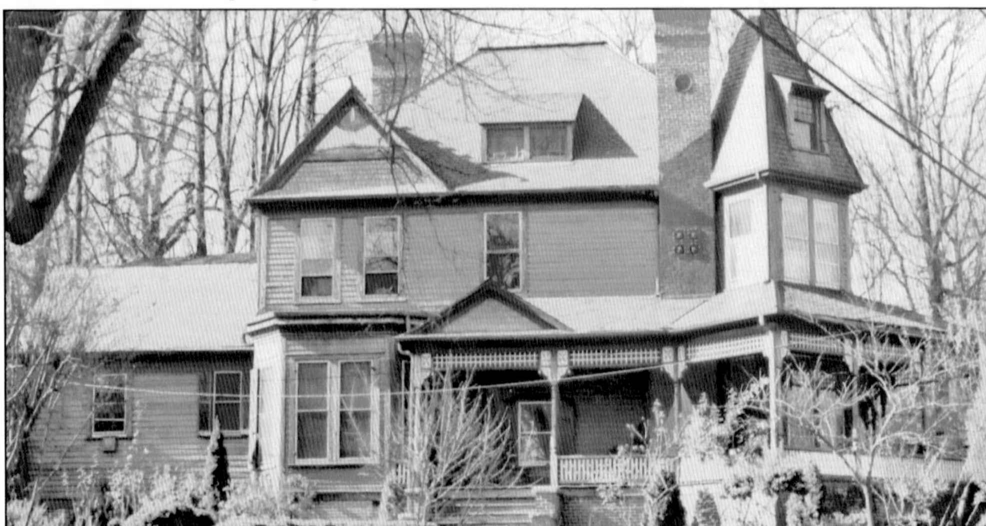

The H.D. Poindexter home is depicted after its move from Fifth Street to 130 West End Boulevard. This outstanding example of a Queen Anne is now painted with Victorian colors. The cottage that stood behind the house at Fifth and Spruce is on its own lot adjacent and to the east of the main house. (Courtesy the author.)

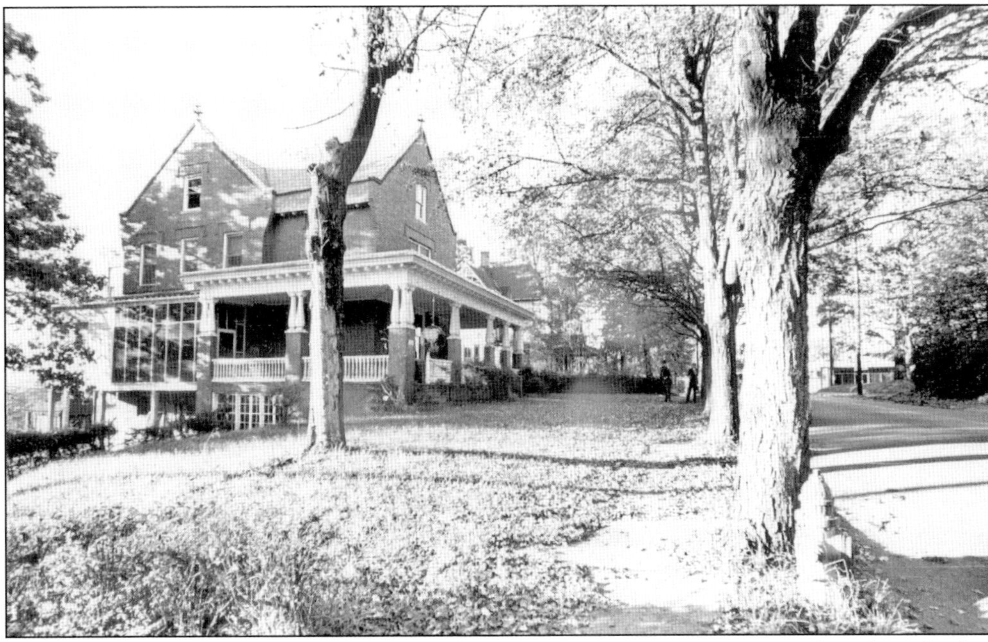

The Benjamin J. Sheppard home, shown here on Summit Street, was purchased in the late 1970s, along with the neighboring Colonel Ludlow home, to form the first bed and breakfast in the West End. The tobacco heritage of the Sheppards can be seen in the detailing of tobacco leaves at the top of the home's porch columns. (Courtesy FCPL.)

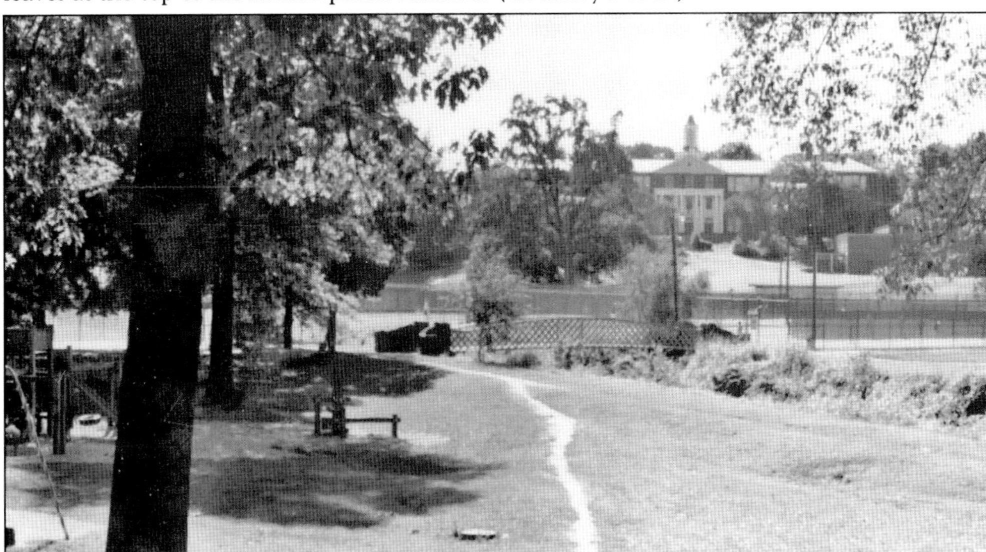

The path from demolition to preservation was not an easy one, and yet converts were made along the way. In 1978, the Petree Stockton law firm began to move their offices to the former C.G. Hill property on the south side of the site of the original Hotel Zinzendorf, west of Grace Court. The zoning loophole crafted in the 1972 negotiations for back-zoning had made this kind of development a likely possibility. However, the firm proved receptive to the sensitivities of neighbors when it acquired the neighboring P. Huber Hanes house in 1985 and renovated it. (Courtesy RPD.)

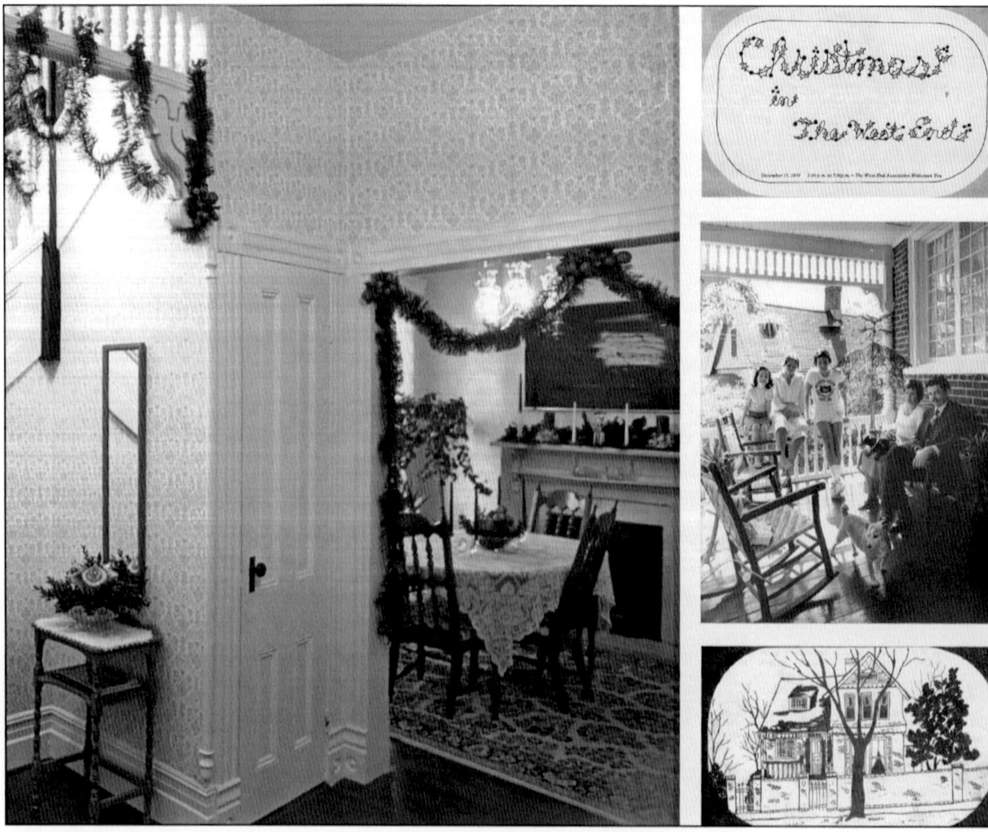

Concurrent with the request to build on the Hill property, West Enders began what has become a community tradition in 1978: the biennial West End Tour of Homes. Always occurring early in the holiday season in December, the tour highlights the best of renovation work in the West End and wraps it in the colors of the season. Above is the Alan Willis family and the Miller-Galloway house at 923 West Fifth on the original tour; below, Barbara Beattie leads a children's chorus in the Brame-Still house at 915 West End Boulevard on a subsequent tour. (Courtesy Juanita Willis and Catherine Hendren.)

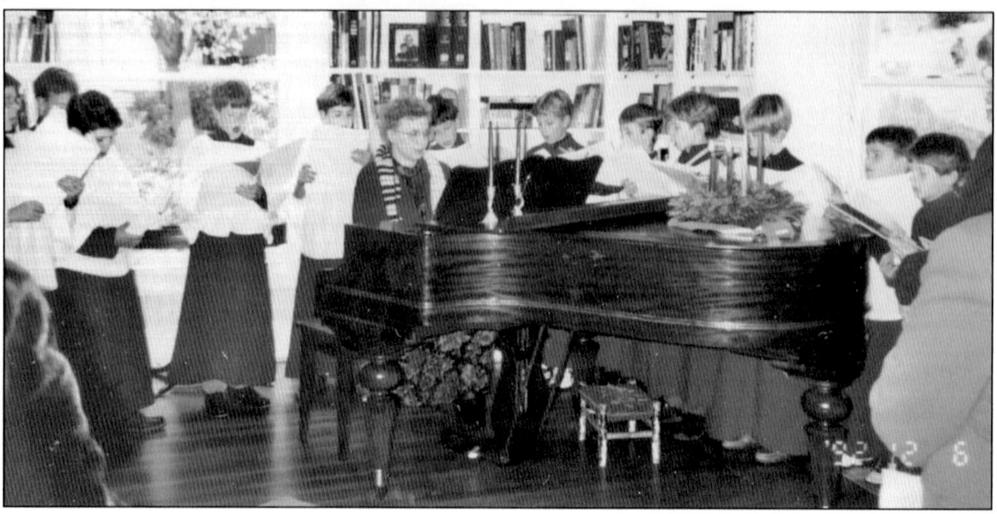

Barbara Smitherman grew up in West End in the Ernest Dalton house at 1209 Clover Street. As a child, she loved the closeness of the community, had been heartbroken by its neglect, and was heartened again by the renewed care of her neighbors. In the early 1980s, she successfully raised over $50,000 for the renovation and restoration of Grace Court and the installation of a new central gazebo. (Courtesy Peter Fox.)

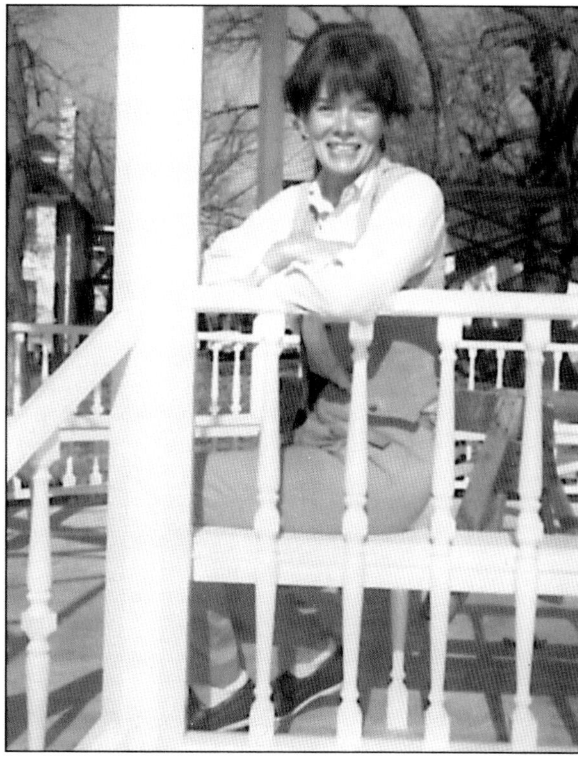

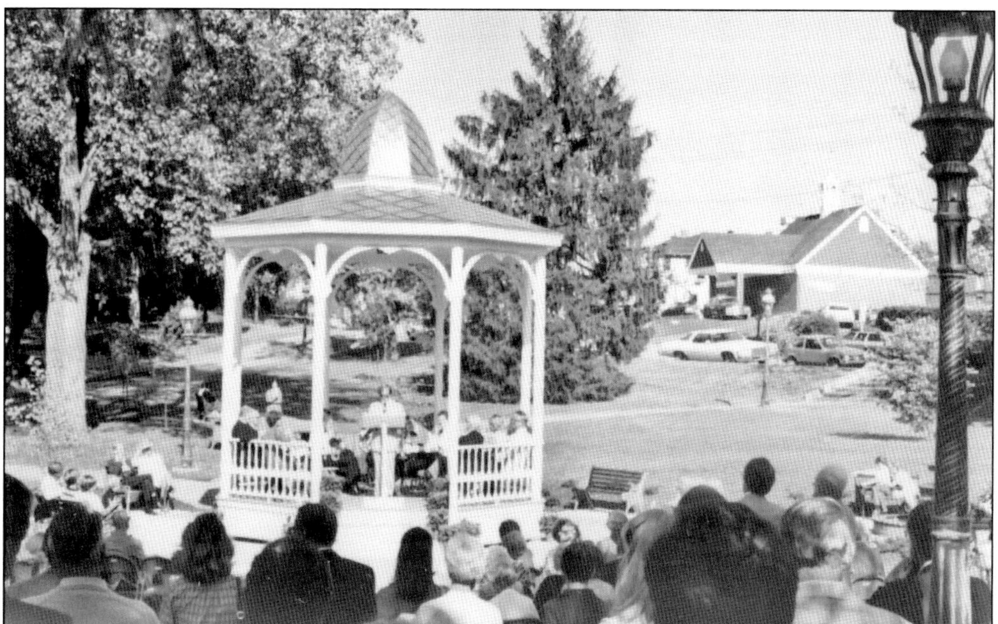

Here is the dedication ceremony for the renovation of Grace Court in 1982. That day, the gazebo sported a copper-colored roof, not the green-colored one it has since acquired. The gazebo is modeled after one in Barre, Vermont, which Smitherman saw on a family trip and was inspired by. The gazebo has been one of the city's most popular spots for weddings for years. (Courtesy RPD.)

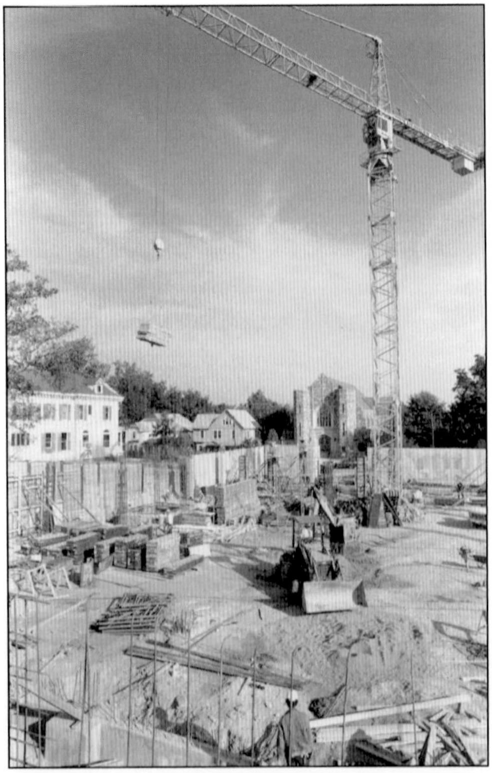

In 1983, Wachovia Bank began construction of its West End Center, a major computing facility for its financial systems. The newspaper commented that with this building, downtown was being redefined westward and that now all of Fifth to Summit Street would be open to commercial development. (Courtesy WCCA.)

The 1909 Rosenbacher house (below left) was by 1986 a lone historic house along this stretch of Fifth Street. In 1985, Dr. Glen Gravlee led a joint West End–Crystal Towers effort, hiring historic preservation consultants Laura Phillips and Gwynne Taylor (insets) to do a survey of properties in order to recognize the neighborhood as a National Register of Historic Places District. (Courtesy CCPB, Laura Phillips, and Gwynne Taylor.)

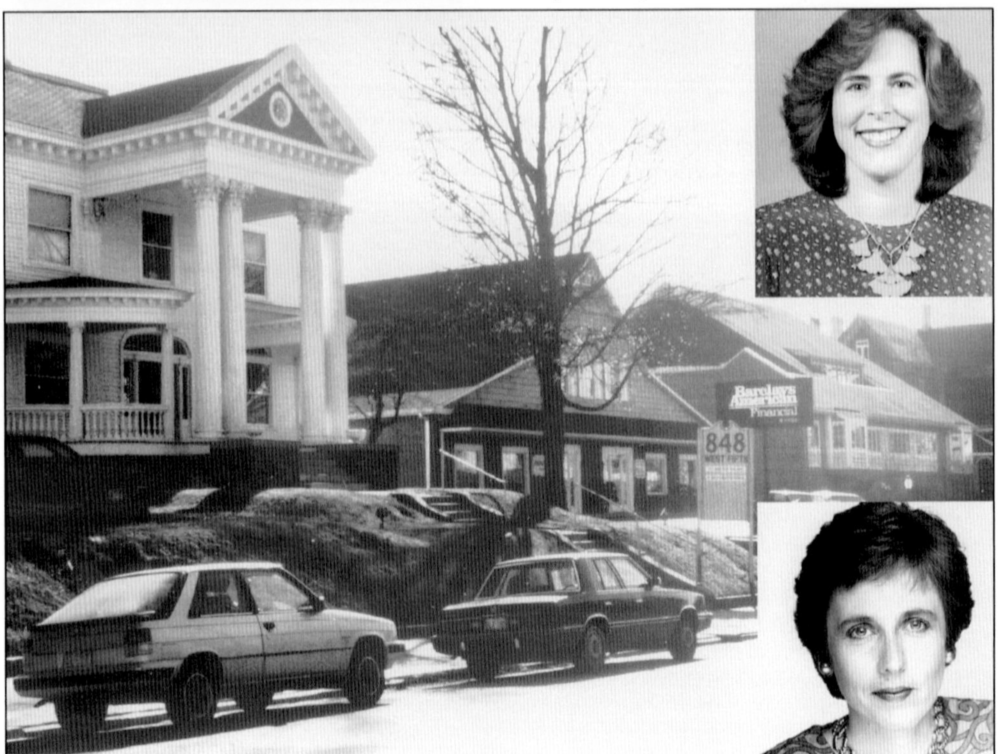

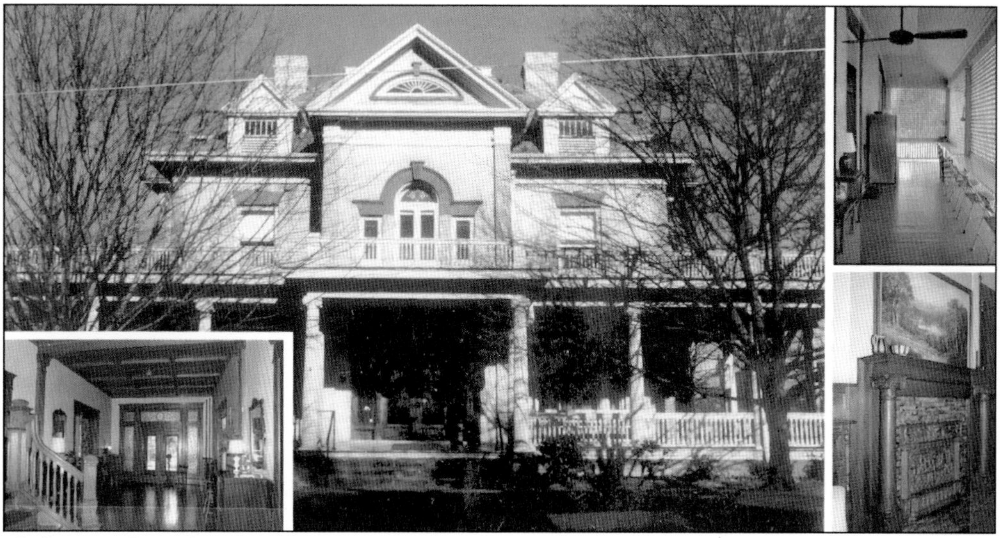

Phillips and Taylor compiled a detailed description of the architecture of each of 600 contributing structures in the area of the West End Hotel and Land Company properties built before 1930 and in the areas along Fourth and Fifth Street where older housing stock still existed. A photographic record of each of these properties is on file in the state archives, as well as locally. Above is the John Coleman home at 533 Summit Street. (Courtesy CCPB.)

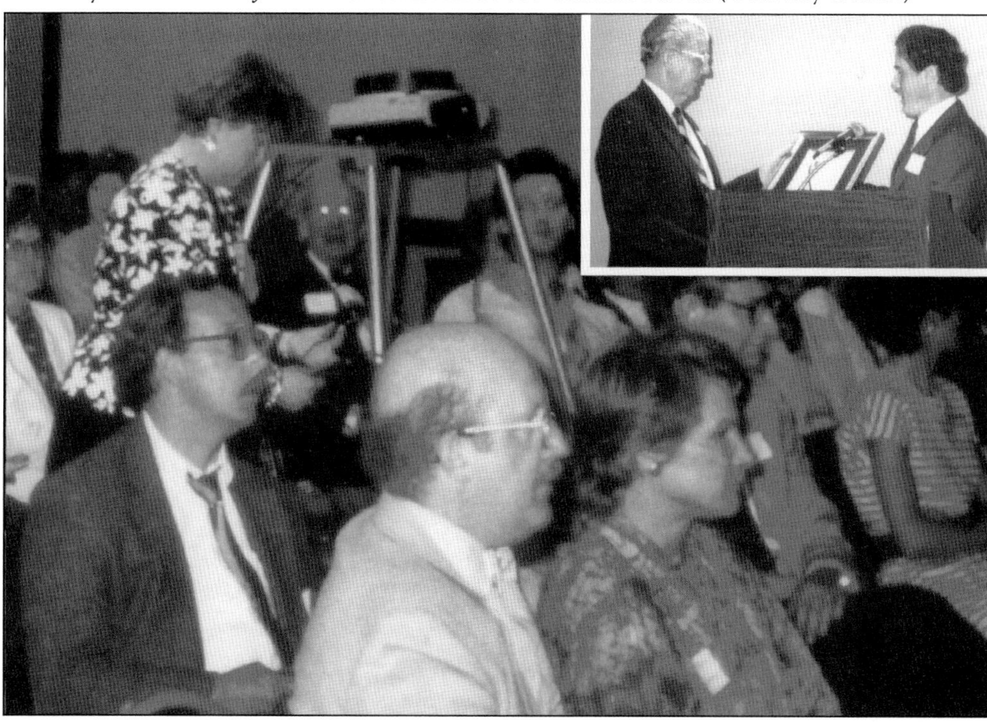

In 1986, West End was afforded National Register status, and in May 1987, neighbors gathered at the Hyatt Hotel to celebrate their achievement and watch Mayor Wayne Corpening receive a state preservation award for the city because of West End's work. In 1993, neighbors agreed to become a Winston-Salem Local Historic District, voluntarily limiting their ability to alter the fronts of their homes. (Courtesy CCPB.)

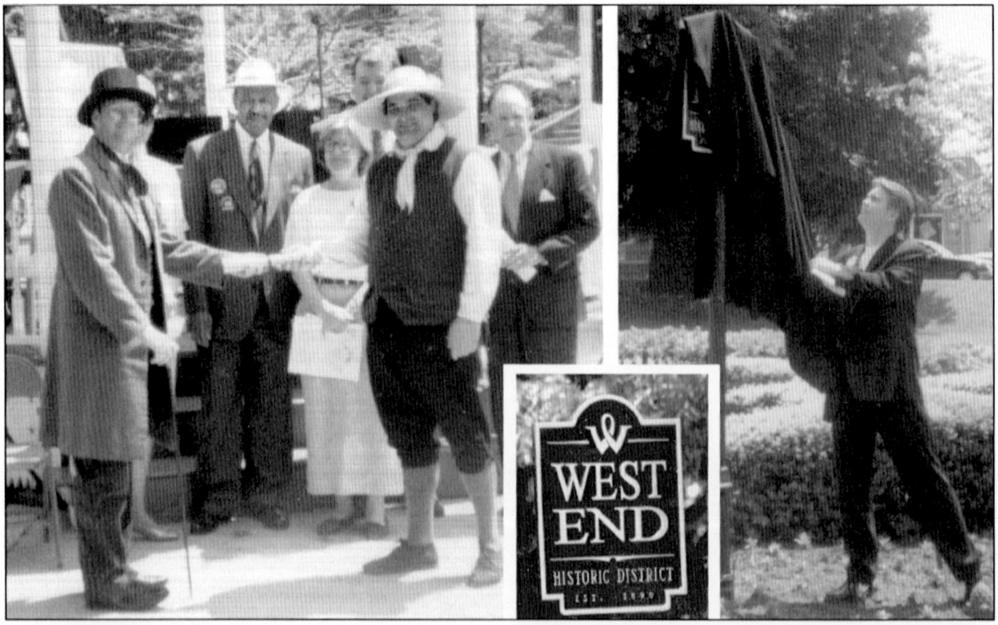

In 1999, the West End Association hosted a party celebrating the 150th anniversary of the founding of Winston and thus the start of Forsyth County. In addition, the association launched a fund-raising effort to install historic district signage around the community and place a time capsule and memorial clock in Grace Court. Mayor Jack Cavanagh presided over the dedication ceremonies in 2000 and was instrumental in assuring the project's success. (All courtesy the author.)

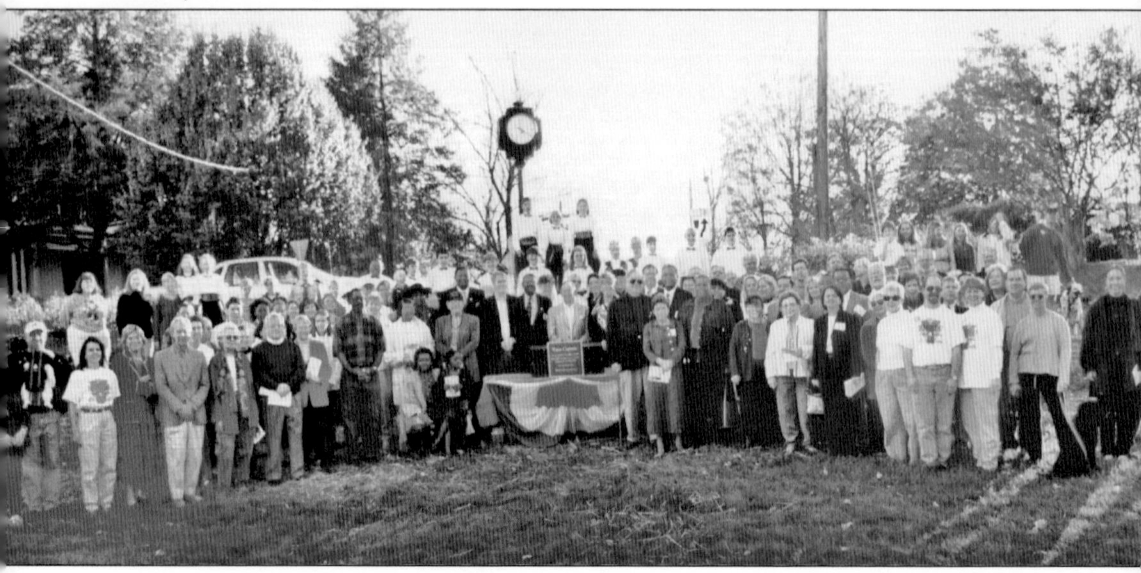

Five

"Winston-Salem's Front Porch" in the New Century

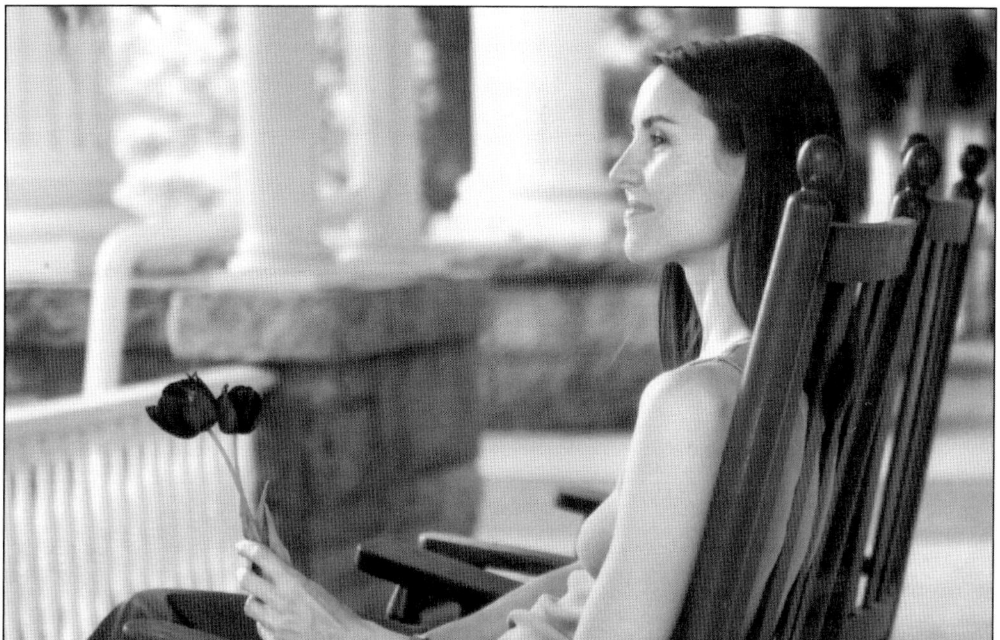

West End today combines a residential neighborhood with professional offices and historic homes with modern commercial development. The neighborhood with hundreds of front porches is a welcoming spot for many doing business and visiting the city. And yet, with all the activity, the area advertised as "Winston-Salem's Front Porch" offers on the street a view of the attractions of another time and place. (Courtesy the author.)

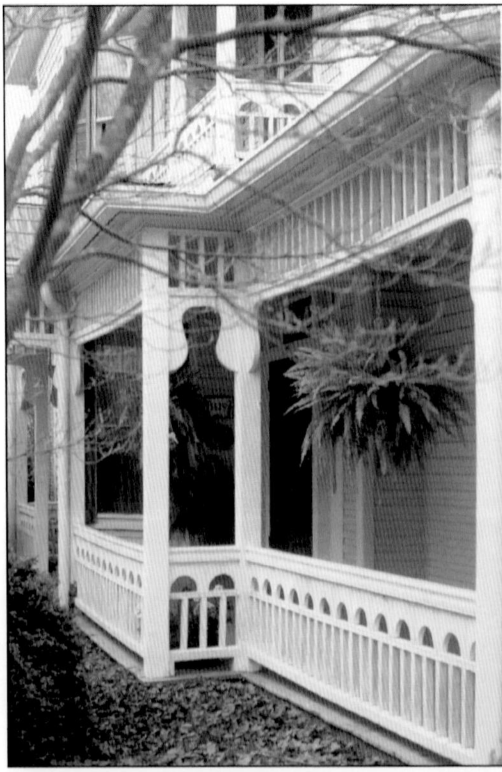

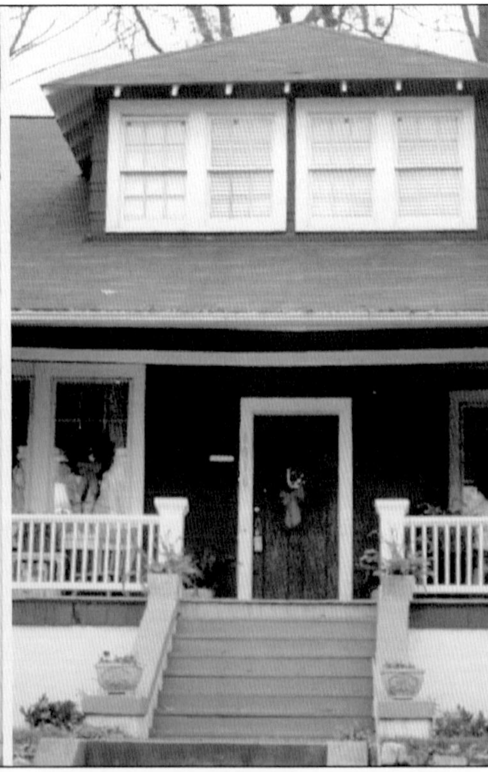

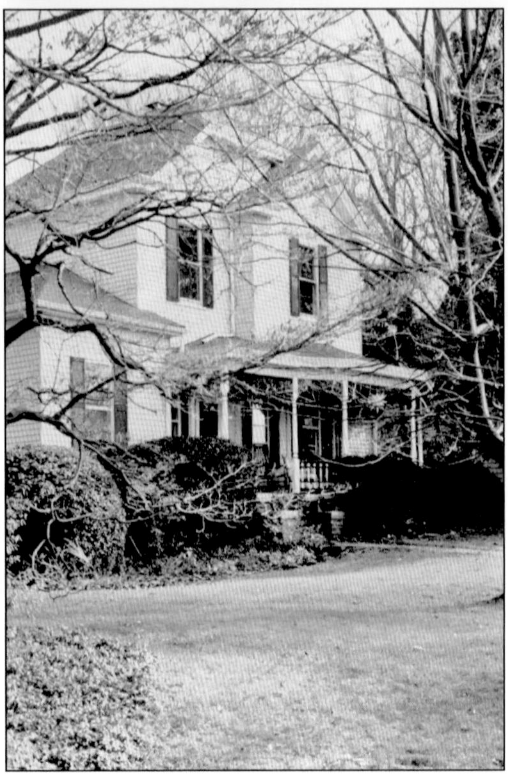

West End remains a pedestrian paradise because of its street layout and four distinctive "front porch" styles—Queen Anne, neoclassical, Colonial Revival, and Craftsman. They offer much inviting detail that can only be appreciated at a slower pace of viewing: across an inner city yard on Spring Street, in the whimsy of porch detailing on Fourth, or in a hillside bungalow "on the Boulevard." (All courtesy the author.)

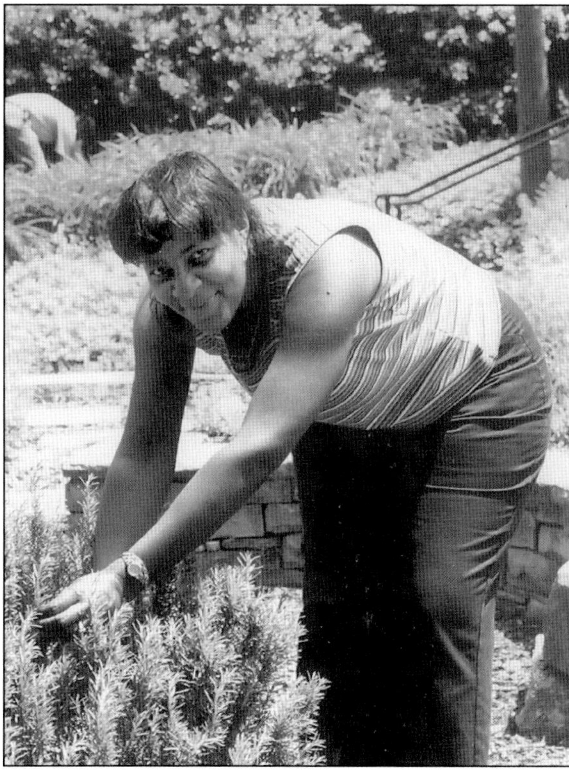

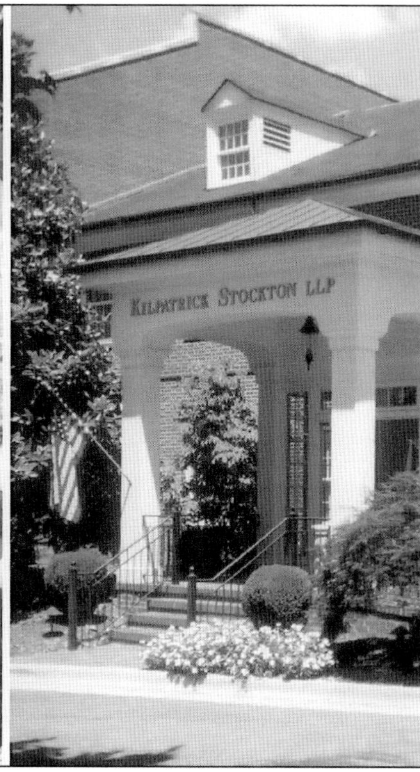

The care in the landscaping of the area is a feature that the smaller lots and intimate pockets of home beauty still bring to the streetscape, but design is given attention in institutional and public spaces, as well. St. Paul's Church is surrounded by gardens, some products of which make it into church dinners. Kilpatrick Stockton takes special pride in their trees and flowerbeds, and Grace Court features an Earline Heath King sculpture of Barbara Smitherman tending flowers in the midst of the park, a remembrance given by the neighborhood association in 1996. (Courtesy of StP, Kilpatrick Stockton LLP, and the author.)

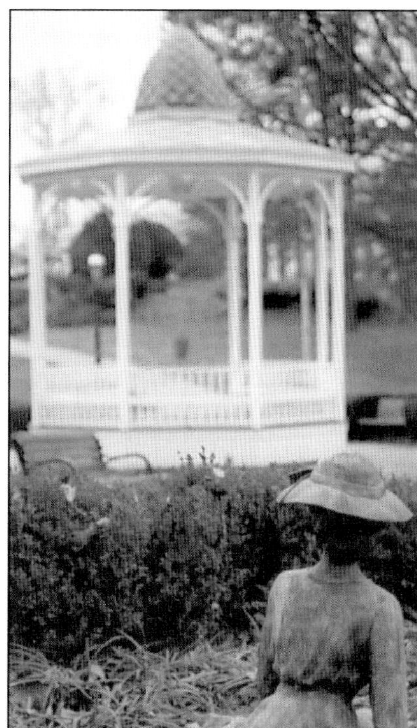

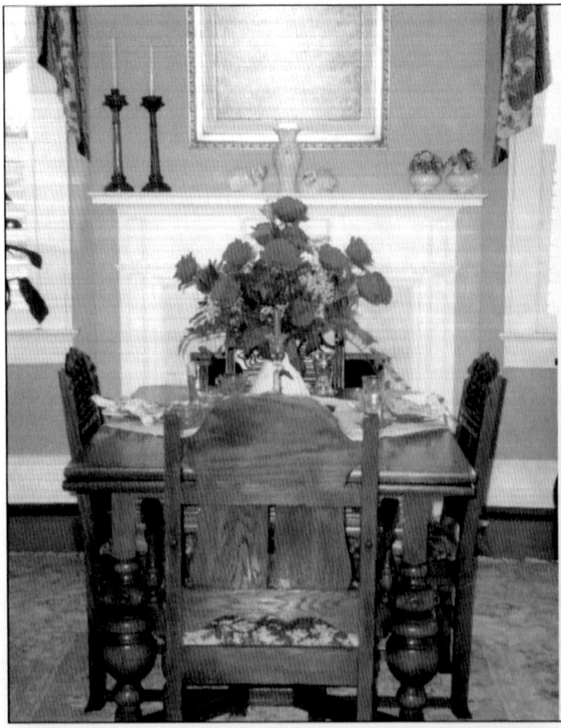

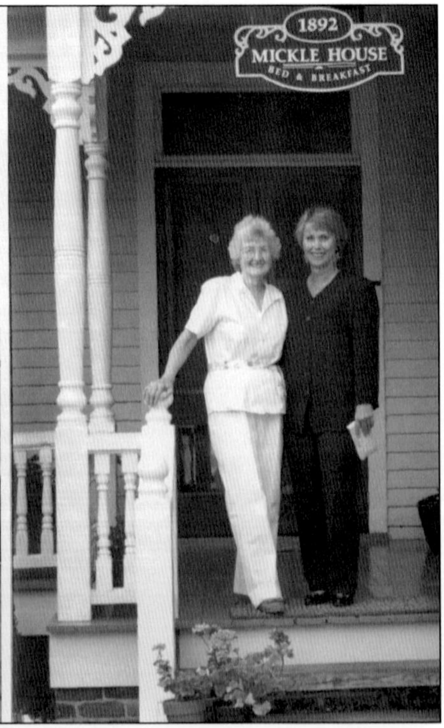

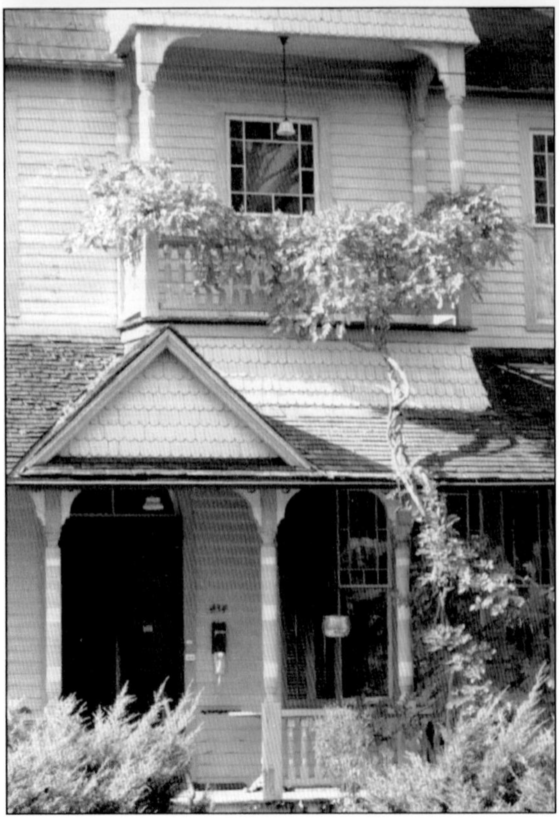

It's not surprising that the intimate, pedestrian-friendly charms of the West End have been home to several bed and breakfasts over the years. Innkeepers take special care to make guests feel at home, as in the furnishings here in the dining room of the Thomas-Welch House on Summit. Barbara Garrison still hears from guests who stayed with her at the Mickle House, though it is now closed as a bed and breakfast. There are few more glorious West End springtime vistas than the blooming wisteria climbing the walls of Colonel Ludlow's house, a part of the Summit Street Inns. (Courtesy of Dave and Marilyn Poorbaugh/ Thomas-Welch B&B, Barbara Garrison, and the author.)

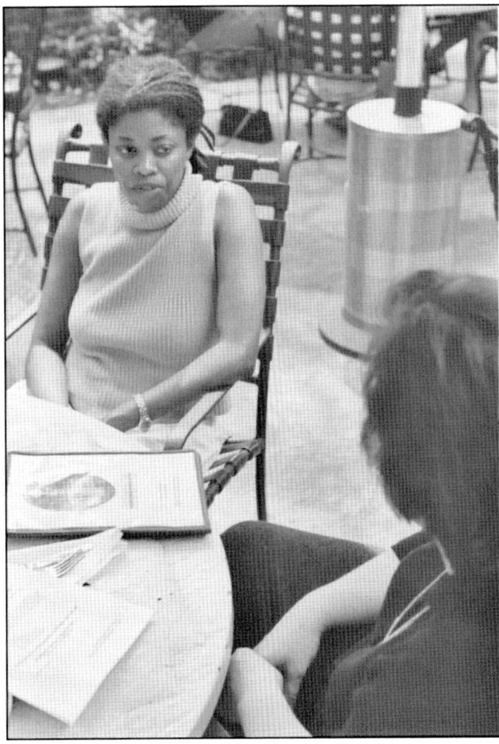

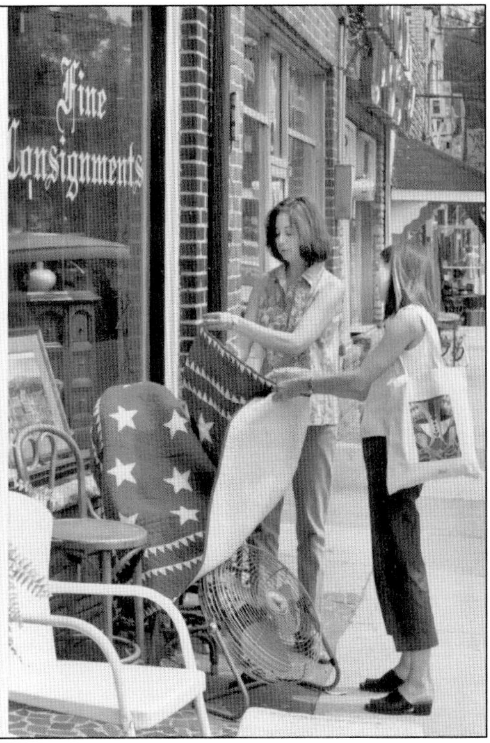

Some of the best of Winston-Salem dining can be found in and around West End, from home cooking to continental cuisine. Antique shops and home furnishings stores fill the curve at Reynolda and West End Boulevard near the arrowhead-shaped Boone Monument, a reminder of the spirit of Daniel Boone if not an actual trail marker. Shops along Burke Street also cater to those with a to-do list of home improvement projects. The West End ArtsFest in 2003 was just the latest in a series of community festivals and events hosted by the neighborhood. (Courtesy the author and Kathleen Ramich.)

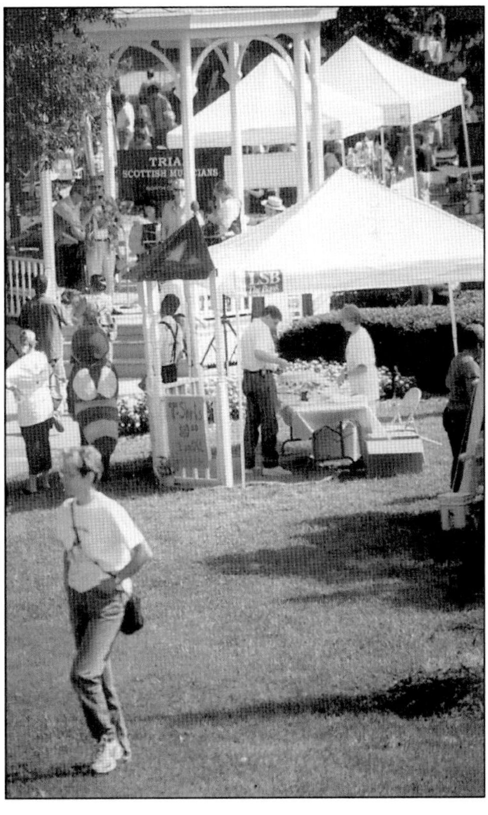

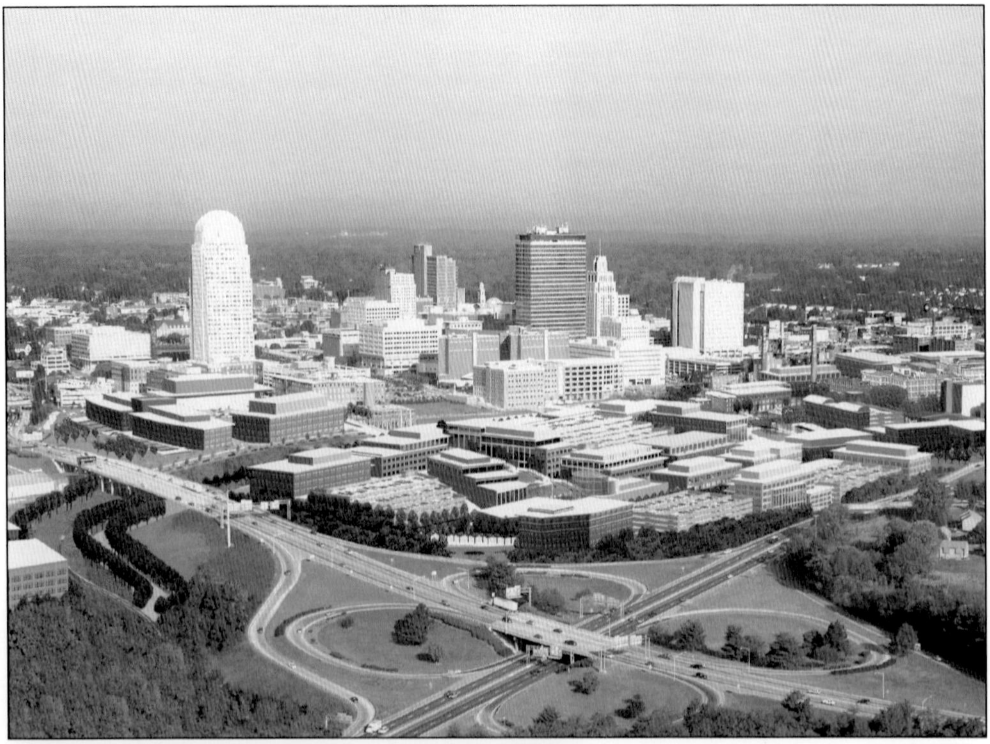

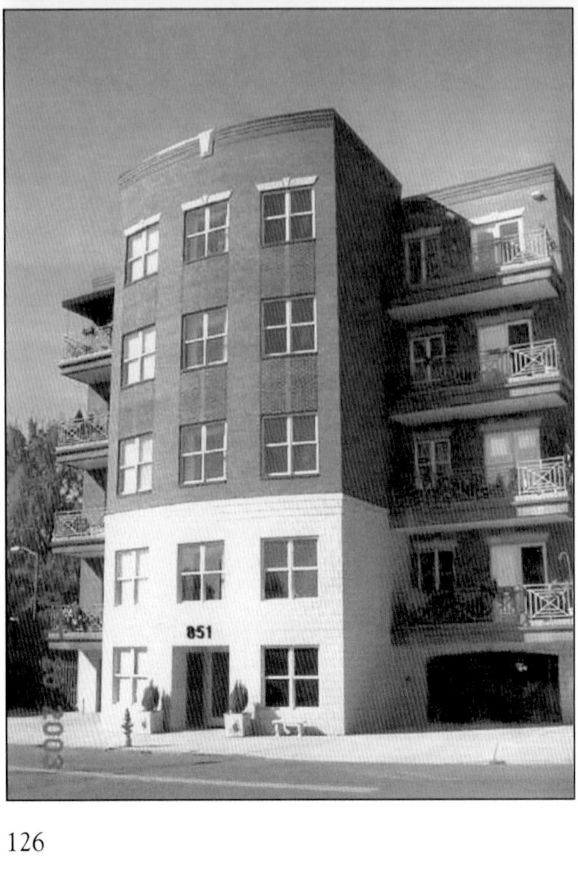

In 2002, Idealliance, a consortium of medical, business, and research interests led by Wake Forest University Health Sciences, announced a 200-acre expansion of the Piedmont Triad Research Park, shown here in a "future version" c. 2023. The development at the intersection of future I-74 and Business I-40, coupled with the Wake Forest University Baptist Medical Center, bookends the West End and downtown with research institutions and their products. Such investments in infrastructure continue to bring interest to West End. The success of JDL Castle's condominium project at 851 West Fourth shows the demand of people for living in a successful urban environment even in a midsize, largely suburban, Southern city. (Courtesy of Idealliance and David Shannon/JDL Castle.)

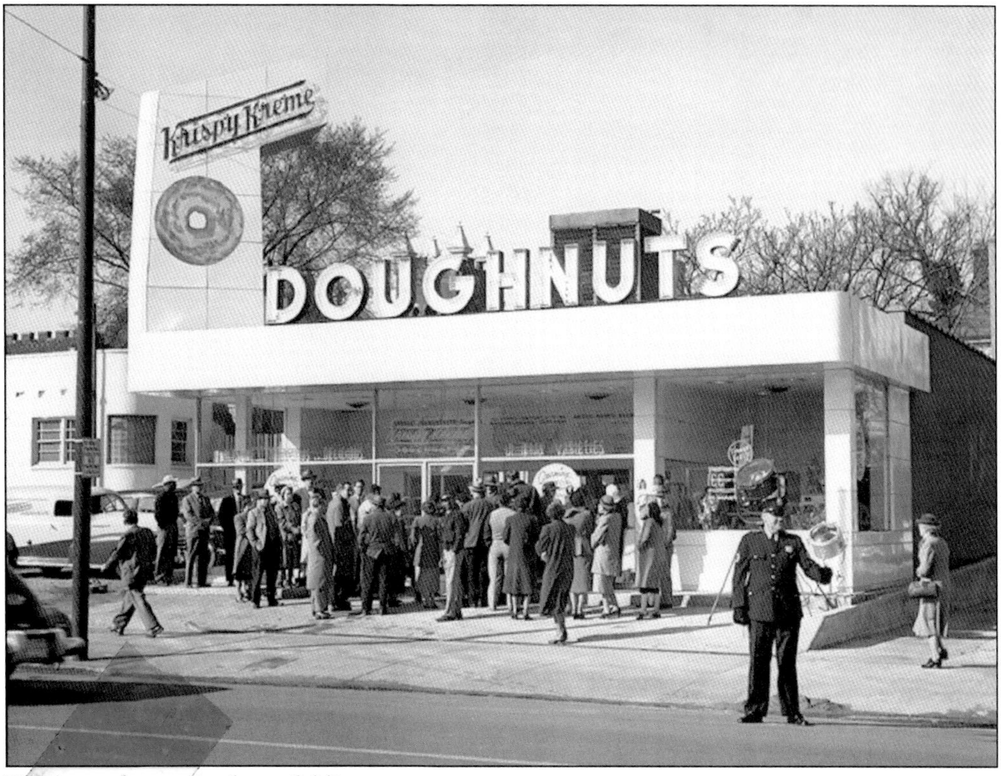

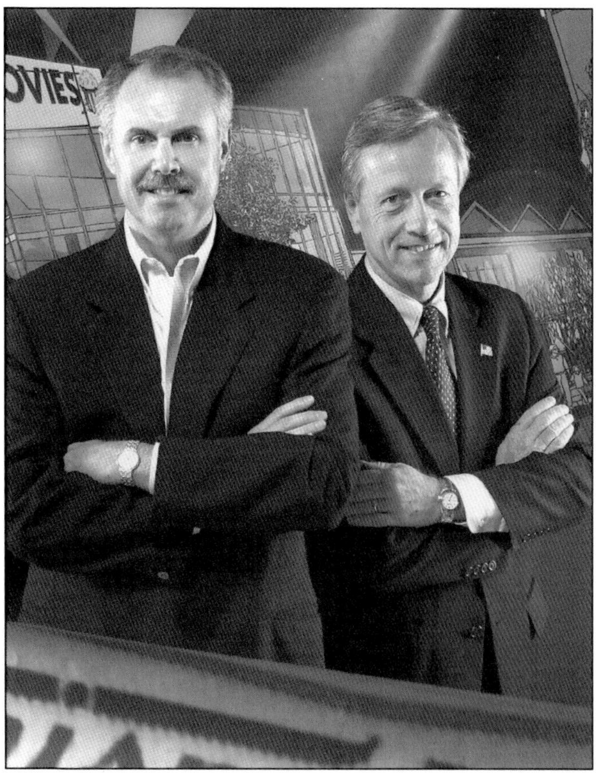

The next chapter in the unfolding story of the neighborhood will involve one of Winston-Salem's sweetest legacies. The Krispy Kreme doughnut was born in a shop in downtown Salem on Main Street in the 1930s. In 2003, the company, whose products are now savored internationally, announced plans to move its headquarters to the southwest corner of Fourth and Broad. Company CEO Scott Livengood, shown at left with Winston-Salem mayor Allen Joines, has committed Krispy Kreme to partner in further retail, residential, and entertainment development of the area in a plan called Unity Place. (Courtesy Krispy Kreme Doughnuts, Inc. and Black Horse Studio, Winston-Salem.)

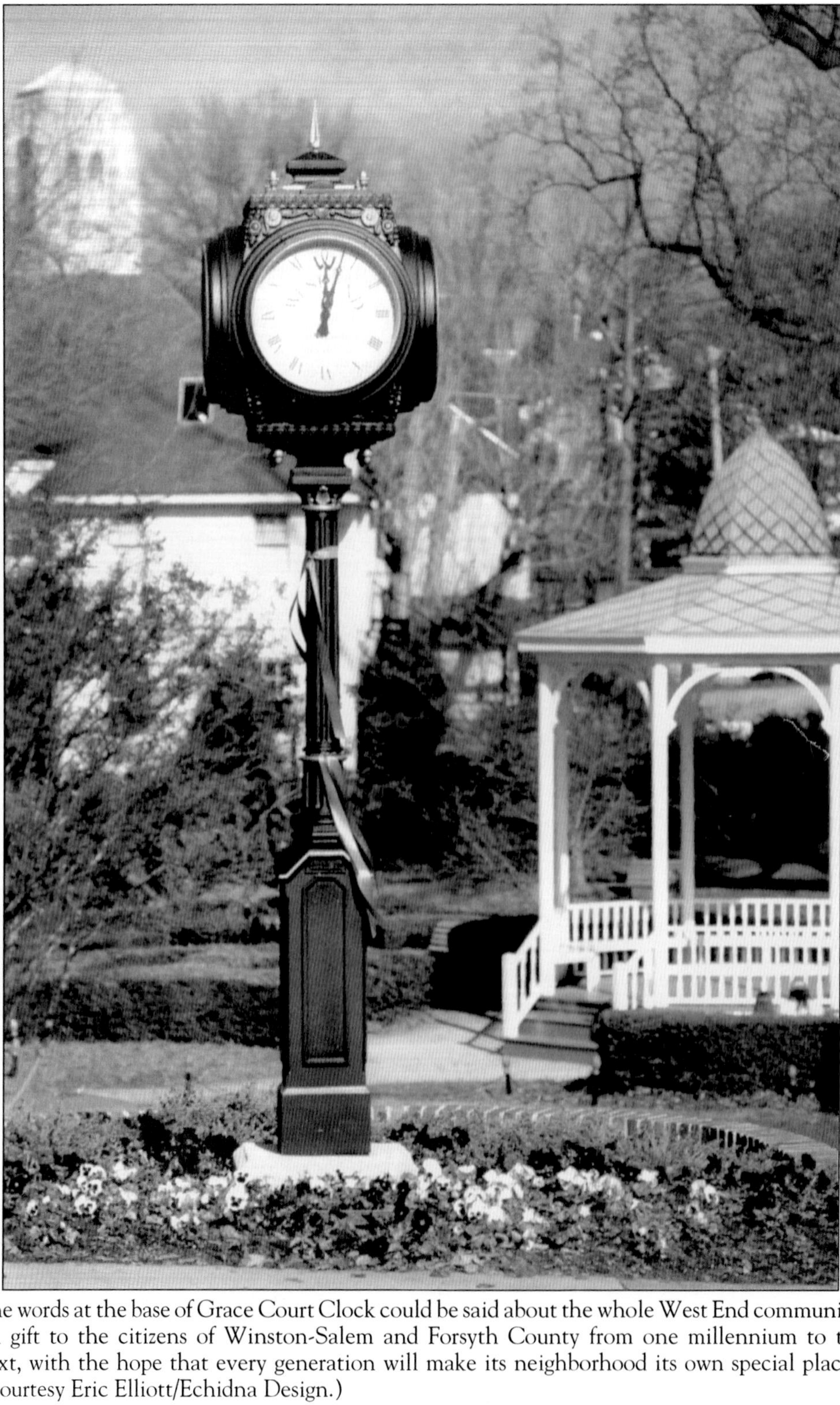

The words at the base of Grace Court Clock could be said about the whole West End community: "A gift to the citizens of Winston-Salem and Forsyth County from one millennium to the next, with the hope that every generation will make its neighborhood its own special place." (Courtesy Eric Elliott/Echidna Design.)